The World is Elsewhere

My Life in Cuba and Other Places

Chris McIvor

W F HOWES LTD

This large print edition published in 2016 by
W F Howes Ltd
Unit 5, St George's House, Rearsby Business Park,
Gaddesby Lane, Rearsby, Leicester LE7 4YH

1 3 5 7 9 10 8 6 4 2

First published in the United Kingdom in 2016
by Sandstone Press Ltd

A CIP catalogue record for this book is available
from the British Library

ISBN 978 1 51003 846 2

Typeset by Palimpsest Book Production Limited,
Falkirk, Stirlingshire

Printed and bound in Great Britain
by TJ International Ltd, Padstow, Cornwall

For my wife, Romana, and our daughter, Zoey.
And for my mother, Rose (1930–2013).

CONTENTS

CONTENTS

PROLOGUE

'Passengers to Casablanca, please board the aircraft,' a voice announced over the intercom. 'We wish you a pleasant flight.' There is a moment at the start of your new life in another country when your decision to move becomes real and irreversible. Up to that point things can change. Perhaps a family tragedy will disrupt your plans. Maybe you will fall and break a leg. But that voice telling you to board your flight has an air of finality, conveying a message that now it is too late to change your mind, that from this moment on there is no turning back.

This was my third flight to start anew in another part of Africa. Twelve years previously I had gone to Sudan as a teacher. Five years later I had travelled to Zimbabwe to start my career as a development worker. Now I was on my way to Morocco wondering, as I had done on those previous occasions, if I had made the right choice to leave familiarity behind. There were routines I had grown used to, work I was comfortable with and people and places I recognized. Most significantly of all, I now had a Zimbabwean wife, several

1

months pregnant, who was unwilling to join me in another country.

Kwadzi had never been less than honest about her reluctance to leave her family behind, the deep roots that tied her to home. She needed familiar surroundings, relatives to interact with and the solidity of a cultural identity that could only be found in a life rooted in one particular place. 'I come from settled people, not nomads,' she had said. 'That's what I want for our child too.'

But she had agreed that my career had to progress from where it was languishing. After seven years with a small British charity providing limited benefits there were practical issues to think about: a pension, financial security and professional development.

'Don't worry,' she had said, when I had agonized over whether to apply for work outside Zimbabwe. 'In Africa, we're used to our husbands spending a few years away from the family. The thing is not to forget that this is where you belong.'

A few months later at Harare airport, her extended family was gathered around to say goodbye. I had a flight to London and then a connection to Casablanca. There had been hugs, handshakes and tears, everyone reminding me that this was only a temporary separation, that we would soon be together again. But I couldn't help thinking that a few years previously I had traded my former way of life for marriage, stability and a home. Was the past now coming to reclaim me? Despite everyone's words of reassurance I had a sense that while one door was opening another was closing, with family and friends on the other side.

'So, why Morocco?' a friend had asked, when I had told him where I was going.

I had shrugged my shoulders as I had done when asked why I had gone to Sudan as a teacher and later to Zimbabwe as an aid worker. 'It chose me rather than the other way round,' I replied, adding that this was the story of my path to date. It always seemed as though once I had decided to leave one country, a new, unfamiliar one would present itself, as if waiting to catch me.

'So you know nothing about where you are going?'

'Well, there's Abdel Karim.'

'Abdel who?'

Abdel Karim El Khattabi was my father's hero and while other children were entertained with tales of Robin Hood, Rob Roy Macgregor and William Tell our childhood was informed by stories of a Moroccan revolutionary who had managed to outsmart an entire foreign army for several decades in North Africa.

It was doubtful whether my father's recollections of who he was and what he had done were entirely accurate. Was he as noble as Dad said he was, robbing the French invaders and distributing their wealth to the poor people of the Rif Mountains in Morocco? My father had 'discovered' Abdel Karim in the reading room of Perth library as a boy, when he had inadvertently picked up a book on African history. Since that time, he had read everything about him that he could find. But the considerable enthusiasm with which he described him left my siblings and I wondering in later years if what we had been exposed to as children was historical fact or something that told us more about the character and rebellious inclinations of my father. Perhaps going to Morocco would give me an opportunity to find out.

'Why Morocco?' had also been asked at the London offices of the British charity I had applied to work for. I had felt intimidated at the interview, not so much by the people asking questions but the sheer scale of the institution I might be joining.

Save the Children occupied a large building in central London and had even converted a school a few miles away for other parts of its operations. There was a canteen for the staff and a finance department that covered an entire floor. I thought of the few individuals huddled over calculators in a shared room in my current organization, our collective excitement when we managed to find a few thousand pounds to add to our funding. In the background information I had been sent about the programme in Morocco, the budget was several million. 'What do they do with so much money?' I had wondered.

A busy office, busy people, phones ringing, serious faces coming out of rooms that displayed the names of every struggling country in the world.

4

The young woman who escorted me said that the principal interviewer was friendly and sympathetic and that I should feel at ease. 'Oh, by the way, she was held hostage a few years ago for a considerable period of time before they released her. Imagine. She still goes back to the same country.' Was there anything I could point to in my own history, I wondered, that could compete with being kidnapped?

But a few weeks later I received a call from one of the interviewers. 'We'd like you to join Save the Children as the country director for our operations in Morocco.'

In London I had been asked about my salary expectations and what terms and conditions of service I expected to receive. Worried that I was being too pushy I had added to the amount I was getting in my current job. No one had reacted and a few days after the phone call I received a copy of my contract.

'That can't be right. They must have made a mistake,' I thought.

Job security and being able to support an expanding family had featured heavily in my decision to move. But compared to what I had been receiving this seemed overly generous. While part of me was relieved that worry about our financial future had been allayed, I had a nagging concern.

Now I was to become a 'professional' aid worker, a tag I had managed to avoid through my decade of low-paid work and volunteerism in Africa.

Would I become seduced by the trappings of office and the lifestyle I would now be able to afford?

I would need to interact with local people, learn the local language, and above all avoid living in the protective bubble that some expatriates seemed content to occupy. As I returned the signed contract I promised myself that I would be vigilant, that I would continue to respect the best advice I had received when embarking on my first journey to Africa. 'Make up your own mind about things. Be open to new experiences. Discard whatever baggage you are carrying with you and leave your preconceptions behind.'

CHAPTER 1

ARRIVAL

'I should tell you I'm a terrible flyer,' the young woman beside me blurted out, interrupting my thoughts a few minutes after we departed Heathrow for Casablanca. Behind her glasses there was a pretty face but the lines of worry around her forehead mirrored the nervous words and shaky voice. She came from London and was headed to Morocco with her daughter to join her husband who had preceded them by a few months to take up a job in the banking sector.

'I love aeroplanes,' the daughter interrupted, a confident ten-year-old who had already quaffed several Cokes before we were even airborne and was frantically signalling the stewardess to bring her some more.

'She knows she can get away with anything. I'm too worried about flying to ever object,' the woman confided, prompting me to reassure her that we would be in Casablanca in no time and that the weather forecast, as far as I knew, had been favourable.

But an hour or so later, somewhere over southern Spain, the pilot announced that we could expect 'bumpy' conditions on our approach to Gibraltar, a point midway to our final destination where some passengers would disembark.

'I knew this would happen,' the woman said.

Not a particularly comfortable flyer myself, I replied that pilots often exaggerated the weather just so passengers would take them seriously when instructed to fasten their seat belts. 'It's nothing to worry about,' I continued, trying to sound more convincing than I felt.

But the word 'bumpy' could hardly describe what we flew into a short while later. The plane began to pitch and roll in a way that I had never experienced before. As thunder and lightning began to crash around us, the chatter in the cabin was replaced by an uncomfortable silence.

The previous day, when I had passed through our office, my boss had told me about a recent experience she had had on a flight. The pilot had announced that there was a technical fault and that he would have to dive to sea level in a steep descent. The oxygen masks had come tumbling out and they were told to fold their arms and keep their heads down.

'I drank my whisky,' she had replied, when I asked her how she had reacted. 'If it's time to go, I reckoned, I might as well get sozzled.'

My own response was much less sanguine. The stewardesses were firmly strapped into their seats. The passengers were ashen-faced. When I glanced at the woman beside me, her terrified expression and white knuckles grasping the armrests, I had to close my eyes. I vowed to myself that if we were to get out of this alive I would be content never to uproot myself ever again.

As we made another attempt to land, the pilot assuring us that everything was under control, my neighbour asked if she could hold my hand. 'Sure,' I replied, 'no problem,' although I noticed that her daughter looked somewhat shocked when we did so.

This attempt to touch down didn't work either and as we began to climb to escape the weather the pilot announced that he had given up on Gibraltar and we would proceed to Casablanca instead. The passengers for the former location would be provided with a return flight the following day. There was loud cheering around us and quite a few animated conversations as to why we had tried to land in the middle of a storm in the first place.

'You can stop holding hands now,' the ten-year-old said when the plane began to level out, adding to her mother that she was reporting her to 'Daddy' as soon as they arrived.

'I couldn't care less what you tell him,' the woman replied, giving me a grateful smile and thanking me for having helped her through the ordeal.

Casablanca, I had been told, was nothing like the romantic backdrop conjured up by the film of the same name. It was a vast, sprawling urban area of around five million people, one of the fastest growing cities on the continent.

It was dark by the time we arrived but, unlike other African locations I had flown into, the lights of its suburbs seemed to go on and on until we finally touched down at the airport. We were relieved to get out of the aeroplane after such a nerve-wracking flight but the heat, even at this hour of the evening, was a shock. I had arrived in the summer months at the height of the Sirocco, a wind that blows from the Sahara conveying the dry, dusty heat of the interior.

Mohammed V airport, named after the current king's father, was large, spacious and modern. The officials were polite but firm, asking me why I had come to Morocco, where I would be staying, and how long I planned to remain. Most of the signs were in Arabic but they addressed me in French and, though it was several years since I had spoken the language when teaching in Algeria, the words came back readily enough.

As I stood in the queue to pass through Immigration I noticed the large photographs of the current ruler displayed on the walls. In many of them King Hassan was dressed in national attire, a long white gown with a traditional Moroccan fez perched on his head. In others he wore a military uniform, an impressive row of medals pinned to his chest. Although the face was unfamiliar, there was a scowl I had seen before, a kind of surliness in his expression that seemed to characterize all the other heads of state whose photographs I had seen in public buildings all over Africa. It was a reminder, to anyone who might have forgotten, of who was in charge.

From my reading I knew that the current king belonged to one of North Africa's oldest dynasties. The Alouites claimed a line of descent to the prophet Mohammed through his daughter Fatima. Their descendants had set up a family empire in the seventeenth century in what was then called the Maghreb, the western limits of Islamic expansion that had included current day Morocco, Algeria and southern Spain.

Being able to trace their descent all the way back to the founder of Islam conferred on the Alouites considerable prestige. It was the same in other North African countries. In the town where I had taught in Sudan, the most respected member of the community claimed the same pedigree. I could still remember the degree of deference that accompanied his presence: the handshakes, the *Salaams*, the bowing and scraping that prevailed whenever he appeared in public.

Popular belief had it that such a lineage conferred on those families who could claim it the power of 'Baraka', an ability to bestow blessings and good fortune on those chosen. Orthodox Muslim scholars challenged this as superstitious and claimed that it had nothing to do with the teachings outlined in the Koran. But despite the controversy, the perception that some individuals possessed special

11

powers was a predominant belief in the part of Sudan where I had lived. Apparently it was common in most parts of Morocco too.

Apart from their religious credentials the modern-day Alouites had other claims to popular loyalty. For a period during the French occupation of the country, they had been deposed, both the current King and his father sent into exile to Corsica, coincidentally Napoleon's birthplace. For the French this had been a blunder. Elevated into champions of freedom and independence from colonial rule, there were riots and demonstrations all over the country demanding their release. Faced with a major insurrection the French caved in. The monarchy was restored and Hassan and Mohamed were released in 1956, their reputations enhanced and a huge fund of popular support available to be cashed in when they needed it.

However, more contemporary Moroccan history seemed to imply that a large part of that good will had now been exhausted. Hassan had taken over from his much loved father in 1962. Modernity, urbanization, the development of mass media and exposure to political ideas from abroad had led to a public clamour, particularly in the cities, for more participative democracy. Worried about his position and determined that the monarchy not be relegated to a merely ceremonial function, King Hassan resisted change, claiming that parliamentary democracy was a foreign idea which would undermine the religious and cultural identity of the country.

Though political parties were tolerated, their leaders were frequently imprisoned, exiled or, if they overstepped the limits by too wide a margin, made to disappear. A wide network of spies and informers kept the population fearful and secretive. 'Be careful what you say,' was the advice of my boss. 'We need to stick to our charitable objectives.' Anything that could be interpreted as interference in the political life of the country, she cautioned, could lead to our expulsion.

Once through Immigration, I was to collect my bags and proceed to the Arrivals hall where someone would be waiting to pick me up. I had been surprised by the orderly queues, the men and women in neat uniforms, the modern-day atmosphere of an airport that was efficient, organized and different from all the other airports I had flown into on the same continent. That perception was short-lived as a moment later I was back in the familiar chaos of public locations in Africa.

There was a press of people waiting for their relatives. Foreign currency dealers rushed forward offering the best rates on the market. Taxi drivers thrust themselves in front of me to insist that they had the most conformable vehicle in the country. 'La, shukran,' I said, no thank you, remembering some of my stock phrases from Sudan. This only resulted in a rapid stream of Arabic I could not understand. 'Merci non,' I attempted instead, which brought a torrent of incomprehensible local French.

Though confused as to how I was to find whoever had been sent to meet me, I was partly relieved by the anonymity that the crowd conferred. Back in the orderly queues of 'Immigration' and 'Baggage Reclaim' the young girl whose mother had been sitting beside me seemed to be glaring in my direction. She had been arguing with her mother ever since we had disembarked. Was it about our holding hands? Suppose her father took the same dim view?

I imagined a scene in the Arrivals hall where in front of everyone I was accused by an irate spouse of inappropriate behaviour. This was not the way I had envisaged my introduction to the country nor to the staff I would have to work with. Thankfully, mother and daughter had disappeared in the throng. To them, I hoped, I had become invisible too.

I was startled a moment later when I heard my name being called above the noise. 'Hey, Mr Chris, is that you?' someone was shouting. 'Don't move. Stay where you are. I'll be with you soon.'

For a few seconds there was the same press of people around me before a space opened up to reveal a young man with a broad smile waving a pair of crutches in front of him which he had used to push everyone aside. When he reached me he kissed me on both cheeks, warmly shook my hand and presented himself as Youssef, the manager of our office in Rabat. 'And this is Mohamed, our driver,' he added, introducing a burly, no-nonsense-looking gentleman who repeated the same greetings before picking up my bags.

'That's a smart move,' I said, pointing to the crutches Youssef was now leaning on. There was no obvious sign of disability and the deft way he had used them to steer a course in my direction indicated a ploy to negotiate Moroccan crowds. 'The next time I come to the airport I'll bring some with me too,' I joked, as the two of them continued to welcome me and offer commiserations when I told them about my nerve-wracking flight.

'So, how did you find me?' I asked, curious as to how I had been identified. It turned out that a photo had been sent the previous week. Youssef waved a page in front of me with my image printed upon it. 'We showed it to some of the other passengers, and would you believe it, someone identified you and told us you were here? Look, there they are. Over there.' He pointed to the woman and the young girl I had been anxious to avoid. To my dismay they were not alone either and I guessed that the large man standing beside them was none other than the father. But when he and his wife waved in my direction I guessed that either nothing had been said or that an adequate explanation had been given of our hand-holding. Somewhat sheepishly, I returned their wave.

The greetings over it was now time to go and I signalled to Youssef to lead the way with his crutches. But as he launched himself forward in the direction of the exit, people moving aside when he bumped into them, I could see to my embarrassment that he was indeed disabled, his legs dragging on the floor behind him.

'I'm so sorry. I didn't realise,' I managed to stutter. 'I thought you were pretending.'

He brushed aside my apology indicating that he had taken no offence. It was only recently, he added, that he had lost the use of his lower limbs after contracting a form of arthritis. 'There is no reason why I shouldn't take advantage,' he grinned. We exited the airport at a brisk pace.

Although Casablanca was by far the largest city in Morocco, Rabat was the administrative capital where embassies, Government Ministries and agency headquarters were located. A couple of hours' drive away, it was where we had our principal office too and where I would be residing for the next few years if everything worked out. Youssef informed me that I would be staying for a few evenings in a hotel until accommodation could be found. He had contacted an agent a few days previously and a selection of properties would be available for inspection.

'Will finding a place be difficult?' I asked, hoping that something could be located soon so I could settle in and concentrate on my work.

He shrugged his shoulders. 'Inshallah, we'll find something by next week.'

I had not spoken Arabic for over ten years but I could still recall the phrases I had regularly used: 'no thanks', 'can you please leave me alone' and 'that is more expensive than the price I have just been offered.' But 'Inshallah' was the most familiar. It prefaced any pronouncements about the future whether later today, tomorrow, next week or the next century. It was an acknowledgement made by all Muslims that nothing would take place without the will of God.

But over and above its religious significance it also served to absolve the person who spoke it of any responsibility for making things happen. I had grown tired of hearing 'Bukra Inshallah' among officials in Sudan when I had been asked to return yet again for a missing document, a misplaced ticket or my salary that never seemed to come on time. Translated as 'tomorrow, by the will of God' it really meant, 'Don't blame me if it is still not here when you come again.' Hearing the phrase used by Youssef brought back a flood of memories, including previous frustrations. Would I have to regain the same equanimity I had acquired in Sudan, the acceptance of inevitable delays and empty promises that was one of the requirements for keeping sane?

Mohammed may well have been an excellent driver by local standards but as he joined his countrymen in weaving in and out of the traffic

17

on the road to Rabat I wondered what was more stressful: attempting to land in a storm in Gibraltar or driving in Morocco. At times the traffic surged forward, then it would grind to a halt for no obvious reason. Mohamed would wind down his window, utter a few curses to whomever was listening, before propelling our vehicle into any of the narrowest of spaces. The distance between us and our neighbours could be measured in inches rather than the obligatory few metres back home. The majority of cars that passed us or that we left behind featured, like badges of honour, the bumps, scratches and dents of previous battles.

Youssef's commentary didn't help. 'Morocco has the highest rate of traffic accidents in North Africa, which probably makes it the worst place in the world to drive. Before every journey I hug my wife and child and pray that I will see them again.'

When Mohammed attempted to overtake another vehicle on a bend in the road with no way of knowing whether there was oncoming traffic Youssef jokingly referred to this manoeuvre as the 'trust in God technique,' clearly a popular practice, judging by the number of times I saw it used.

'Can't he just wait to see if the road ahead is clear?' I asked hopefully. 'I really don't mind arriving late.' But that remark was greeted with an expression that said there was no point in trying to challenge such deeply ingrained behaviour.

Khartoum had been the noisiest city I had ever experienced in terms of traffic. There was no minute that passed without the blare of car horns and the shouts of remonstrating drivers. But Morocco was a close second. Even when we were stuck on the road and going nowhere Mohammed would press the horn. To me it sounded angry and aggressive but when I said so to Youssef, he disputed my judgement.

'I know in your country you sound the horn when you are about to have an accident. But here there are lots of different messages that are being conveyed such as "please proceed", "may I go in front of you?", "out of my way" or "are you as bored as I am sitting in this queue going nowhere?" Cars in Morocco speak to each other,' he claimed, adding that over and above French and Arabic this was a third language I needed to learn if I intended to drive.

Although it was late by the time we arrived in Rabat I was in no mood to retire and go to sleep. Between the flight and the drive my nerves were frayed and I wanted a restful and more auspicious conclusion to my first day in Morocco. 'Can we go somewhere?' I suggested to Youssef as he accompanied me to the hotel reception. 'But let's walk if we can. I've had enough of anything that flies or moves on wheels.'

The hotel was near the Medina, the old quarter of the city, where cars and bicycles were not permitted and where the only transport allowed seemed to be donkeys. Every second shop had

19

tables and chairs in front where scores of patrons drank tea and coffee and smoked oriental pipes called 'Sheeshas' which tinged the air with perfumed smoke.

As we headed to Youssef's favourite café there was something familiar in the slow, ambulatory pace of the people around us, the effusive greetings that were taking place among the passers-by, the fact that no one seemed in any rush to conclude their business. The markets of Sudan and Algeria were similar. They were not only the commercial hubs of towns and cities but meeting places for people to hang out and socialize, to relax with others and to spend time staring at everyone else doing exactly the same thing.

Youssef also confirmed that buying and selling in Morocco, as in other parts of the region, was not simply a financial transaction. I would have to learn how to negotiate and haggle even if I didn't feel like it.

'Don't be surprised if the person you want to buy something from wants to argue over the price. Really it's an invitation to have a conversation, to prolong the interaction beyond handing over a few coins. Don't accept the first thing he says either, even if you're happy with the price. That's like telling someone you don't want to talk to them.'

At the spice section of the Medina the smells of coriander, cumin, paprika, turmeric, ginger and cardamoms, displayed along an entire street in large, open piles, evoked strong memories of the many other markets I had visited in North Africa. All I had to do was close my eyes and breathe the air to return to Dongola, El Geneina, Khartoum and El Golea.

'Where I come from,' I said to Youssef, 'you buy spices because they are on your shopping list. Here, you buy them because you can't avoid them.'

The café where Youssef spent much of his spare time was at the other end of the market, a walk he seemed to have no problem in undertaking. We were headed to a place called the Oudiyah and he explained that this was the original fort around which the city had later developed. It dated back to the twelfth century when one of the most famous rulers of the country, Sultan Moulay Ismail, decided to establish a trading settlement on the Atlantic coast. The fort he had constructed had been transformed into a residential quarter of narrow, winding streets and apartments set into the original walls. Quaint and picturesque, it had become fashionable to live in and when I asked if I might be able to find something here Youssef shook his head and said that the asking prices were considerably beyond what even a country director working for an international agency could afford.

A few minutes later we sat down at a table on a terrace that offered a spectacular view of old Rabat. The sea pounded somewhere below us, and along the coast a few miles away was the port of Sallee, on the other side of the Bou Regreg River that separated the two communities. Sallee I had heard of before. It was one of the ports used by the infamous Moroccan corsairs, pirates who had plundered the coastal settlements of southern Europe for several centuries during the height of the conflict between Muslims and Christians. It had also been the port that Robinson Crusoe had mentioned in his memoirs, where he had been captured and kept as a slave for several years before making his escape to embark on the rest of his adventures.

Although the two communities were only a few miles apart Youssef claimed that they might as well have belonged to two different countries. Sallee was a strongly religious, conservative community where traditionally outsiders were not welcome. Rabat, large parts of which had been built and administered by the French during the height of their occupation, was much more outward-looking and cosmopolitan.

'A few decades ago you could not have entered Sallee unless you were a Muslim. Even today people will stare at you with some hostility if they think you are a foreigner. Unlike the market we have just passed through, most of the women there are heavily veiled. The men have long, black beards and constantly count their prayer beads as they go about their business. Mohammed, our driver, comes from that side of the river. That probably explains why he trusts more in God than I do when he's driving.'

Obviously a regular, judging by the greetings of the other patrons and the fact that our waiter deposited a pot of tea and a *sheesha* in front of us without even asking for our order, Youssef was clearly at home. It was not hard to see why. The heat that had accompanied us ever since I had arrived had been dispersed by a cool breeze that blew off the Atlantic. The history of the buildings around us, the special view, the friendly locals who came up to shake my hand and the lingering smells of the spice market had indeed soothed my nerves, turning what had been a difficult and stressful day into something more relaxing.

As I sat back, sipping green tea with mint and lots of sugar, and puffing away on the traditional pipe, I reflected that the journey had not been the pleasant transition I had hoped for. I also thought with some apprehension of the frequent trips I would have to make on Moroccan roads to visit our projects in different parts of the country. Ever since my departure from Harare I had thought with pain of the family I had left and the home that was now thousands of miles away. Had I made the right choice? Was I foolish to have left all that behind?

These questions would clearly not be answered in my first day, week or even month. I would need much more time to be able to come to any conclusions about the decision I had made. But as Youssef raised his glass to welcome me to my new life in Morocco, along with trepidation at having abandoned what I was used to, there was a familiar sense of anticipation, an excitement about the future waiting to be discovered.

'I'm happy to be here,' I replied, raising my glass in response, and for the first time in several months I felt this might turn out to be true.

CHAPTER 2

KHEMISSET

Sudan had provided my first experience of Africa and so it was the one I remembered most: the anticipation on arrival, the apprehension too, the sights, sounds and smells of a country whose difference from my own had turned out to be even greater than what I had imagined. There were many things I recalled in later years that had made it seem 'exotic', but a few particularly stood out.

During my first excursion onto the streets of Khartoum, amid the press of people, the busy traffic, the sheer weight of a large city going about its business, I could remember the momentary pause when a long line of camels had suddenly appeared on the main street, seemingly oblivious to what was going on around them. The men on top, wrapped in their headscarves and indifferent to the gesticulations of the drivers who had had to let them pass, had clearly acquired the same aloofness as their animals.

I also vividly recalled on my first morning jerking awake at around five o'clock to the call to prayer emanating from a mosque on the other side of the road. It had lasted for several minutes and despite some irritation at the early hour I could appreciate the novelty.

'Come to prayer. Come to peace. Come to God,' a Sudanese friend later translated the Arabic for me. Every day of the three years I lived in that country I listened at the same hour to the same message and never grew tired of it.

So despite my fatigue after an exhausting journey, despite the expectations of a busy day ahead there was something familiar and reassuring when I was jolted from sleep on my first morning in Morocco, exactly as I had been in Sudan a decade earlier. Youssef had been almost apologetic the previous evening when he pointed out the numerous mosques on our way back to the hotel. Moroccans, he said, were a deeply religious people and there was no part of any village, town or city from which it was possible to escape the call to prayer first thing in the morning and last thing at night.

'Well, we don't have camels on the streets of Rabat,' he responded when I told him about my memories of Sudan. 'But being woken up before dawn is definitely something we can arrange for you.'

Peter was the outgoing country director, a tall Irishman who had been in Morocco for several years and whose fluency in numerous languages had been remarked on in London. Thankfully it was not something I was expected to emulate. I guessed from what Youssef had told me that he must be something of a Spartan in his habits. He had transformed a small back room in the office into his residence which he then had to vacate every day when the staff came to work. He was drinking tea with Youssef when I arrived and rose to shake my hand and welcome me to my new job.

Methodical and ordered, he provided me with a set of reports on our projects, a practical update on the country and extensive notes on the state of our finances which he recommended I become familiar with as soon as possible. There was a timetable too for the next few days marked out in detail. This included a meeting at one of the key Ministries later that morning, and an introduction to how business was generally conducted. 'Best for you to jump in at the deep end, I think. You'll need this too,' he added, handing me a tie. 'Moroccans like formality.'

Youssef had alerted me the previous evening to the compulsion his countrymen felt to negotiate, to spend hours haggling over the sale of an item even if they had little intention of buying it. A quaint, amusing custom if you had the time to indulge, I had not expected to encounter it in a Government establishment where Peter had spent many months trying to reach an agreement.

I had visited many Ministries in Africa: part of the role of being an aid worker involved numerous interactions with officials in the Ministries of

Health, Education, Social Welfare, Youth Employment, Sports and Culture, Immigration, and Foreign Affairs. Generally, the offices were sparse, formal places that encouraged quick, businesslike transactions. You were in and out in five minutes before the next delegation from another agency turned up to discuss their affairs.

The office we were ushered into later that morning was of a different character entirely. It had rich furnishings, deep sofas, piled carpets and chandeliers. There were paintings of old Morocco on the walls and one in particular stood out, an image of the Sultan holding court among a group of obsequious-looking ambassadors. The message was not lost. Here was a place where decisions were not made lightly, and where it was the prerogative of whoever presided to change their minds whenever it took their fancy.

The two officials who were waiting for us were polite and friendly. They welcomed me to their country, guided us to comfortable chairs and signalled to someone waiting at the door to bring tea and coffee. When we all sat down they were effusive in their appreciation of our organization, congratulating Peter for all his hard work during the past few years. They were also keen to conclude a deal on the matter under discussion, an agreement by the Government of Morocco to a package of aid we were proposing to deliver over the next few years.

'Does that mean we can sign the actual contract?'

Peter ventured, momentarily sounding more hopeful than before we entered.

There was a brief silence. 'Would you like some more tea?' one of them asked, refilling our glasses before we had a chance to decline or accept.

'There are a few more details we still need to clarify,' the other one said, encouraging us to help ourselves to the sweets that had also appeared on the table in front of us. 'The size of the budget for one thing. We think it is not enough.'

From Peter's expression I could see the effort he was making to maintain his self-control, to maintain the same calm and composed demeanour of the officials. I guessed that the message he now conveyed had been repeated on many other occasions: that funds were fixed, that the proposal had been written with their prior input many months ago, that it would be very difficult now to go back to the donor and ask for more money. Polite and smiling, nodding their heads as he spoke, I could see that they had already anticipated these words, that they had their counter-arguments ready, that this was a game where they were the professionals and we the amateurs. Thirty minutes later we exited their office no further forward than when we had entered.

Peter pulled off his tie in the car, his frustration evident. He would now have to consult our headquarters to see if we could increase the funds being offered. 'Welcome to your new job,' he remarked wryly.

Having been several years in Morocco, he was now planning to travel for a few months in Europe before choosing another post, and he was looking forward to not having to make any decisions apart from where his next stop should be on his holiday itinerary. 'There is much about this country I will miss but the inscrutability of the Moroccan character, the way that public officials behave like vendors selling you a carpet, are things I am happy to leave behind.'

The following morning Youssef picked me up at the hotel. With Peter stranded in the office to finalize the terms of the agreement we had tried to negotiate, he was unable to accompany us to Khemisset, the town where we had one of our biggest projects. My apprehension must have been apparent since Youssef informed me before I had a chance to speak that he had had words with our driver. 'Don't worry. I've asked him to be more careful. I can't guarantee the behaviour of other people on the road but at least it won't be us overtaking on corners.'

The two-hour journey to Khemisset took us away from the coast and towards the interior, through a dry, dusty landscape of open plains and occasional forest that reminded me of southern Italy and parts of Greece. There were olives that grew here too, and something I had not expected in a Muslim country: cork to insert in bottles of wine that they also produced for a limited local consumption.

When I asked him, Youssef claimed that agriculture had been neglected, that after independence when land had been seized from French farmers, a few wealthy Moroccans had benefited rather than the anticipated wider population. At the same time, the focus on industrialization, manufacturing and tourism had deprived agriculture of the investment it needed. Morocco's role as a former exporter of produce to the region and to southern Europe had declined. Now unable to feed itself, a large part of its annual budget went into importing the very foodstuffs it had previously exported.

'Although no one officially admits it, the only agricultural commodity we now excel in is cannabis,' he continued, adding that Morocco was now one of the world's principal exporters. I had heard about this before and had read that a large area of the country, in the same Rif Mountains that Abdel Krim had resolutely defended against the French, was given over to its production. The local population jealously guarded their rights to grow it. Since they had cultivated it for centuries and since little else could flourish on their impoverished soil, they saw no reason to stop doing so. I remarked to Youssef that, in a café in Amsterdam I had once visited, it was several varieties of Moroccan hashish that had dominated the menu.

Occasionally we passed through small towns and villages with names prefaced by terms like 'Sidi',

'Abu' and 'Ain' which indicated a predominant Arab history and identity. Youssef explained that the population of the country was divided between Arabs and Berbers. The latter were the indigenous inhabitants of Morocco and Algeria who had been pushed into the arid mountains and hostile deserts of both countries by the waves of Arab invaders who had arrived on the back of the Islamic expansion of the 8th and 9th centuries. The latter had populated the coastal areas and the more fertile plains, a division of the land that had become an obstacle to good relations between the two communities ever since, although Youssef pointed out that considerable intermarriage had taken place and that the line between both populations was frequently blurred.

One thing I noticed about these settlements was the unfinished, half-built quality to all of them. Most of the houses were only partially completed with vacant spaces for windows and doors and bits of concrete protruding from the roofs to indicate a section still not done.

'You have to remember that families are different here than where you come from,' Youssef explained when I wondered why. 'Here you will find many generations in one household. When people have money they invest in an extension to their property so that they can have enough space for new family members. In that sense no house is ever really finished. We just add onto it when resources become available.'

He added that unfinished property was also exempt from local taxes so even those who could afford to do so never bothered to finish them completely. This in turn left a shortage of municipal funds for communal services such as garbage collection, water distribution and provision of electricity. It resulted in a temporary, almost abandoned quality to parts of the towns we passed through and shabbiness in the public spaces that belonged to no one.

But I was cautioned not to make too quick a judgement based on outward appearances. 'You'll see a huge difference between what people have inside their homes and what you would expect from the outside. There's another reason for this too. Our religion cautions us not to display wealth in a way that will attract jealousy and ill feelings. So something that looks extremely modest on the outside might be a palace once you enter.'

With agriculture a limited option and with the high rates of unemployment that prevailed, I asked Youssef where people found the money to extend their homes, to furnish them to the standard he had described and to pay for the expensive satellite dishes that bristled from their walls. He replied that the area we were passing through was a significant exporter of migrant labour to southern Europe, and that the money to keep these communities functioning came through remittances from family members working abroad.

Official estimates indicated one million Moroccans

working overseas. But these were the ones who were legal. A further three million, Youssef claimed, were illegally resident in Spain, Portugal, France and Italy. As he related the hardships that these people faced – the hazardous journey by boat across the Straits of Gibraltar, the intimidation by the police if they were caught without documents, the discrimination that they encountered and the harsh working conditions in sweatshops in Paris and Madrid – I was reminded of a similar situation in parts of Zimbabwe where I had encountered communities that almost entirely comprised women, children and old men. The men of working age had gone to the mines and commercial farms of South Africa. The meagre amounts of money they sent home to their families seemed inadequate compensation for the difficulties they faced.

Youssef shrugged in the same way people in Zimbabwe had done when I had asked them whether the sacrifices involved in migration were worth it. 'If it's the only way to support your family, to earn enough money to be able to marry, to afford further studies, to buy a car, then there really isn't an alternative, is there?'

Although Khemisset had its fair share of houses and buildings still in various stages of construction, it was bigger than the other settlements we had passed through and had more of an established permanency about it. It was one of the principal centres for the manufacture of Moroccan 'killims', brightly coloured carpets common to most households and much in demand among tourists too. Along the main street the reds, purples, blues and yellows of the products on display gave the town an almost festive presence, a feature complemented by the same proliferation of coffee shops and 'Sheesha' dens I had seen in the Medina of Rabat.

Cathy was from London, had a thick Cockney accent and, as I was to discover on numerous occasions, had no problem speaking her mind. She was sitting in our office in Khemisset when I arrived, sipping tea with the staff, eating croissants and, judging by the levity, keeping everyone amused. 'Don't stand up,' she said when I entered, 'he's only the new country director.'

I was unsure of the etiquette in terms of greetings between men and women in Morocco, aware that in some Muslim countries it was bad practice for the former to proffer a hand. But as I walked around the room nodding stiffly to the female staff in front of me, I could sense some surprise and confusion. Cathy, who was doing the introductions, whispered to me to lighten up. 'You read the wrong guidebook for this country,' she said, when I told her why I was being so formal. 'It's only the king who doesn't shake hands with anyone.'

Najia was the manager of our programme in Khemisset. Like Cathy she had a self-confident, informal manner that put everyone at ease. She had worked for the organization for an impressive twenty years and remarked that she had lost count of the country directors she had encountered. 'I'm sure I'll get through several more by the time I finish,' she joked, a remark which further lightened the atmosphere, dispelling the nervousness over meeting the new boss.

Back in London I had received a briefing on our work but I was keen to know more, to find out what had taken place in the past that had determined our current priorities. As we sat together after the introductions and a tour of the premises were over, I asked Najia and Cathy to share with me our history. How had we started? What had brought us to the country in the first place?

Although I was aware that Morocco experienced earthquakes I had not realised that on occasion these were major events, causing levels of destruction that I had not associated with North Africa. Some thirty years previously one had struck the town of Agadir in the far south. A third of the population numbering around twenty thousand had perished in the first few minutes. The rest had relocated to makeshift camps where cholera and other diseases, lack of food and inadequate water had threatened to raise the death toll even further. Our organization had responded with a relief programme and had later constructed an orphanage.

This disaster had closely followed on the heels of another. 'We had thought that we had been punished enough, that our troubles were over,' Najia added, 'but it seemed that God had other plans.'

A few months previously hundreds of people in the central part of Morocco had suddenly become paralysed. Overnight, men, women and children lost the use of their arms and legs. They could not move or speak. The centre of the outbreak was in two of the country's oldest cities, Fez and Meknes, both of them a few hours' drive north-east of Khemisset. I was shocked to hear that the epidemic at its peak had affected over ten thousand people. It was only a few months later, after an internationally assisted investigation, that the source had been identified.

Some merchants had purchased engine oil from an American military base near Casablanca. They had mixed some of this with edible cooking oil in order to increase their profits and then sold it in the markets of the two cities. Contaminants in the oil, which had been used to flush out the engines of military jets, had affected the nervous system of those who had consumed it.

In the aftermath of the disaster and the investigation that had followed, the merchants involved were sentenced to death. This was later commuted to lengthy prison sentences, an act of clemency by the King that had not been popular. Although a percentage of the ten thousand victims eventually recovered, a significant number had never regained the full use of their limbs. They had become permanently disabled and it was in response to their needs that our organization had established a more long-term presence.

'At that time it was standard practice for agencies like ours to construct orphanages and other facilities,' Cathy continued. 'In fact our original programme in Khemisset involved the establishment of a multi-million-pound residential centre for disabled children who came from all corners of the country. For years it was one of our biggest projects worldwide and the King himself visited several times.'

But good intentions and lots of money were not a substitute for adequate foresight. The Khemisset centre and the other establishments we had helped to support were unsustainable. Removed from the financial realities of what the Moroccan state could afford, they had been dependent on foreign funds. When those began to dry up, the question arose as to what would happen to the children.

'They had nowhere to go. The Khemisset centre, for example, had become their home and family. Having lost all contact with where they came from, what were they supposed to do?'

Najia concurred and went on to say that removing disabled children from their families and communities contributed to another difficulty. 'If you ask a disabled person what their biggest obstacle is they will often tell you that it is not their impairment. It is the prejudice they face from the people around them, the fact that they are excluded from normal life. So if you establish a residential facility you can end up depriving the community of an opportunity to realize that disabled people are no different. In fact, you only serve to reinforce the perception that they should be kept apart.'

As a result of this lesson the team in Khemisset had designed a different approach. They now promoted a programme where families were encouraged to care for children with disabilities within their home environments. Neighbours and local volunteers were trained to provide additional support. Schools were encouraged to assimilate disabled children whenever possible.

Had our previous programme, therefore, been a mistake? Both Cathy and Najia were cautious about making that judgement. The residential model of care was what had been deemed appropriate at the time. The centre had had its success stories too. Some of the children who had passed through it had acquired the skills, confidence and opportunities to lead productive lives, achieving positions of influence in Moroccan society. That had helped to confront prejudice too.

'There is no such thing as a perfect project,' Cathy concluded. 'In ten years' time someone looking back at what we are doing today will point out how it could have been improved. If development work were so simple, we wouldn't still be debating how best to do it.'

It was time for my first visit outside our offices and, as Najia described where we were headed and who we would be seeing, my nervousness increased. She had talked at length about the prejudice and discrimination that our programme was trying to dispel. People with disabilities needed to be treated as equals. That meant they were not to be perceived as victims, as objects of charity but as people with rights, aspirations and wishes as valid and important as anyone else's. Yet what about my own attitudes? Weren't they similar to those they were challenging?

A memory came back from many years ago, buried somewhere in the back of my mind in a file marked 'Things you would rather forget'. I had registered for student work at a centre for the disabled on the outskirts of the city where I was studying. At the end of my first day I had handed in my resignation and had barely avoided running out of the facility. It wasn't about the residents. There was no antagonism, hostility or unkindness. It was about me and the fact that I was unable to see beyond their disabilities to the human beings behind them. My feelings of shock, pity and gratitude that I was not like them were stronger than emotions that would have been more helpful. Now I wondered if my reaction, after twenty years, would be different. Maybe the very people that our organization was supporting would realise that its director had the same prejudice as so many others.

'I don't want to intrude,' I said, as we drove the short distance to the meeting. 'I understand if some families are sensitive to newcomers. If you think it's better for me not to attend, it's not a problem. I know the team is doing an excellent job.'

'How would you know that if you haven't seen the work we do?' Cathy replied with her characteristic bluntness. 'Besides, you're the country director. No one will think you're intruding.'

The house we arrived at belonged to one of the wealthier families in town. They had a disabled daughter and, as we exited the car, Najia mentioned that it was interesting to see how a common issue had united people across the divisions of wealth, status and privilege that normally separated them. The mothers who attended these meetings came from all classes of society, their usual isolation from each other temporarily cast aside, united in facing the challenge of bringing up a disabled child.

There was a group of around forty mothers and children. Najia introduced me, explaining who I was and that I would be observing some activities so I could see the programme in action. The mothers nodded and smiled, but I felt awkward sitting in a corner wondering how I should behave. I buried myself in my notebook as the meeting commenced, pretending to jot down my observations.

Although the children had barely glanced at me

41

when I entered they became more curious as time progressed. One young girl crawled over to where I was sitting and fixed me in a curious stare, as if I were some strange creature that had suddenly appeared. She set up a noisy racket a few moments later, pointing in my direction so that everyone stopped what they were doing to look at me. Was I supposed to ignore her? Should I display some interest? In the end I did nothing, continuing to look awkward as my face turned red. Finally, the girl stood up, grabbed my notebook and pen and proceeded to scribble on the page I had been working on, a perfect imitation of what I had been doing. Everyone laughed as my new companion rolled around on the floor in a fit of giggles. As I grinned back as best I could I knew the ice had been broken.

'Well done,' Najia said when we left a short while later. 'They seemed to like you.'

I confessed I had been nervous and worried as to how I should behave, and related the story of my previous experience and my lack of perseverance in confronting a situation it had been easier to run away from.

She replied that the first step in confronting attitudes that were not helpful to those we were supporting was to acknowledge their presence in ourselves. She had been no different when she first started working with people with disabilities. She too had felt shock and pity and gratitude that God had not given her such afflictions.

'My family sometimes says to me, "Najia, how can you stand such work? How can you bear to see these children every day with all their pain and suffering?" I tell them how this work has inspired me and helped to make me a better person. I often feel that I have received more than I have given. That's what has kept me going for twenty years and I hope for twenty more, Inshallah.'

That evening we stayed in Khemisset. Our meetings had ended late and I said to Youssef that I was not prepared to endure another night-time journey when the traffic was more dangerous. The hotel we were to stay at seemed comfortable enough but the receptionist warned us that the plumbing was being repaired, hence no water in the showers. 'You can try the local Hamam,' he replied when I asked him where I could wash. 'Just ask someone on the street and they will point you the way.'

'Hamams' or communal bathhouses were famous in Morocco. There was a whole page in my guidebook devoted to the subject. Some of them dated back hundreds of years, established at a time when piped water in private houses was unheard of. It was even claimed that their original precursors in North Africa were the Roman baths that had been established in their colonies along the coast. In later years and in keeping with Islamic injunctions around cleanliness and purity before praying, many had been built near mosques. I had read that they catered for both men and women, but in conformity with the same religious tradition there were separate hours for attendance.

But the language in my guidebook was cautious too, something less than an enthusiastic endorsement. 'Hamams have no frills. They can be dark and poorly lit . . . Be careful where you step. Don't be surprised to find dead skin and clumps of hair floating on pools of water on the floor . . . For the curious and intrepid traveller they are a must. But bring your sense of humour with you.'

Somewhat apprehensive, but armed with a recommendation from Youssef, who claimed he had been going to his local Hamam for years and had suffered no ill effects, I ventured out of the hotel a short while later. After taking directions I found myself in front of a shabby building a few blocks away. A passer-by assured me that this was indeed the place I was looking for. He pointed to a sign in Arabic above the door and repeated the word 'Hamam' over and over to make sure I had understood. Remembering what I had been told about not judging a place by its exterior, I took a breath and stepped inside.

'Poorly lit' turned out to be accurate. Behind a desk I could make out a surly-looking attendant presiding over a pile of towels. He barely raised his eyes when I entered and shrugged his shoulders when I asked him how much it cost. After I handed him a few coins he gave me a towel, a bar of soap and something that looked like a wire brush for scouring pots and pans. Then from a large bucket beside him he extracted a substance that looked like mud and deposited some in a plastic bowl. From the motions he made around his head when I asked him what it was for I guessed that it must be a type of local shampoo. Thankfully it did not smell as bad as it looked. 'Ghassoul' he said when he handed it to me, the only word he uttered during our interaction.

Escorted to a room where I was to deposit my clothes, I was directed down another corridor at the end of which was the Hamam itself. The area I finally entered was as poorly lit as the rest of the place. As I inched forward, inspecting the floor in front of me for clumps of hair and dead skin, I could see some bodies lying around on flat, wooden benches. But any thoughts I had of asking someone for directions or guidance evaporated when I heard them snoring away. They were out for the count and I was on my own.

The water was abundant and the heat considerable. Standing under one of the showers I lathered myself as best I could with the soap. The black mud I ignored. The wire brush I also discarded deciding that it was too abrasive to be comfortable. Clean was good enough, I thought. No need to overdo it.

A short while later I was lying on one of the vacant wooden benches, allowing myself to drift off, when a large gentleman stopped in front of me and began a conversation I couldn't understand. When he saw the items I had deposited on the floor he went over to pick them up, continuing his voluble Arabic in a tone of some admonition. Had I taken his place? Had I offended the Hamam rules in some way?

I was about to offer an apology and explain as best I could that this was my first time in such a place, that I was not sure of the etiquette and procedures, when he grabbed the towel I had wrapped around myself and tossed it to one side. Pushed flat against the bench, I was too surprised to register any objection when he poured the entire contents of his bucket of water over me. This was too much, I thought to myself. No matter what I had done wrong this was excessive. But when he took the brush and began to scrub my back, arms and legs I knew that I was not being assaulted but cleaned. 'Just lie back and enjoy it,' I said to myself. 'You are having an authentic Moroccan experience.'

But 'enjoyable' was not the word I would have used to describe it. The brush was as rough as it looked and when he started on my face I felt that my skin was being scraped off. Every so often he would point with considerable enthusiasm to the dirt that was being washed away, a cue for him to scrub even harder. My feeble protestations that

I was now clean enough were ignored, as were my objections when the mud was lathered into my hair and rubbed in with the same vigour. Would there be permanent damage? Would I come out of this place the same as when I went in? By the time it was all finished, my skin on fire and red patches all over my body, I had already decided that my first experience of a Hamam would be my last.

Half an hour later I was back in the hotel contemplating my crimson face and the red bruises that had not gone away. When I joined Youssef and Cathy for dinner they asked me with some concern what had happened. 'Looks as if you had an argument with your razor.'

I described my encounter in the bathhouse and my confusion as to how something so painful and unpleasant could have become such a strong cultural tradition. But they were both adamant I would return.

'The first time is always the worst,' Cathy continued. 'I can remember running out of the place I went to and swearing that I would never repeat the experience. You mightn't think so now but tomorrow you'll wake up feeling refreshed and relaxed and cleaner than you have ever felt before. I bet you'll be a regular customer in no time.'

I insisted that I wouldn't. As I ate, occasionally glancing in the mirror opposite at my pink cheeks and pained expression, I said to myself that while one visit was adventurous, returning a second time would be foolish. 'No victim willingly goes back to their place of torture,' I said, as my companions speculated as to how long I would stick with that decision.

CHAPTER 3

BETWEEN THE DESERT
AND THE SEA

Harare had been the most spacious city I had lived in with numerous parks, houses with large gardens, wide streets and shopping malls where you did not have to push and shove to get where you were going. The countryside was vast and imposing, the few scattered villages and an occasional farm only reinforcing the impression that the inhabitants were temporary visitors. It was the land that endured. There were many places in Zimbabwe where you could be on your own and after a few months in Morocco I began to miss that occasional solitude, the opportunity to escape the clamour.

'But there is plenty of space in this country,' Youssef replied when I told him over coffee one evening that I was still searching for somewhere that was not crowded. We were sitting in our usual café in the Medina, where he came to relax and I to ask questions.

'Then where?' I asked, adding that I had spent a great deal of time looking for somewhere I would not be jostled, hassled to buy a carpet or a plastic camel, or petitioned for my address in Scotland so I could become someone's pen pal.

'It's in that direction,' he responded, pointing behind him. 'It's called the Sahara and that's where you'll find all the space you need.'

A thousand kilometres inland to the desert seemed a long way to travel to enjoy some tranquillity and so at weekends I would venture onto the roads and explore beyond the confines of the city to see what I could find. But it seemed that Youssef had been right; I would have to go much further afield. Although Casablanca was some one hundred kilometres south of Rabat they were joined by an unbroken line of settlements along the coast.

There was open space out to sea but even to find a place to sit and enjoy the prospect I had to push my way through boys fishing on rocks, families out for a stroll, stray dogs tracking my progress and vendors selling popcorn and cans of Pepsi. I fancied at times that those I bumped into during these weekend expeditions were on the same quest as I: to find somewhere they could look around, see no one and bask in the experience.

If I thought that Rabat was crowded, then Casablanca was nothing short of intimidating. On my first visit there I had asked the driver for a tour. As we drove around with Youssef enthusing about the grandiose buildings, the train station that stretched for several blocks, the famous cathedral at its centre, the large Suq that could have swallowed a small town, I realised that not all African cities were the conglomeration of disparate villages and isolated suburbs that I was familiar with. As we crawled through the traffic my overriding impression was that five million people had been packed into a space that should have held only a fraction of that number.

During our tour Youssef had pointed with pride to one of the city's most famous landmarks, the Hassan II Mosque that had been completed earlier that year after a decade of construction. It was reputed to have the tallest minaret in the world, one which aircraft had to navigate around.

I was astounded when he added that its prayer hall could accommodate twenty-five thousand people. Another eighty thousand could fit into the surrounding courtyard. But what could prompt one hundred and five thousand people to pray together, I wondered. Weren't small congregations encouraged? And what about praying on one's own? 'You'll just have to accept the fact that Moroccans prefer to be in large groups,' Youssef said as we walked around and as he continued to marvel at the volume of people that could be packed in.

Larbi was our representative in Casablanca, an affable man in his forties who, like Najia, had worked for our organization for many years. Having lived in the city all his life he was able to elaborate on its history. I was surprised to hear that less than a hundred years ago it had numbered only a few thousand inhabitants, and been little more than an isolated backwater predominantly settled by Spanish merchants. Prior to that the Portuguese had built a small fort and a refuelling station for their fleets travelling south along the coast. They had called their settlement 'Casa Blanca' or 'White House', a name that had stuck ever since.

Under the French occupancy at the start of the twentieth century and in keeping with their intention to have a deep-water port that could handle trade with the eastern seaboard of the United States, it had expanded rapidly. Larbi explained that the French had wilfully neglected many other parts of the country while favouring their new city, heavily investing in industry and infrastructure which had fuelled an influx from rural areas ever since.

Now it was the country's biggest metropolis by far and what was worrying was that its population continued to grow at a pace that far outstripped its ability to handle it. Larbi described the nightmare of travelling to work in the morning and returning home at night, a journey that in terms of distance was not much more than a few kilometres but could take several hours as hundreds of thousands of commuters clogged the arteries of the city.

Another consequence of overcrowding was that a significant percentage of Casablanca's inhabitants lived in informal settlements or slums, more romantically expressed in French by the term 'bidonville'. There were many of these and, from the window of Larbi's office, he pointed to one that we were going to visit where some of our beneficiaries resided.

'Is it safe?' I asked, as I looked out on a large expanse of tin roofs and dilapidated wooden constructions stretching for a considerable distance. I had seen informal settlements in Harare and Khartoum and I had been warned that once inside, I was fair game for thieves and touts and bored residents looking for entertainment. But Larbi assured me that I would be fine. The principal risk was getting lost inside the maze of streets where there were no defining landmarks.

Our entrance barely provoked a reaction among the people we had to squeeze past. Everyone seemed occupied: there were young girls with buckets on their heads collecting water from a broken standpipe; there were men repairing bicycles and hammering away at tin cans to transform them into something functional. Since cars could not penetrate the narrow spaces between the dwellings, goods were transported by handcart. Young boys ferried charcoal, fruit, vegetables, bits of metal and bags of rubbish, occasionally shouting a warning to let them pass or an announcement that their items were for sale.

There was an industry about the place that I had not expected. When Larbi explained that different parts of the settlement specialized in

53

different services: recycling, carpentry, repair of electrical goods, currency exchange, sale of clothes, I realised how self-contained and distinct it was from the rest of the city. There were attempts at orderliness too. The tin doors to the different dwellings had numbers painted on them and, as we reached a small crossroads where several paths intersected, there was a wooden sign indicating the suburb of 'Tangiers' in one direction and 'Marrakesh' in another.

A short while later our path was blocked by some donkeys being driven in the opposite direction. There was no space to press ourselves into and I presumed we would have to backtrack to let them pass. But Larbi knocked on the door of the nearest dwelling and when it was opened by a young boy he spoke a few words to see if we could step inside.

There was an old man in the room and after several greetings and an explanation as to why we were there he invited us to sit down, motioning to the boy to fetch us some tea. We declined the offer, thanking him for his hospitality, and indicated that once the donkeys had passed we needed to proceed.

The furnishings were meagre. All that separated this household from the next was a few centimetres of thin board. As we sat making polite conversation the sound of the people in the street outside echoed through the walls. Privacy was clearly a luxury that residents of this place could not afford.

There must be a skill required to living here, I said to Larbi after we exited, a spirit of neighbourliness, patience and communality to get through the hassles of sharing a confined space with so many others. I thought with some guilt too about my own search for peace and quiet. All I had to do was find a room in my ample apartment, close the doors and windows and enjoy all the isolation I needed.

Over the course of this visit and several others to different parts of Casablanca I had a chance to see the scale and magnitude of informal settlements in the city. Harare had slums but nothing on this scale. Khartoum when I had been there had shanty towns to accommodate war refugees and economic migrants from other parts of Sudan. But the authorities there had been careful to hide them from view, not wishing to offend middle class sensibilities or foreign visitors with a reminder of the poverty that afflicted many in the country.

Here it seemed different. On another occasion, sitting with Larbi in his vehicle after we had just visited another of our project locations, I asked him why Casablanca's 'bidonvilles' were frequently no more than a stone's throw from some richer suburb, where large houses, wide streets, spacious parks and malls offered a disturbing contrast.

'Because they need each other,' he replied. The residents of informal settlements provided the cheap labour that the wealthier parts of the city required to function. It was they who swept the streets, fixed the plumbing, tended the gardens and cleaned the houses of the better off. The fact that they weren't expelled to some distant location where their poverty was not so evident was due to the fact that the city's ailing transport network could not shunt them back and forth with any efficiency to where their employment was needed.

On several occasions when public clamour and political expediency demanded it, slum areas were flattened and their populations expelled. Housing had even been constructed on the outskirts of the city to provide alternatives. But invariably the same evicted population would return to where work or other economic opportunities were closer at hand. 'After a few years the areas that were demolished are back to what they were. The rich need the poor to clean up after them. They complain of course. They say that slum dwellers are thieves, criminals and are not to be trusted. But they are the first to call for them to return when they have been evicted, since they can't do without them when they leave.'

It was on another weekend jaunt, this time north of Rabat, that I finally found what I was looking for. Half an hour outside the city towards the town of Kenitra I came across a barely visible sign on the road with a picture of sand dunes and waves painted upon it. The beaches I had visited to date were always packed with people so I was not expecting anything different at the end of the track I turned onto. But a few minutes later I was parked in front of the ocean with a large expanse of sand stretching to the horizon and apart from a few isolated boats out to sea there was no one else in sight.

'Maybe there is something wrong with this place,' I speculated as I took my first walk in the country with no one around to disturb me. But despite my looking for them there were no signs I could see that marked this out as a prohibited area. Perhaps the distance from the city combined with the relatively cold weather, warm enough for me but winter for Moroccans, accounted for the fact that the location was deserted. As I progressed further with nothing but the sounds of the waves crashing against the shore, a few curious seagulls flying overhead and miles of empty space in either direction, I reckoned that I had found my refuge, that the noise and bustle of the city would now become a lot more tolerable because I had an alternative to escape to.

I came back the following weekend and then the weekends after that. Occasionally there would be another vehicle in the space where I parked but the beach was always big enough to make sure that I never bumped into another visitor. Having warned me about being on my own, I decided not to tell Youssef about the location I had found. 'There are reasons why some places are empty of people,' he had said, 'and none of them are good ones.' I had dismissed his remark at the time as a well intentioned but excessive concern for my welfare and further proof, if it were needed, that Moroccans were only comfortable in each other's company.

The fishermen I had seen on that first day generally kept out to sea but as I became a regular they would occasionally wave in my direction if they were close enough inshore to spot me. It was only after several months that I actually encountered one of them in person. He was an old man with a weathered face and watery eyes and when our paths intersected he stopped in front of me, uttered a 'good morning' in Arabic and asked if I could spare him a cigarette. When I indicated that I didn't smoke he grinned and shrugged his shoulders, to signal that it was more in hope than expectation that he had asked. Whatever livelihood he derived from fishing, I thought, must have been meagre judging by his patched-up clothes, lack of footwear and the flimsy-looking rod slung across his shoulder.

Having completed the obligatory greetings, I was about to pass and proceed with my walk when he signalled me to stop. He wanted to show me something. From a bag he was carrying he produced an enormous fish, laying it out with considerable pride on the ground in front of me. Then he pointed out to sea to make sure I knew where he had just caught it. I inspected it with admiration, wondering at the same time how he was able to catch a fish of that size with such meagre equipment.

In tolerable French he then announced that it was mine for only one hundred dirhams. It was too big, he added, to carry all the way home. He pointed to the far end of the beach and uttered the name of what I presumed was his village. The fish, he continued, had exhausted him and he picked up his rod and gave me a demonstration of how he had barely managed to land it.

Compared to the price of the fish I purchased in Rabat I was being offered a bargain. But I remembered the recommendation in my guidebook about the importance of negotiation. 'Offer a quarter of what you are being asked for and expect to pay half. That way you will both be happy.' It was the same advice that Youssef had given me when I had first arrived. So congratulating myself on being so savvy I responded that his fish was not as big as the ones I could purchase in my local market. Then I prodded it dismissively with my foot and said that I was only prepared to pay a generous thirty-five dirhams.

There was a moment of silence, presumably as he worked out in his head the likelihood of fetching a higher price in his village weighed against the hassle of having to transport the fish home. But unlike the always composed, expressionless faces of the merchants I had dealt with to date when arguing over the price of something, he seemed upset, if not offended by my reaction.

Shaking his head, he pointed towards a black object a short distance away, a tyre that I presumed had been washed up on the sand like the other bits of waste I occasionally stumbled upon during my walks along the beach. He motioned me to follow him and as we approached it, he told me that this was what he used to ferry himself to deeper water where the fish were located. In this makeshift 'boat' with his legs dangling from a harness that had been fitted inside it, all there was between him and the bottom of the ocean when he ventured upon it was no more than a few centimetres of thin, flimsy rubber.

As some sizable waves crashed in front of us I realised how dangerous it was out there and how every time he took to the sea he was putting his life at risk. My refusal to offer him a decent price for what was no doubt a rare catch seemed miserly and mean-spirited and I felt embarrassed that I had assumed he was trying to cheat me. 'A hundred dirhams it is,' I announced when he began to put the fish back in the bag it had been wrapped in.

When I gave him the money he took my hand, placed it on his lips and announced that Allah would bless me for having helped him out that morning. He insisted too on coming back with me to the car, claiming that the fish was too big for me to carry on my own and that this was part of the deal we had agreed to. I watched him for some time after he said goodbye, walking towards his village with his rubber tyre trailing from a rope behind him. 'You need to get rid of that stupid guidebook,' I said to myself, resolving that any advice I received in future was there to be weighed up and considered rather than simply accepted without question.

'I hope you didn't get ripped off,' Youssef said the following day at the office, when I handed him a large slice of the fish I had purchased, since it was too much for me to consume on my own. He had told me on a previous occasion that if I wanted to visit the local market to buy anything I should contact him beforehand, since the sight of a foreigner on their own would double the price of whatever was being sold.

I didn't tell him about the circumstances of my purchase, not wanting to disclose where I disappeared to every weekend. Instead I thanked him for his concern but reassured him that he had no need to worry on my account, that this time the transaction had been a fair one. 'I paid what I had to. Buyer and seller are both happy.'

Until my encounter with the fisherman I had been quite possessive about the beach. While the reason I had not mentioned the location to Youssef was because I did not want him to worry about my safety, my motive for not disclosing what I had found to anyone else was that I did not want my private space to be invaded. Selfishly I reckoned that the secret once out could lead to a surge of unwelcome visitors. But in the weeks that followed that meeting I walked along the beach feeling more like a guest than a proprietor. By placing themselves at risk every day in the hazardous waters of the sea around that coast I realised that the fishermen had a much more substantial claim than I to any kind of ownership.

Although I never saw the old man again I often wondered about him: whether he had made another such catch as the one that had introduced us, whether he had traded his tyre for something more substantial, whether he had abandoned his dangerous occupation altogether. I had also decided that if any of his companions were to approach me with another fish for sale I would agree to whatever price they asked, a payment not only for whatever they might be selling but for their 'permission' to intrude into their territory.

A few weekends later, during another of my walks, I spotted two figures in the distance emerging from the dunes that sloped down to the sea along that part of the coast. I presumed that as on previous occasions they would have launched themselves into the water by the time I arrived at the place where they had been standing. But when they turned in my direction instead and began to walk towards me I thought that this time my luck might be in, that another opportunity would present itself for a mutually profitable transaction.

I did not pay much attention when a short distance away they split up, one moving to the edge of the water while the other cut a path slightly inland so that I was headed somewhere between them. But when I waved a hand in greeting and neither of them responded a warning bell began to ring. For the first time since I had been coming here I realised how isolated it was, how anything might happen and no one would be around to help me. Should I turn around and run away? Should I veer off in another direction? But as quickly as my concern arose I brushed it aside as an overreaction, an unfortunate echo of Youssef's warnings that bad things only happened to people when they were on their own.

They were young men in their early twenties I guessed when I found myself only a few metres away. They were not selling fish and did not look as if they had an intention to catch any either. Neither of them had a rod. There was no tyre dragging from a rope behind them. Both of them wore slightly shabby suits more appropriate for a city than a beach, I thought, and several sizes too big for them as if they had once belonged to someone else.

I greeted them in Arabic and when that elicited no response I tried again in French. But they remained impassive as if still figuring out what to say or do. One of them was smoking and I did not like the way he exchanged glances with the other, at the same time looking in front of and behind him as if to make sure that no one else was around. They must be strangers, I decided. If they were at all familiar with this place they wouldn't have bothered to check for other people.

When I moved to pass and the taller, thinner one blocked me I knew for certain that I was in trouble. Discarding his cigarette, he undid some buttons on his jacket, just enough to make sure that I could see the handle of a knife in his inside pocket. The other had circled round to cut off my retreat. No words were exchanged for a while as I stood in front of them, wondering what it was they wanted. I was carrying nothing. All I had was my beachwear: shorts, shoes and a T-shirt, nothing that was of any value.

For a moment I thought of running away but I was tired after my walk. I remembered the advice in my country director's handbook, a huge tome I had been asked to read before I started my job. There was a section dealing with thefts, robberies and hold-ups. 'Hand over what you have,' it said. 'No property is worth your life.' The other thing that dissuaded me was the thought that Moroccans were excellent runners. The young men looked fit. The long distance champion of the world at that very moment in time came from this country. So instead of bolting I put my hands in the air in a gesture of resignation, motioning them to take whatever of my possessions they fancied.

The one who seemed to be in charge pointed to my pockets, indicating that I should turn them out. I had nothing but a few dirhams, since my wallet was back in the car. I handed them over. Then he pointed to my watch which I removed and handed to him too. As he inspected it with his friend I could see that they were not impressed. It was a cheap affair that I had bought a few months previously at Heathrow Airport. I had a habit of losing my watches and so for the last few years I had never invested in anything of value. For a moment I felt embarrassed that I had nothing on me that was worth taking.

'What about your running shoes?' I thought to myself, as our stand-off continued. They were Nike trainers I had purchased in London before I had left for Morocco and they were still in reasonable condition. From the prices I had seen in Rabat market for that brand of footwear I knew they were a coveted possession so I pointed towards them, indicating that they were the most valuable thing I had on me that morning. When the one in front of me nodded his head and motioned me to take them off I prayed that they would be a decent fit. Thankfully our feet were the same size and as he trotted around while his friend whistled in admiration he seemed pleased. I knew then that the worst thing that could happen to me that morning would be an uncomfortable walk back to my car along the beach with no shoes.

After they had congratulated each other on finally having found something worth taking I was given a signal to go back in the direction from which I had come. They seemed almost apologetic when they waved me away. But I had only taken a few steps when I heard a shout behind me. I was being called back to where they were standing. Had they changed their minds? Was something worse about to happen? I raised my hands again in the air indicating that there was nothing left, that apart from my shorts and T-shirt they had taken everything I had.

But this was not the reason I had been summoned. The one I had given my Nikes to was pointing to my feet and then to the end of the beach where I still had to go, as if alerting me to a fact I already knew that across the pebble strewn sand it would not be a pleasant stroll. He then picked up the somewhat shabby sandals he had tossed aside when he had taken my shoes and in a gesture that was unequivocal indicated that they were mine if I wanted them.

I had made no gesture of defiance during the whole episode. I had not attempted to run away. I had handed over whatever coins I had in my possession and the watch on my wrist without any fuss. I had even given them my shoes without being asked. But this offer of his discarded footwear irked me almost more than the actual robbery. By accepting them I would be acknowledging that little more than an exchange of goods had taken place that morning, rather than a forced, intimidating seizure of my property. That would be taking docility too far.

Without uttering a word, I marched off as stoically as I could back in the direction I had come. I tried not to stumble on the hard stones or to show any discomfort. I could hear a few muttered comments behind me and something that sounded like laughter but I did not offer them the satisfaction of turning around. When I finally did so a considerable while later they had disappeared and my beach had once again returned to its former, isolated splendour.

'Maybe you'll listen to me in future,' Youssef said with some condescension the following day when he noticed my limping around the office and I told him what had happened. If the beach was empty of people it was for a good reason. Hadn't he warned me about being on my own? There was little point in reporting the matter to the authorities, he added. The robbers would have long since disappeared and in any case shoes and a cheap watch would hardly merit an investigation. The only thing the police would have told me would be a repetition of his own good advice, namely that visiting deserted places was foolish and was only asking for trouble.

Probably noticing that I was upset he told me that it could have been much worse, that I could have lost much more than a few paltry items. I replied that I couldn't care less about the meagre possessions that had been taken, that they were easily replaced. What had gone forever was my weekend refuge, the place I had found where I could be alone for a few hours to recharge my batteries and relax in a beautiful, isolated location. Now there was just the city and the noise and traffic and constant press of people and no moment where I could be on my own.

Adopting a less preacherly tone he placed a friendly hand on my shoulder. 'Look, we all appreciate some peace and quiet occasionally. You are not the only one who needs some space. So why don't you do what Moroccans do when they want to be by themselves?'

'What's that?' I asked with some scepticism, thinking he was about to advise me to travel to the Sahara, a weekend's journey just to get there.

'Take a deep breath. Close your eyes. Pretend that the people around you have disappeared and enjoy your privacy that way.' He assured me that with practice, noise and distraction could be made to disappear, that unwelcome interruptions could simply be ignored. More importantly, he added, was that it was perfectly safe, that I did not need physical isolation to be on my own. 'And when you open your eyes again,' he said in a tone of voice that left me wondering if he was poking fun, 'you will have all your possessions still with you, including your shoes.'

CHAPTER 4

THE RED CITY

The 'Marrakesh Express' was a train that linked Tangiers on the north-east coast of the country with Morocco's most southerly city on the fringes of the Sahara. It was also the name of a song I had listened to in my teens, although I had never been sure whether it referred to an actual train or a different kind of journey altogether. To experience the Marrakesh Express, one friend had claimed, you did not need to travel to North Africa at all but simply sit at home and be transported in a smoky haze.

Keen to avoid the hassles and dangers of road travel from Rabat to Marrakesh I decided to book a ticket. Expecting it to be late, as per most other schedules in the country, I arrived at the station only a few minutes before its intended departure. But there it was, smart and gleaming on the platform, and an announcement that any passengers should get on board immediately.

Unlike the words of the song there was nothing chaotic about it. An inspector entered the empty compartment where I was sitting, punched my ticket and wished me a pleasant journey. A vendor pushing a trolley sold me an excellent cup of coffee. Every so often over the speakers our next destination was announced. There was no evidence of the goats, chickens and dogs that I had expected. Moreover, unlike trains in my own part of the world, this one seemed to be on time.

'May I sit here?' another passenger asked shortly after we had departed, pointing to all the empty seats around me. Kurt, who came from Germany, took no offence, when after motioning him to take a place, I mentioned that I had been hoping for the company of some locals to tell me about all the places we would pass through.

Middle-aged, neat and precise, there was something of the teacher about him in the formal manner in which he spoke, the way he brushed his seat before he sat down, his justification for opening the window so that we would have some fresh air. 'Closed spaces are full of germs,' he said. 'Every half hour we will open the window for five minutes to keep the air fresh, no? That way there will be no sniffles tomorrow.'

But there was a concession to a different history too in his ponytail and the colourful T-shirt he was wearing, emblazoned with an image of Jimi Hendrix. As he had twenty-five years' experience of visiting Morocco behind him, I was keen to know about the changes he had noticed and what it was that continued to fascinate him about a country that he claimed to have adopted as a second home.

'I have to admit that I was something of a hippy in those days,' he replied, when I asked him how he had first discovered Morocco and what had prompted him to come. Easier to get to than India, hashish was just as available. The food was cheap, the hotels inexpensive. And of course it was in vogue to frequent the same hangout as rock stars, artists and writers who espoused the same irreverent, drug-induced lifestyle.

As for the Marrakesh Express, twenty-five years ago it had offered a very different experience. He had travelled third class, not only because that was all he could afford on his meagre budget but part of the hippy ethos at the time was to hang out with the locals. As he described the colourful company, the other passengers who had shared their food, the chickens that had rooted around the luggage and the spaced-out travellers from Europe, it all sounded a far cry from the neat, sanitized version we were now seated in.

Kurt was a civil servant back in Germany, so I was not surprised to hear that he did not miss the fact that in those days the train was always late, that frequently they would be stuck for hours in a remote siding waiting for some mechanical problem to be fixed. Although he still listened to the music that had influenced much of his youth and remained convinced that Jimi Hendrix, who had spent several months in Morocco composing some of his songs, was the greatest guitarist of all time, he added that there was something false and contrived in the way his generation had interacted with the country. Having become a favoured location for young drop-outs from Western society, Morocco had become what they wanted it to be, rather than what it really was.

'Few of us bothered to learn the local language. We knew nothing about its history. The places we visited were all chosen because of the availability of hashish and hotels where no one would bother us while we smoked it. Most of the writers who made Morocco famous perceived it through a haze of drugs and alcohol. It became a country of our imagination, which meant that we missed many of the other things it had to offer.'

'But why Morocco? Why not some other country that was warm and cheap?' I asked.

According to Kurt, what they were looking for was a society significantly different from their own, so that they could turn it into an exotic escape.

In that regard, he added, the hippies, though perhaps more benign in their judgement of the locals, were not that dissimilar from colonialists who had been blind to the reality of the places they occupied. Showing a real interest in the country and its people, taking time to understand them and their culture, was never part of their agenda. 'A friend of mine who used to come here a lot said that he treated this country with a mixture of reverence and disdain, emotions which prevented him from seeing what was there. I believe that was the same for most of us.'

Kurt went on to add that a few years after Morocco had acquired its dubious reputation the authorities became concerned about the image of their country its visitors were projecting. Increasingly dependent on trade with Europe and regarded as a key ally of the US in the Middle East, the Government was becoming sensitive to pressure around the liberal availability of drugs and their export to northern markets.

At the same time the country was keen to develop a tourism industry that brought cash into the economy. 'Maybe some wealthy rock stars had money to spend but the rest of us never had more than a few coins in our pockets for basic food, cheap hotels and inexpensive drugs. Some of the locals began to get hostile too, worried that we were corrupting their society with our loose morals and behaviour. I can remember one year arriving in Tangiers by boat with my rucksack, a small amount of money and my long hair. I was told to go home and only return when I looked more decent. That's when I knew that an era had ended.'

According to Kurt, many of his fellow travellers received similar notice and so, following in the footsteps of their icons, they travelled to Bali and Goa instead, in search of the same diversions that had prompted them to come to Morocco. For a number of years he had also kept away, too busy ridding himself of his drug habit, pursuing his studies and becoming respectable.

But something had prompted him to come back. 'I felt I had missed an opportunity. Here was this wonderful country I had visited so many times yet never really seen. Maybe by becoming more curious I wanted to make amends for all those wasted years.'

I asked if it was Marrakesh that kept bringing him back. As we got closer to the city I could see him become more animated, looking out of the window and pointing at the various landmarks that signalled our imminent arrival. Earlier he had described its startling red walls and houses, the backdrop of the Atlas Mountains rising behind it, the famous palaces, gardens and markets that dated back hundreds of years. It was the same enthusiastic endorsement I had heard from Cathy who claimed that it was her favourite location in the country, a place that was different from any she had visited in her extensive travels.

While Kurt was similarly appreciative of its historical attractions it was something else that explained his enthusiasm for returning so frequently. A few years previously he had befriended a Moroccan family in the city. As he had no family of his own back in Germany they had 'adopted' him and so it was something of a homecoming he experienced every year when he spent a month enjoying their friendship, company and hospitality.

'When I first came here the only time I interacted with Moroccans was when I wanted to buy something, usually to get a high. But a country never really opens up until you get to know its people. Monuments are interesting. Museums too. There are plenty in Marrakesh to keep you busy. You'll enjoy the sights, sounds and smells of a place that is unlike any other you've encountered before. But history and famous buildings can become a kind of addiction too,' he said, as we pulled into the station. 'It's other people who will cure you of that habit.'

Marrakesh was one of our principal programme locations. We had an office there, a small team of workers employed on a disability project and a house we rented to save on hotel bills when visitors like Cathy, Youssef and I came to stay. It was the end of summer when I arrived but Kurt had warned me that the days would still be unpleasant, and that evening was the time to explore the city and enjoy some relief from the forty-degree heat. To add to the discomfort was the sand and dust, clouds of it that at this time of year could leave visibility restricted to only a few metres and clog up car filters, air conditioning units and nostrils.

It was the last city before the Sahara and Kurt had explained that when it was built by the Almoravids they had not considered climate. Wealth in the eleventh century came across the desert in the form of gold, slaves and salt from further south and so a garrison town was needed to control the lucrative trade with the rest of Africa.

That meant it was directly in the path not only of the trans-Saharan caravans but of the Sirocco too, the dry wind I had first encountered stepping off the plane in Casablanca. When it blew it could last for several days at a time, leaving the city shrouded in a blanket of thick dust that kept everyone indoors until it had passed.

Its sand and heat notwithstanding, after a week in Marrakesh I began to understand something of its appeal. Although it was busy, noisy and full of the same congested traffic as Casablanca and Rabat it offered a more entertaining sideshow as a distraction.

There were several animal markets distributed within the city which meant that vehicles constantly competed with long lines of camels, donkey and goats vying for the same space. The Berber shepherds, easily identified by the colourful garments adorning the women and the traditional grey and brown hooded cloaks worn by the men, came from the nearby mountains. They blithely ignored the blaring horns and remonstrations of the drivers whenever they blocked the roads, as if they and their animals had more right than the more recent intruders.

Walking through the streets in the relative cool of the evenings I would bump into the city's considerable population of touts and beggars, but in Marrakesh they seemed to have a more extensive repertoire of pleas and entreaties than their counterparts elsewhere. The street children in particular would put on a show. They would stand in a group outside the restaurant where I ate most evenings, raising their hands to their mouths, mournfully rubbing their stomachs and pointing to my food before being chased away by the waiters. Whenever their appeals were rewarded, the incredible change in their expressions, the way that misery and imminent starvation were transformed into boisterous hilarity after receiving a few coins, invariably left me amused.

There were islands of respite too from the city's noise and bustling vitality. Perhaps to make up for its climatic disadvantages the sultans and their viziers had constructed extensive parks where irrigation watered large areas of palm trees and vibrant greenery, even permitting a few lakes and fountains. In the hours immediately before and after sunset these gardens were a favourite haunt of families and couples taking a stroll and, though many of them were surrounded by busy, crowded suburbs, they were extensive enough to permit one to imagine that the rest of the world was far away.

At the centre of Marrakesh was 'Jemma El Fna' square, a large, open space where impromptu cafés, open-air restaurants, conjurers, acrobats, snake charmers and other performers kept crowds of visitors fed and entertained. Although the exact meaning of its name was disputed, my guidebook claimed that 'Place of the Dead' was the most literal translation, although hardly congruous with the level of activity, noise and drama that took place there every evening.

Like its name the exact history of the square was disputed, but early records indicated that it was almost as old as the city itself. Indeed, it offered a real sense of stepping back in time as dancing monkeys, walking lizards and snakes coiled around the necks of their owners attracted the attention of the scores of people milling around.

The largest crowds were drawn by the storytellers and it was in their section of the square that people tended to linger. Although I could barely understand a word of what was being said it was clear that the raconteurs were skilled and practised in the art of delivery. There were oohs and aahs throughout the performance, silence when the story demanded it and applause for the actions of the hero when it was merited.

The storytellers were dressed in elaborate outfits too, some in blue and red velvet, all garishly attired to set them apart. Even when not performing they seemed separate and unique, as if they belonged to an exclusive and private guild whose membership conferred a certain aloofness and other-worldly quality to their demeanour. They never collected the offerings at the end of their performances. Young boys would walk around instead to gather the coins and notes extended towards them. The storytellers would relax in indifferent silence some distance away, as if financial reward was the least important part of what had transpired.

It was however commerce not entertainment that was at the heart of the city, the strongest link between its past and present. The square where people congregated for their evening recreation was surrounded on all sides by the famous Suq of Marrakesh, the city's principal market reputed to be the biggest in North Africa. My guidebook claimed that within its considerable territory you could purchase anything you wanted: from ancient antiquities to modern-day car parts, from every kind of food and beverage to carpets from distant Iran and Afghanistan.

Entering the Suq was an ordeal. There were hundreds of stalls arranged in different sections and outside each someone seemed to be employed full time to convince passers-by, especially foreigners, to come and look and purchase the best bargain in the city. Their persistence frequently strayed into a pushiness that was intimidating, worse if one displayed any interest whatsoever. Acceptance of an invitation to browse was always interpreted as an intention to buy. Whenever I put my hands up to signal that I was not interested in any of the shoes, slippers, scarves, carpets or books that had been laid out in front of me, offence was taken and the polite, friendly interaction turned into cajoling, haggling and irritation.

After several exploratory visits I had had enough, preferring the relative anonymity of Jemma el Fna to the chaos and hassle of the Suq. From the roof top cafés that offered a vantage point, I would sip my tea and observe other distraught foreigners emerge from some section of the market pursued by packs of persistent salesmen.

'Glad it's not me down there,' I said to Kurt one evening as we sat above the square watching the chaos. We had exchanged numbers and agreed to meet. He had brought a member of his adopted family with him, a young man called Ahmed, a teacher in one of the local schools who spoke excellent English.

Every Moroccan I had met sooner or later during our first conversation asked me about my impressions of their country and then the city, town or village they came from. So when Ahmed enquired, I enthused about what I had seen so far, in particular the vitality of Marrakesh, the sense of history and the people who were friendly and colourful. But when I observed that the main market, one of the city's most famous attractions, was not for the fainthearted and that it had exhausted my patience after only two encounters, he replied that it did not have to be like that. My experience, while typical of foreigners, was due to the fact that I had not yet learned how to properly negotiate. 'You are looking at things in the wrong manner.'

'What do you mean?' I asked, pointing out that all I had done was keep my eyes open. Even without signalling any interest in buying I had still been accosted.

Ahmed laughed. 'Your eyes can have a will of

their own. They don't just see. They can be attracted to something even without your noticing.' He added that the slightest flicker of interest, a signal that I had found something attractive, was exactly what the vendors were looking for, something they had been trained to identify. The moment they spotted it they turned into predators and I became a potential client rather than simply a passer-by.

I was still confused. 'So the only way I can walk around the market without being hassled is to keep my eyes closed? I'd end up bumping into everything.'

But Ahmed insisted there was a skill to be learned: just as a Moroccan needed help to understand the metro system in London or Paris, in the same way visitors needed help to negotiate the Suq. 'There is an ability to see without looking,' he added cryptically. 'This will allow you to register a range of goods without indicating any desire to purchase, even if it's exactly the thing you're looking for.'

Echoing what Youssef had told me, he added that if any salesman thought that a potential customer really wanted the item under discussion the price significantly increased. 'You have to pretend indifference and acquire an attitude that indicates that, if you were to walk away with nothing, it wouldn't bother you in the slightest, in fact you would prefer it. You have to make the salesman think you're doing him a favour.'

As I was still not convinced by his argument and wondering how it was possible to walk around not focused on anything, Ahmed offered to escort me around the market for an hour to show me what he was talking about. Kurt urged me to accept. He had had a similar lesson and claimed that it had helped him to enjoy a part of the city that he too had previously kept away from.

A short distance inside the Suq we came to a halt. 'What I want you to do,' said Ahmed, 'is to walk up that street in front of us as quickly as you can. Don't stop anywhere. Don't stare. Just behave as if your sole purpose is to get from one place to another without getting distracted. I'll be behind you. When we get to the end I want you to tell me everything you've seen.'

The list of items I had managed to register in those few minutes was meagre. I had noticed some jewellery stores with gold rings and necklaces, some stalls selling leather bags and shoes, and a few places with carpets and cushions. But Ahmed was able to remark on the different colours of the bags and shoes, had seen a wider variety of jewellery and added jackets, purses, wallets, slippers, silk scarves and *killims* from Khemisset. All of this was confirmed when we returned more slowly along the same route, but not at such a pedestrian pace as to attract the interest of the vendors.

Such a skill, which he claimed could be acquired after only a few more visits, meant that while I would see what I needed, no one else would pick up any sign of interest. That in turn meant I would largely be left alone, until of course I had decided on what I wanted.

On the subject of 'negotiation' he had advice too, this time not about coming away with the best bargain but about the pleasure of purchasing something through an engagement with the vendor. That was one of the real attractions of buying in the Suq, he said, as opposed to a store where items were labelled and sales were conducted with minimal interaction. Wasn't something appreciated all the more if one could recall the conversations around it, the arguments that had been traded about its value, and the satisfaction in believing that, through one's own powers of persuasion, eloquence and diplomacy, the price had been reduced?

'Don't worry about whether you might have paid more than someone else,' he added. 'If you're happy with the final price and if the vendor agrees then no one has lost face, no one has lost their dignity. In our culture that's what successful buying and selling is all about.'

Michael was an Irishman in his early thirties, and somewhat ungraciously my first thought when introduced to him was that here was someone who needed a good bath. He was dressed in a traditional *burnous*, a heavy woollen cloak worn by the locals that doubled up as a blanket or sleeping bag in cold weather. With a rucksack strapped to his shoulder and a somewhat fidgety, animated manner, he recalled for me the spaced-out travellers that Kurt had described. He was sitting with Cathy in our favourite café above Jemma El Fna square and, as I joined them, I thought to myself that I would have a discreet word with her later about the company she chose to hang out with.

But first impressions are either entirely accurate or entirely erroneous and after a short while in Michael's company I realised that I had been wide of the mark. He was a writer and anthropologist and for large parts of the past few years had been studying transhumance in the mountains behind Marrakesh. According to him, this area of North Africa was one of the few remaining parts of the world where this was still practised, where small groups of people roamed with their herds of sheep and goats between different grazing grounds as winter and summer transitioned into each other.

Like Kurt he had been adopted by a family. He spent several months of the year in their company, experiencing the same hardships and noting his observations on the dynamics within their household and between them and their wider clan. I was aware that nomadic communities were often mistrustful of outsiders and wary of anyone trying to penetrate their closed societies. Michael admitted that he had struggled at first, that acceptance had been slow and that he was constantly tested as to his endurance in keeping up with the family while they were on the move.

As if aware of my initial impression, he pointed to his utilitarian clothes and the somewhat grubby bag where he kept his belongings. 'Of course if I had turned up in a suit and tie I probably would have been told to get lost a long time ago. I have to confess though that at times I dream of clean clothes and a warm bath. Maybe I enjoy them all the more for having done without them for long periods of time.'

About to conclude his study, Michael had one final trip to make. He was headed back to a small town in the mountains where he had arranged to meet up with his family for their last journey together. As he described the curious children, the women who teased him and the brothers he had made friends with, I could sense that beyond the anthropological interest there was an emotional attachment too. 'Of course it's difficult not to become close when you spend so much time together and you face the same struggles. I don't know whether this feeling is reciprocated. Though they seem to be happy enough when we meet, their lifestyle doesn't permit much sentiment or emotional attachment. Generally these are luxuries they can't afford.'

'Why don't we give him a lift?' Cathy interjected when Michael mentioned his bus would depart the following morning. We had a few days' holiday and had already planned to cross over the Atlas mountains to the desert beyond. The market town that Michael needed to get to was only a small detour. I nodded my agreement, glad that we would have some more time with him. We arranged to meet the following day at his hotel, a place that Cathy later characterized as a place that was as utilitarian as his clothes.

From Marrakesh, the Atlas mountains, when visible, had looked like a pleasant backdrop, a range of hills occasionally topped with snow. But as we approached, they looked more and more formidable, a solid wall that rose in front of us, dividing the land. On one side were the vast agricultural plains that stretched to the coast, the more fertile parts of the country where Morocco's cities were located. On the other side were the beginnings of the desert, a sparsely-inhabited landscape of isolated communities sustained by the seasonal rivers and streams that flowed from the peaks behind them.

According to Michael, the Atlas Mountains were not just a geographical barrier. They marked the limits in Morocco of what its various kings and sultans had effectively controlled. 'For almost a thousand years there was an inner and outer Morocco. One part was called "Bled El Makhzen" or "Land of Taxes". The other part comprising the mountains and the beginnings of the Sahara on the other side was called "Bled Es Siba" or "Land without Laws." This area was presided over by independent chiefs who only paid homage to the king whenever it suited them.'

There was an interesting adjunct to this division of the country into one half that was supposedly enlightened and the other that was characterized as barbaric. Michael pointed out that nearly every dynasty that had ruled Morocco: the Almoravids, the Almohads, the Sassanids, the Hafsids and others who had been responsible for establishing its great towns and cities, had their origins in the same desert communities where the absence of civilized behaviour was thought to be most prevalent.

'Are you familiar with the writings of Ibn Khaldun?' he asked, as we continued on the road towards the mountains. I nodded but added that it was only a fleeting acquaintance with his philosophy, back at university in England. I was aware that he was a medieval Islamic historian who had travelled extensively in North Africa in the fourteenth century and part of his time had been spent in Morocco where he had reflected on the factors that caused the rise and fall of its numerous empires.

According to Michael, it was evidence of what had happened during the few years he had spent in Fez when one of the country's ruling dynasties had been overthrown, that prompted Ibn Khaldun's principal thesis that 'civilization' was inherently unstable. The ease of life that came from living in towns and cities, he had claimed, led to a corruption of morals. The rulers became more fixated on maintaining their extravagant lifestyles than ruling fairly, forgetting where their ancestors had come from only a few generations in the past. Meanwhile, their subjects fought and squabbled over wealth and privileges that were unequally shared, further weakening the coherence and stability of the state.

Renewal and regeneration only came from groups of people who were not subject to the same distractions. Ibn Khaldun had argued that because of their shared hardships in facing a harsh environment, the spirit of cohesion among desert and mountain dwellers was more advanced than that found among their counterparts in towns and cities. In Morocco that meant that it was the tribes of the Bled Es Siba who were responsible for the removal of old, tyrannical regimes which had lost the allegiance and support of the people they were supposed to protect.

Then the cycle would repeat itself. Once a new dynasty was founded, the seeds of its later destruction were inevitably sown. It had struck me when I had first read about it that Ibn Khaldun's philosophy presented a bleak characterization of human nature and society. But as Michael recounted the names of the various ruling families that had once presided over the country before they were overthrown, it was easier to understand where the historian's pessimism had come from and to sympathize with his argument that only change was permanent.

For the first few hours the road from Marrakesh had passed through areas of considerable greenery: fields planted with wheat, plantations of palm trees, estates where large machines irrigated rows and rows of vegetables. But as we began our ascent into the mountains the change in environment was dramatic. The palm trees changed to smaller outcrops of pine and conifer, the landscape became rockier and though agriculture was still present the fields looked as if they required much more work and attention to make them productive.

There was a shift in climate too. We had departed the city in T-shirts but as we climbed the steep, winding road towards the Tizi n'Tichka Pass we had donned sweaters, then jackets, then switched on the car heater. An hour further on and the road itself was carpeted in a thin layer of snow. It was not unheard of, Michael commented, for the Pass to be blocked altogether. The previous year he had waited for several weeks before he was able to find a lift back to Marrakesh, since winter storms had made much of the route impassable.

Like the weather and the vegetation, the villages here were unlike those we had driven through earlier. They were enclosed, fortress-like affairs with houses clustered together behind thick stone walls and only narrow openings between them for people and donkeys to squeeze through. There was a difference too in the way that the women appeared in public without the head scarves we had seen earlier and without the half-averted glances of their counterparts nearer to the city. Many were riding donkeys and at one section of road we had trailed behind a group for almost twenty minutes as they continued chatting among themselves, refusing to let us pass until they felt inclined to do so.

'Why are the children not at school?' I asked, as we encountered yet another group of them waving plastic bags of apples, pears and mulberries.

Michael explained that in Berber regions like this one many communities resented that the language of educational instruction was Arabic. 'Much of the time the children don't understand a word of what is being taught since many of the teachers come from outside the area. There is a move to introduce more subjects in the local language but progress is slow and until that happens a lot of children will simply stay away.'

Youssef had previously explained the division of the country into Arab and Berber regions and my guidebook had a few paragraphs to offer on that subject too. But since he had several years of traversing these mountains behind him and a detailed knowledge of Morocco's history, I asked Michael for his views on a community that seemed to have jealously guarded its cultural, linguistic and social independence. They seemed somewhat aggressive too, judging by the indignant shouts of the children when we passed by without stopping to purchase what they had on offer. They would wave their sticks as if we had no right to ignore them, our progress frequently accompanied by a clatter of small stones on the back of the car.

The history of the Berbers, Michael explained, was a matter of considerable conjecture, since early records that referred to them were written by outsiders. These documents were frequently characterized by hostility since they reflected the viewpoint of people who were trying to subjugate them, whether it was Greeks, Romans, Phoenicians, Arabs, Turks or Europeans. In fact, the term 'Berber' was a derogatory label deriving from the Latin word for 'Barbarian' and used to name the indigenous people of North Africa when the Romans had begun to invade their territory. 'Among themselves they prefer the term "Imazaghen". The translations vary but generally it means "free men" or "noble men".'

At one stage the Berbers occupied most of North Africa, from Morocco in the far west as far as the Nile in Egypt. They had communities too that penetrated much further south, well into the Sahara. Their language differed according to territory but, according to Michael, it had a common root that allowed them to more or less understand each other across national borders. Many governments had imposed restrictions on the use of Berber in an attempt to diffuse their sense of nationalism and their calls for greater autonomy. Arabic and

French had been imposed in schools and there were instances in the past when people had been arrested and fined for speaking their local language in public.

It was the wave of Arab invasions that commenced around the middle of the eighth century that proved the most defining moment in Berber history. Despite their initial resistance, they were increasingly pushed back from the fertile lowlands and coasts they had once inhabited, to the mountains and deserts that the newcomers showed little interest or aptitude in conquering. An uneasy accommodation had developed between the two groups over the following centuries, made easier by the conversion of the Berbers to the Islam that the Arabs had brought with them. In fact, it was often under the banner of that religion that they rose in revolt, a case of the ideology of the conquerors coming back to haunt them.

While much of the terrain that Berber communities were forced to inhabit was harsh and uncompromising, they occupied positions of key strategic importance. So while agriculture was less productive than on the lands they had vacated, raiding caravans or imposing taxes on merchants who wanted to pass through their territory to conduct trade across the Sahara provided substantial revenues. Some of the tribal chiefs who presided over a mountain pass or a desert oasis that the caravans were forced to use became fabulously wealthy as a result.

Irritated by their lost revenues the various Sultans of Morocco conducted punitive expeditions against these chiefs. But none of their military forays ever succeeded in reaching the ultimate objective of defeating them. At first sight of the Imperial army, the tribesmen would disappear into the remoter, more inaccessible parts of their territory. Their houses might be razed, women and children seized as slaves, but invariably after the soldiers disappeared the men would return to resume their previous, insolent disregard of central authority.

In keeping with the topic under discussion, Michael pointed out that we had now entered the lands of the Glaouis, one of the most influential Berber families in Morocco. We had crossed over the Tizi n'Tichka Pass and had entered a plateau with high peaks all around us; there was little but stones and rocks for scenery and occasionally an impoverished collection of houses that called itself a village. If this area had once been 'fabulously wealthy' then none of its former glory was evident.

A short distance beyond the Pass, Michael pointed to a sign marking a side road to 'The Kasbah of Telouet'. This was the ancestral home of the family he had referred to and, although it was in the opposite direction from where we were headed, it was well worth the one or two hours to get there, he claimed. Cathy, who had visited before, confirmed his opinion and, since we had no fixed timetable to adhere to, I welcomed the detour.

'So what would prompt anyone to establish their home here of all places?' I asked Michael sometime later, as the scenery around us showed little sign of altering from the stark, depressing landscape we had entered earlier. There was a tin mine somewhere along the road, he replied, and nearer to the Kasbah some agriculture had permitted the growth of more substantial villages. But the family castle at Telouet was primarily located where it was, not because of any nearby resources but because of its position. The valley we were in was one of only a few that penetrated the mountains and that meant that whoever controlled it could levy taxes and impose conditions on all who sought to pass through it.

Michael added that in this regard Telouet was no different from the scores of other Kasbahs dotted across the mountains. The Glaouis had been no more powerful or influential than the many other tribal leaders who derived a livelihood from commanding a strategic position. Sometime towards the end of the nineteenth century, however, an event had occurred that had dramatically changed their fortunes, transforming them from a minor Berber chieftainship into the most powerful clan in the country.

After one of his frequent expeditions to punish the desert tribes who had refused to show him allegiance, the then Sultan of Morocco, Moulay

Hassan, and his army had become stranded in a winter storm on their return to Marrakesh. His situation was precarious not only because of the extreme weather but because of the attacks by his enemies as he retreated. Some of the local chiefs had refused to offer him refuge but in a shrewd move the Glaoui family had opened their doors, calculating that the rewards for doing so would outweigh the hostility of some of the tribes they would have offended.

In return for having saved him, the Sultan appointed the then head of the family, Madani Glaoui, as the local Caid or lord, the officially recognized administrator of the region. He was given more territory at the same time. But the most significant gift he received was not the extra land or the new title but a powerful cannon, a German-made artillery piece that was one of only a few in the country. The enhanced firepower this provided them at a time when only antiquated muskets and swords prevailed, as well as the mythical prestige it was said to confer on whoever owned it, allowed the Glaouis over the next decade to subjugate most of the Atlas Mountains and a considerable number of the desert communities beyond them.

The family's prosperity and influence extended even further during the early years of the French occupation when they were rewarded for siding with them and putting down various rebellions. 'It was said they were the de-facto rulers of Morocco,'

Michael continued. 'They wined and dined with Presidents of France. They were courted by ambassadors and heads of state. They might not have had the royal title but everyone understood that the Sultan was hostage to their interests.'

Although the Glaouis acquired mansions in Morocco and estates in France and Spain, they did not forget their ancestral home. The Kasbah at Telouet was renovated, extended and transformed. Despite its stony location a golf course was established. It even had its own cinema where film stars from Hollywood were invited to introduce their movies. Guests were provided with sumptuous rooms and entertained with mock battles and pageants that they could observe from their balconies. As Michael continued his description, it sounded like something out of *The Thousand and One Nights,* a place where Western visitors could have all their preconceptions about the fabulous Orient confirmed. Presiding over it all like some mythical potentate was the patriarch of the family, reminding everyone, in case they had forgotten, who held the real power in the country.

But in keeping with Ibn Khaldun's philosophy, the good fortune the Glaouis had enjoyed disappeared as dramatically as it had arisen. The shrewd calculation they had made to support the Sultan when he was stranded in their territory was reversed when they sided with the occupying power against his descendant and as public clamour for independence arose during the 1950s. When the French capitulated and the Sultan was returned from exile, the fate of the family was sealed. Once they were stripped of their positions, possessions and power by the new Government, the head of the family, Thami Glaoui, died in straitened circumstances in Marrakesh a few years later. Michael added that there was even a word to describe their abandonment by their former benefactors. 'Glaousier' was now part of the French language, meaning 'to be double crossed' or 'betrayed.'

From a distance the Kasbah dominated the skyline. I was struck by the drama of its setting, its size and scale, the blackness of its walls that added to its mystery. As we neared, vast flocks of birds could also be seen circling above its battlements. I asked Michael what could sustain them in an environment that seemed so devoid of vegetation. He explained that each year when the snows appeared and then melted, the carcasses of the sheep and goats that had been lost in the winter storms would be exposed. Whenever that happened vultures, crows and other carrion arrived in large numbers to gorge themselves on the remains.

But up close it was clear that Telouet has seen better days. The walls were crumbling in places. Large sections of the roof had fallen in. There were goats wandering around a large space in front of it that apparently had once been part of its extensive gardens. Outside the main entrance, an imposing gateway with a bolted wooden door, we found an old man with a set of keys. He indicated that for a few coins he was prepared to let us in and show us around, a favour on his part he added, since no one had phoned ahead to let him know he would be having visitors.

Much of our tour consisted in avoiding places where we could fall through the floor. From its heyday in the 1950s until now, a period of less than forty years, it had reached a state of collapse. This surprised me since in other parts of Morocco there were buildings centuries older that were better preserved.

There were two reasons, our guide responded, when I asked him about the level of deterioration. The principal building materials in the mountains were mud and straw baked in the sun since wood was too scarce to fire bricks. This meant that unless the walls were regularly maintained and repaired they were subject to a fairly rapid decay. The other factor was to do with the significance of Telouet as the symbol of the Glaouis. Shorty after their demise it had been stripped of anything that was considered valuable or useful. Part of this was due to simple profiteering and plunder. But the principal motive on the part of the authorities was to remove any vestiges of the power that had once controlled Morocco.

After an hour of gingerly stepping on floorboards and climbing stairs that creaked and groaned as we ascended them, the old man announced that he had now exhausted his set of keys. We had only seen a fraction of its numerous rooms but he added that the rest was off-limits. The previous year a tourist had been injured exploring another part of the Kasbah. The local Government in Marrakesh had sent a delegation to survey the property and to specify which parts were safe to visit and those that were too dangerous. 'Don't worry,' he said, as we exited. 'One empty room is the same as the next. You aren't missing anything.'

At a small café in the village opposite, the full extent of how the mighty had fallen was brought home to us as we sat drinking tea. The proprietor who served us had lived in the area all his life. When I asked him what the Kasbah had been like in its prime he echoed much of what Michael had previously described: its extensive gardens, the foreign dignitaries arriving in limousines, the hundreds of employees who had maintained the property, the pride the local people felt in having their tribal leader as the most important person in the country. Now the only visitors were a few tourists like us come to inspect the ruins. The only villagers left were old men and women unable to accompany their sons and daughters to the towns and cities to which they had all migrated.

I had pointed to a section of the Kasbah wall covered in what seemed to be an extensive coat of white paint. Was this the start of a programme of renovation perhaps, an attempt by the authorities to forget past history and return the place to something approaching its former glory? He had burst out laughing. 'Those white streaks on the walls are shit from the birds that fly over Telouet. No, my friend. No one wants this place restored. The rest of Morocco is happy enough to leave us to the crows and vultures.'

CHAPTER 5

BLED ES SIBA

We dropped Michael off the next day at a village in the mountains. He was tranquilly sipping tea in a small café when we left him. It was entirely possible that if we returned a few weeks later he would still be there. The arrangement he had made with his family seemed to me to be remarkably loose. These were nomads on the move. The territory was huge. What if they had changed their minds? All there had been was a conversation that had taken place months previously and during the period in between, no possibility of further communication.

But Michael brushed aside my concern. A few words in the local market was all that was needed. The message that he was there, he claimed, would ripple outwards like waves in a pond. His conviction was based on past experience when they had come to a similar agreement. 'Don't worry, sooner or later we will find each other.'

As we said our goodbyes I had to admit to myself a moment of jealousy. Despite the hardships that Michael had described – the long treks every day, the rough terrain, the plummeting temperatures

101

at night in the mountains, the chores he was expected to carry out – I envied him the close relationship he had forged with his family. I also recognized that the effort he had made, including foregoing clean clothes and a warm bath, was a precondition for them opening up their lives to him. No one would reveal themselves to an outsider without feeling they could be trusted, and it was to Michael's credit that he had achieved that rapport.

When I had been a teacher in a remote community in northern Sudan for several years, I had felt that a similar door had opened. I learned then that none of this was automatic. Shared difficulties, enough time to establish relationships, a willingness to listen and patience were all necessary for social barriers to break down – the initial wariness that characterized interactions between people from different cultures.

Now my interactions with local people had become increasingly fleeting and usually mediated through the transactions associated with dispensing charity. I had begun to notice this in Zimbabwe in terms of the dynamics that arose when people found out I was the representative of an aid organization. To compensate, and because my organization was flexible enough to permit it, I spent most of my time out of the office trying to find out more about the lives of the people we were helping. While part of my motivation arose from a desire to improve the quality of our assistance it was also because of that same curiosity that had prompted me to this lifestyle in the first place. Why be there at all if not to understand another culture?

In Morocco I was part of a bigger operation. We had more resources and with that responsibility came more bureaucracy, administration and time behind a desk. That meant less opportunity to meet with communities and manifest the levels of interest that would have allowed them to genuinely open up to us.

'And the thing is, when we do engage with people, our questions are often loaded, designed to extract information to justify a particular project,' I had said to my two companions the previous evening in the small guest house we ended up in after our detour to Telouet. 'Sure, part of our work might be modified, a few aspects changed but the parameters of our interaction have already been fixed. I worry sometimes that aid workers are becoming more like missionaries than anthropologists because our own beliefs about the best interests of our beneficiaries dominate the relationship. Even worse, frequently we get it wrong.'

I had shared with them a discussion I had had the previous month with a young man in Casablanca that had highlighted something of what I was attempting to explain. Mohammed was one of the former participants in a programme we had established to help children with disabilities. He was a regular visitor to our office where he would help out with various tasks, make himself useful or simply hang around for the sake of the company he enjoyed.

I was interested to hear about his past involvement with our organization and Mohammed in turn seemed keen to respond to my questions. 'I was selected because of this,' he said, pointing to the caliper that had been fitted to one of his legs. 'I had polio as a child which left me disabled. I still need a walking stick to move around.'

He went on to say that he belonged to a family of seven other children and that his father, who had now passed away, was out of work when Mohammed contracted his illness. As a result of their poverty, none of them could attend school. 'That all changed when I was selected. My school fees were covered. I visited a surgeon who managed to straighten my legs so that I could walk. I even received clothes. I can remember thinking at the time, "Why me? Why have I been chosen?"'

As part of the programme he had been sponsored by a family in England and in return for their financial contributions he wrote regular letters to thank them and give them an update on how he was progressing with their help. 'Our communications became more frequent. They seemed really interested in how I was getting on. Sometimes at different times of the year I would also receive some gifts that they sent through the office here. But that was when the problems started,' Mohammed added, taking a deep breath.

'Remember, we were a poor family. My brothers

and sisters watched me go to school while they had to stay at home and work. I received all these gifts when on their own birthdays they would get nothing. My parents told me to share and I did, but it was clear I was the one with everything. They would gang up on me. Sometimes I would be beaten. I understand why. I'm not blaming them. I would have done the same myself. So you see, while I got a life I also lost my family.'

That was not the worst of it, and as Mohammed continued I could see him became more agitated, so that I asked him if he wanted to go on. But he insisted on telling his story.

'One year I was told that my parents in England wanted me to visit them. I could hardly believe it. God had smiled on me again. But I was worried too. I had never been outside Casablanca. The only people I knew were my family and some relatives, a few friends at school and the staff in the office. What would they think of me? What would happen if I was not what they expected?'

He had travelled with some other children to London where they were picked up by their sponsors. He had never imagined a house like the one where he stayed. He had his own bed and his own room. Back in Casablanca he shared a small space with his four brothers.

'I was supposed to stay with them for some time. But one morning they said they had something important to tell me. Our relationship hadn't worked out and they thought it best for everyone if I went home. I wondered what I had done wrong. I had not stolen anything. I had done my best to be polite. I had even learned to eat with a knife and fork and not use my hands like we did at home. But when I asked them what I had done they just shrugged their shoulders and said nothing, only repeating that it was best for me to leave.'

Mohammed took another deep breath and there were tears in his eyes when he continued. 'And so a month before I was due to come home I was back in Casablanca with my family. My brothers and sisters told me I must have done something bad. Why else would I have been sent away?, they said. For the rest of my childhood I carried that guilt around with me, the feeling that it was my fault. It's only in recent years that I have stopped blaming myself, that I realised that the problem was not with me but with them.'

When I had begun to apologise to Mohammed for what had happened to him he had stopped me. He was thankful to the organization for the opportunities it had given him, for his chance at education and for the medical treatment that had allowed him to walk again. But after he spoke I wondered about the emotional scars he had been left with. There was the distance that had been created between him and his family as a result of charity that had been blind to the consequences of singling out specific people without consideration of the reality of their world.

'I can't help thinking that much of this could

have been avoided if we had taken more time to ask people about the kinds of interventions that would have benefited them,' I had said the previous evening. 'Unless we take the time to be more involved then these are the results. When I asked Mohammed if anyone had ever spoken to him about what was happening in his family, about the conflicts between him and his brothers and sisters, he replied that that was not part of the relation-ship established between the organization and those they helped. No one had asked for their opinions and they did not think it was their place to offer them either.'

Cathy was as shocked as I had been and pointed out that the one-way flow of communication between aid agencies and the people they assisted was thankfully changing. The community-based project she was heading was about finding out from people with disabilities themselves, including chil-dren, what they wanted, and what would best suit them in their local context. 'What happened to Mohammed can't be excused,' she continued, 'but lessons have been learned. Individuals are no longer singled out for special favours that will alienate them from their families or communities.'

While she acknowledged that it was important to listen, she had a different take on just how much people in our profession could afford to step over boundaries. 'You can't shelve your own value system completely. Of course aid workers should not be like former missionaries who were wilfully ignorant about who they were saving. But we're not anthropologists either, who have the luxury of taking notes and writing academic articles for fellow professionals. We can't pretend scientific distance when we're in the business of trying to help people.'

Echoing a previous conversation we had had, when I first asked her about her work in Khemisset, she added that aid was frequently messy, experimental and often influenced by events that could not have been envisaged before a project started. But these were not reasons why it should not be attempted. The most important thing was to be flexible and to learn from mistakes, not to assume they would never happen again.

I was aware that Morocco had established itself as a popular location for hosting Hollywood movies. Its relatively developed infrastructure, its exotic backdrops and an accommodating bureaucracy were some of the reasons it had become a favoured destination. Sometime previously I had been asked by one of Cathy's friends whether I would like to be an extra in a film they were shooting. The location was the same part of the country we were now travelling in.

Dana was an American woman who had lived in Marrakesh for many years. She had retained an engaging southern drawl and combined with her good looks, her considerable charm and an exuberant, outgoing personality, it did not surprise me when she had mentioned she was involved with the movie industry. 'Would you be so kind as to turn your head so I can see your profile more clearly?' she asked, taking a few seconds to examine my face from different angles. 'Perfect. You look just the person we need. We pay thirty dollars a day and require you for two weeks.'

'So what's the film about?' I asked, my curiosity piqued.

'It's a film about the life and death of John the Baptist. We're desperate to find some thuggish looking soldiers.' She was at pains to point out that my normal appearance was perfectly benign but from a certain angle and with just the right make-up she was sure I could fit the part.

As I had never acted before part of me was tempted but the thought of being spotted by friends back home in such a role cooled my enthusiasm. Besides, I did not have the two weeks to spare. Dana, who had already started looking around the neighbouring tables, assured us that despite my refusal we would be welcome to visit the set and see for ourselves how a film was made. 'It will be shot in a village called Ait Benhaddou, on the other side of the mountains from Marrakesh. It's a fabulous place. Lots of movies have been set there. You have to see it to believe it.'

Our trip south had not coincided with the shooting of her film but a few hours after leaving Michael in his village we found ourselves approaching the location. From a distance I could understand why it had been chosen. The background was perfect: snow-covered mountains, palm trees along a river, a train of camels on the road below us and dramatic red walls and houses that looked centuries old. In fact, the town itself, so my guidebook claimed, dated back some five hundred years and was a fine example of a traditional Moroccan 'ksar'. These were protected settlements, ubiquitous in the mountains where feuds between rival groups were common. Surrounded by high walls, its buildings were clustered together in circles around an imposing central tower, the last place of refuge if the outer fortifications were ever breached.

Unlike the ruins of Telouet, Ait Benhaddou seemed remarkably intact and well preserved. I said to Cathy that it looked exactly like something out of the movies. She laughed and replied that that statement was truer than I could imagine. 'Wait and see,' she added, when I asked her what she had meant.

Much closer and it was as if the town had dissolved like a mirage. Though the buildings were still there most of them were empty. The only people in evidence were some workmen hammering away at the walls of various houses and erecting some painted wooden facades made to look like old historical battlements. It was clear that these were props for the next film. While sections of what I presumed were the original town still remained, its emptiness, the absence of people, its

contrived tidiness and its manufactured appearance had turned it into exactly what it had looked
like when we had approached, a film set for an
exotic movie.

There were several cafés and a small restaurant
on the side of a valley, dispersed along the road
to offer the best view. Our tour over sooner than
I had expected, we decided to have lunch there.
A bus had also pulled up just as we arrived,
disgorging a group of tourists who seemed happy
enough to click their cameras and observe from a
distance the place they had come to see. I noticed
that the guide who was with them showed little
interest in escorting them any closer.

'But where are the inhabitants?' I asked the
waiter who served us, a young man who said that
he was from the area.

He replied that only a handful of families still
remained in the original *ksar*. The rest had been
moved to a location a mile or so away on the other
side of the river, to a modern village that had been
constructed for them around the same time that
the film industry became interested in their
settlement.

We could see nothing of this from where we sat.
He remarked that the site of their new village had
partly been chosen so that it did not interfere
either with the view that the tourists came to
photograph or conflict with the images the film
crews wanted. Television antennae protruding
from houses, street lights for the residents, cafés

blaring noisy Arab music and cars instead of donkeys and camels were not appropriate for the settings required by films like 'Lawrence of Arabia', 'Sodom and Gomorrah' and 'The Last Temptation of Christ'. Ait Benhaddou was required to be biblical and untouched by modernity which meant that it was better if no one lived there to spoil the illusion.

The waiter seemed confused by my question when I asked him if the original inhabitants of the town resented what I considered to be blatant manipulation, their history frozen in time to satisfy the requirements of the film industry. 'Don't you feel that you are being exploited? They want to photograph your community but they don't want you in the picture. That seems offensive to me.'

'But that's what brings us jobs and I for one am not complaining,' he replied. Had I noticed what the other nearby villages were like? I had to admit that they were quite impoverished, bedraggled collections of houses, with historical ruins that hinted they had once seen better days. He nodded his head as if I was confirming his point.

'A few years ago I would have had to leave this place to find work. Now I can stay here. We have proper houses, electricity and a school for our children. We would have had none of that if it weren't for these people,' he said, pointing to the tourists who like ourselves were sitting down having lunch and occasionally clicking away at the view. 'You've seen the other towns. The people there envy us our good fortune and wish they had the same.'

Cathy dismissed my indignant tone when I complained in the car later about the town's lack of authenticity and my concern about the way in which its history had been recreated and preserved to meet the needs of tourism and a foreign-owned movie industry. 'So what if poor people market their past and sell it to the highest bidder? You were the one who remarked last night that people were insufficiently consulted about what they wanted. No doubt they have good reasons for their choices, even if your sensibilities are offended and you don't like the decisions they end up making.'

'What are these small, white houses with stubbly bits poking out of them?' Cathy asked, after we had seen a number of them in various communities we had passed on our route beyond the mountains. They were situated on the edge of villages, generally on the desert side of the road, among rows of upturned stones and slabs of rock that we understood to be local graveyards.

From my time in Sudan and Algeria I recognized them as the tombs of Muslim saints. The 'Marabouts' of North Africa were a key feature of an alternative Islamic tradition, a movement that focused more on mysticism and attaining closeness to God than compliance with the juristic, formulaic aspects of the religion.

Those who achieved enlightenment were reputed to have special powers that could confer blessings called 'Baraka' on others. On their death they were buried in these small, white buildings which in turn became sites of pilgrimage for those who wanted a special favour. I mentioned to Cathy that at the edge of the community where I had lived during my time as a teacher in southern Algeria there was one such tomb. On certain days of the year hundreds of women, some of whom had travelled from distant towns and cities, would gather there in the hope that the intercession of the saint, prompted by various gifts of perfume and sweets, would allow them not only to conceive a child but to choose its gender.

On the outskirts of Tamegroute, a small town situated along the valley that the road had tracked ever since we had left the mountains, we came across a procession blocking the road. Men, women and children were singing, dancing and making their way toward another white building, much like the tombs we had seen earlier. But this one was grander, had a fresh coat of paint and the trees and bushes around it had been festooned with brightly coloured ribbons.

Unable to proceed further, I parked the car and managed to find someone who was happy enough to tell us what was happening. We had arrived on a day when the death of the most famous Marabout of the region was being commemorated. The crowd before us, he said, would swell later that evening to many thousands more. There would be visitors not only from towns and cities in other parts of Morocco but from countries like Tunisia and Algeria much further afield. Did we know, he asked with some pride, that Tamegroute hosted not just one of these saints but a total of eight? In fact, it was the historical centre for one of Islam's largest mystical or 'Sufi' orders that dated back hundreds of years.

'So what is this saint famous for?' I asked, pointing to the tomb around which the crowd was gathered.

'You're lucky,' he whispered, pointing to Cathy. 'If you say the right prayer this evening your wife will be pregnant tomorrow morning.'

At a small café where we had lunch, Cathy, who had been perusing her guidebook, confirmed that Tamegroute indeed had eight Marabouts. 'It says here that one of them was not only a religious teacher but a physician too. Apparently he had a special interest in curing people with mental disabilities. There is still a centre here that helps people with this problem. Let's see if we can visit,' she said, her professional curiosity aroused.

I was less enthusiastic. In Sudan on the outskirts of the town where I had lived, there was an establishment that claimed similar credentials. A colleague had invited me to visit and what I had seen had not convinced me that they had found anything remotely like a cure. Part of the treatment consisted in beating the inmates with sticks inscribed with passages of the Koran.

'It drives out the devils that have made them mad,' one of the attendants had said, an argument that did little to convince me that he knew what he was talking about. The patients did not look as if they were benefiting either.

'Does it work?' my colleague had asked him.

'Of course. That's why they're quiet,' he had replied.

But Cathy was not dissuaded by my past experience. 'My book says that it is well worth a visit. So don't be so squeamish. In any case, what's happened to your curiosity?' she teased.

The centre was not far away and a few minutes later we were knocking at the door of a building that looked more like a library or school than a hospital, or thankfully the 'prison' I had envisaged. The old man who answered had no objection to our looking around and politely answered our questions as he escorted us through various rooms and halls. The few patients we saw, both men and women, were busy with their chores of maintaining the centre: washing clothes, scrubbing floors and in the kitchen chopping vegetables and scouring pots and pans.

When I asked him about their treatment the old man, who confessed that he himself had been a patient, indicated that what we saw in front of us constituted a large part of what was on offer. Participating in the life of a religious community through service and contribution, being exposed to the teachings of their founder through reading

116

texts or hearing the words of their current Sheikh, replaced the drugs and medical prescriptions provided in other more secular establishments.

He added that mental illness had been identified by their founder as a symptom of spiritual neglect, an indication that the patient had grown distant from their true religious nature. So prayer, devotion and helping others were more effective than any physical interventions. 'I finished my treatment many years ago,' he said, 'at least for my mental problems. But I have stayed on here to continue my religious journey. That will only finish when God calls me home.'

The scholarly, monastic character of the centre was further confirmed when our guide informed us that it also had a famous library which held a collection of over four thousand precious texts and manuscripts which dated back hundreds of years. 'I'm sorry I can't let you see them,' he said, as we peered through the window of another building where we could discern rows and rows of books and special glass cases to protect the most fragile. The manuscripts were so valuable, he added, that special permission was required from an office in Marrakesh to peruse them more closely.

A previous head of the order, the old man continued, had made it his mission to preserve a body of literature from throughout the Islamic world that was in danger of being lost through neglect, ignorance or in some cases wilful destruction by religious bigots who believed that reading books led to heresy. For much of his life he had scoured the towns and cities of North Africa, the Middle East and even parts of Europe to find them. The collection he had established included one of the oldest copies of the Koran inscribed on gazelle skin and reputed to date back to the eleventh century. There were works of medieval philosophers, jurists, astronomers, mathematicians, medical practitioners and mystics. At one time hundreds of scholars from all over the Muslim world had made their pilgrimage to Tamegroute to study its texts and then return to their own communities to disseminate what they had learned.

As we gazed through the windows at the large, vacant room and the empty tables and chairs, it was clear that the library had seen busier days. The old man ruefully confirmed that the only visitors it had now were a few academics and tourists like us who were curious to see some ancient relics. Its centrality as a place of learning had long since disappeared. There was an abandoned, bereft atmosphere about it that was echoed in the words of our guide when he claimed that what had once been the most famous centre of enlightenment in North Africa had turned into a museum.

'Our Sheikh tells us that we need to reconcile ourselves to the fact that nothing is permanent, that every human achievement no matter how grand, like famous buildings, monuments or palaces, will one day disappear and be replaced by others. But it is difficult for some of us to accept that the world has moved on,' he confided as he shook hands and as we thanked him for his informative tour. 'That is a lesson I am still learning and another of the reasons why I will not leave this place until I have done so.'

It had been our intention to continue our journey that day to the town of M'hamid before our plan was hijacked by the gathering that had first prompted our interest and then our detour to the religious centre. Well into the afternoon we decided to stay on since I was reluctant to continue by night along a road I did not know. Accommodation was not easy to find since the town was packed with people come to enjoy the festivities, but eventually we were directed to a small guesthouse where rooms were still available, basic and Spartan but clean enough to be acceptable.

The celebrants started congregating shortly after the sunset prayers when the streets, that in the heat of the day had largely been empty, became filled to a point where it was difficult to move around. Back in Sudan where similar celebrations had taken place during the high points of the Muslim calendar I had always been intrigued by the easy mix of the religious and secular. Here it was no different. There was little sign of piety or asceticism in the conspicuous consumption of food outside the numerous stalls that had appeared, offering everything from skewered lamb, fried livers and steaming mutton to sweets and popcorn covered in sticky syrup. The entertainers were out too: the storytellers, snake charmers, acrobats, conjurers and clowns that Jemma El Fna hosted every evening, and judging by the crowds of adults and children around them, were just as popular in Tamegroute.

The noise, excitement and intensity continued beyond the centres of entertainment to the vicinity of the saint's tomb where the throng was thickest. The singing, dancing and drumming had increased to another level. But on the faces of the men who were shuffling back and forth as they clapped their hands uttering various praises in honour of their Sheikh, the expressions were not of amusement but of concentration, as if they had entered a different realm where their jerking bodies had transported them. Occasionally one of them would fall down in some kind of trance to be carried to one side by a group of minders. There were women too, ululating, clapping their hands and moving back and forth in the same coordinated movement. As in Sudan I was struck by the contrast between this charged, communal outpouring of sentiment and the more sedate, reserved and constrained gatherings that occurred in the mosques every day where none of this emotion was visible.

'Where is everyone?' I asked Cathy the following morning after we had gone in search of a place to have breakfast. The entertainers had disappeared. The stalls had been dismantled. The flags and ribbons that had been draped from various buildings had been taken down. The streets were almost empty and Tamegroute had returned to the same sleepy indolence we had found in the other communities we had passed beyond the mountains, as if what had happened the previous evening was only a temporary aberration.

'Maybe they're busy producing babies,' Cathy remarked as we walked around the deserted town. It was only outside the tomb of its saint that the bottles of perfume and the bits of cloth still tied to the trees around it confirmed last night's festivities.

Back in the guesthouse the proprietor offered us tea and coffee when we told him that we had been unsuccessful in finding a place that was open. When I mentioned to him my surprise that only a few hours after its biggest event the town had transformed into something unrecognizable, he said that what we saw now was much more typical of Tamegroute. 'Apart from the eight days when our saints are remembered and a few days after Ramadan, when everyone visits everyone else to celebrate the end of the fast, nothing much takes place here,' he said, shrugging his shoulders in a kind of apology. 'But occasionally other things do happen,' he added, as if trying to soften that judgement, 'like that time we had our famous visitor.'

In Marrakesh another of Cathy's friends had told us that the previous year an artist from Europe had arrived in southern Morocco with several lorries packed with ice to create a sculpture in the desert. At the time I had thought he was either

121

joking or had misinterpreted a rumour. But as the proprietor confirmed his story I asked him the same question that had come to mind back then; what could have prompted someone to have embarked on such a crazy undertaking?

According to the proprietor, the sculptor, whom he believed came from Holland, had arrived with an entourage comprising some helpers and a film crew brought to record the event. The lorries had deposited their ice in the middle of Tamegroute central square and then in front of the stunned inhabitants he had begun to chisel away. 'He called the sculpture the Three Marabouts although what they had to do with our saints was not clear to us. We could see some shapes eventually emerge from the ice so he seemed to know what he was doing. Then we just sat back and watched them melt.'

'How long did they last in the heat?' I asked, mindful of the fact that Tamegroute exceeded even Marrakesh in terms of its daytime temperatures.

'Longer than most of us expected, I have to admit,' he replied. 'It was clear that he had brought a lot of ice with him. About two days I think. I can remember arriving in the square on the third morning and all that was left was a puddle of water.'

As to what message the artist was trying to convey, the proprietor shrugged his shoulders, indicating that it had perplexed the townspeople ever since. 'Maybe he was trying to say something about change and impermanence,' I suggested, remembering the conversation we had had the previous day with the old man who had guided us around the centre and what he had said about the remaining part of his spiritual journey.

But the proprietor, clearly a more practical man, pointed out that this was something the villagers did not need to be reminded about since it was a key part of the teachings they were exposed to as a result of hosting some of the most famous Marabouts in North Africa. 'Many of us wondered about the amount of money it must have cost him and all those other people to come here. He could have left some of that behind instead. Or why not finance a small ice factory for our community? What I thought about when I watched that ice melt in front of us was the number of cold drinks we could have had in Tamegroute for several weeks if it hadn't all been wasted.'

Quite where the Sahara began in Morocco was difficult to say with several towns and settlements anxious to claim that honour. At the foot of the mountains on our descent from Ait Benhaddou we had come across a large mural painted on a wall near the road, depicting camels and sand dunes and welcoming us to the desert. But an hour later at the town of Ourzazate, the provincial capital, there was another sign indicating that the gateway to the Sahara was at a place called Zagora still some two hundred kilometres away. Meanwhile the guidebook that Cathy was reading expressed a different opinion. The desert proper could only be found at a place called M'hamid on the border with Algeria, another few hundred kilometres beyond Zagora on the same road south.

Whether it was actually the Sahara or not, the motif of sand dunes, nomads and camels played itself out in the marketing of the area for visitors. At the hotel in Ourzazate, where we had spent an evening, one of the entertainments on offer was a visit to an encampment half an hour's drive away. For a price that was quoted in dollars one was offered an authentic desert experience, including nomadic cuisine, camel racing and a pageant re-enacting an historic battle between warring tribes. Another tour at the same hotel offered a more ambitious two-day journey to visit some 'real' sand dunes, which prompted me to ask whether the ones we had seen earlier that day had been manufactured.

These words, 'real', 'authentic' and 'genuine' appeared frequently in the brochures, posters and hoardings we had come across, as well as in the words of the tourism officials and touts who hassled us at breakfast, lunch and dinner with various offers of excursions and expeditions. Whenever I saw or heard these adjectives I knew that another set of illusions was being peddled. What I had seen at Ait Benhaddou still rankled, combined with the fact that this was not the image of the Sahara I had held and cherished for many years after my first encounter with the desert in Sudan. I tried to explain this to Cathy when she asked me why I sounded so indignant, and why I was being such a purist. 'I don't like the fact that one of the few places on the planet that has not yet been tamed is being turned into an amusement park for visitors who are offered a taste from the luxury of their airconditioned vehicles. They don't appreciate that it is not to be treated lightly. It's about respect. That was the prevalent attitude among the communities in Sudan and Algeria where I lived. Tourism has a habit of turning something special and different into the banal and ordinary. That's what I object to.'

I related to Cathy a journey I had once made across the Sahara while I was based in southern Algeria. I had travelled on a lorry carrying dates from the town where I was a teacher to the markets of Nigeria where they fetched a higher price. On hearing my interest in crossing the desert I had been offered assistance by one of the merchants I had befriended in the town where I was living. He had placed me under the protection of his son who would accompany me on the two-week trip to where they were headed.

Along the track we had followed for several days I had been surprised by the numerous car wrecks we had passed, the hollowed-out remains of vehicles that had tried to cross the desert and never made it. According to my chaperone, there was a lucrative market for cars from Europe in the countries of West Africa and in an attempt to capitalize on that opportunity many attempted the crossing. A fair number, he said, perished in the attempt, ill-prepared for what they would find.

It was more comfortable travelling by night than during the heat of the day and one evening we had come across a young French couple stranded in their car. We had found them because of their flashing headlights that our driver had spotted, a matter of extreme good luck for them since they had lost their way and were far from any recognizable track they could have followed. They had been there for several days and had almost given up hope of being rescued. We helped them repair their vehicle and then we guided them to the safety of the border where they would find a convoy going south.

My guide was angry about the lack of respect shown by outsiders towards an environment he had now traversed many times. 'They come here thinking that the Sahara is like something familiar. But the desert is not like one of their beaches back home. Every year we have tourists getting lost, needing to be rescued, sometimes dying in their cars because they did not carry enough water. What is wrong with them?'

As to the community most familiar with the desert, the nomads of the Sahara, I had had some fleeting encounters. I had come across them in the markets of northern Sudan, selling their goats and camels and haggling over the items they wanted in return, convinced as always that the local merchants were trying to rip them off. I mentioned to Cathy that there was considerable suspicion between town dwellers and nomadic communities throughout North Africa fuelled by conflicts over land and territory. But on the part of the former there was a grudging respect for the hardships the latter endured and the lifestyles they chose to persist with. They were brash and dismissive when I had seen them but their swagger was appealing, the way they comported themselves as if the land they walked on belonged to them. Somehow I could not reconcile that memory of a proud, self-enclosed and independent people with the thought of them performing tricks on their camels for the sake of a few coins.

Cathy this time had listened patiently to my tirade. Perhaps she had grown used to my sounding off and thought it best to let me get it out of my system. When she spoke it was to voice the argument she had made previously about not being critical of people who had little option around the choices they made due to financial necessity.

'What you have just said seems to say more about the image you have of these people than the reality of what they face on the ground. Aren't their livelihoods under threat? Isn't the world they inhabit changing?'

She pointed out that the lorry I had travelled on probably transported more goods in a matter of days across the Sahara than a nomadic caravan could carry in weeks if not months. There had been droughts in recent decades which had impacted the size of their herds of goats and camels. From what she had heard many nomadic communities had been forced to settle in towns and villages because the livelihoods that had sustained them for generations were no longer viable.

'So perhaps the tourism you frown upon is one of the few things that brings them any revenue. And perhaps entertaining foreign visitors is the price they are prepared to pay to maintain their lifestyles a little longer.'

M'hamid, the small town at the end of the road before the 'real' Sahara, was dusty, hot and had a frontier feel about it: an impression reinforced by the military barracks that guarded its entrance and the men with guns who were walking around. We were stopped at a roadblock before we were allowed to proceed. The soldiers who asked for our papers were friendly and polite but curious as to why we were there.

'Zagora and Ourzazate are much more interesting,' one of them said. 'They have historical monuments, old castles and good hotels. Here, there is nothing but a few buildings, a small oasis and some miles further on the Algerians.' He had concluded the latter part of his statement by spitting on the ground. 'You should save yourselves the trouble and turn back now.'

In a small, central square where we parked our

car a short while later, the men sipping coffee in front of their stores barely glanced at us as we passed. The few goods they had on display, utilitarian household items for the most part, were clearly aimed at a local audience. Not having to fend off offers of carpets, daggers, leather bags and expeditions was a novelty. Even at the small café where we sat down after our walk around the streets, the waiter seemed reluctant to stir himself from his morning nap to serve us.

We had heard that M'hamid was a prime location from which to explore the surrounding desert and had been told that there were several places in town that offered excursions. But during our walk we had seen no gaudy offices with large billboards and neon signs. I had brushed aside Cathy's previous interest in taking one of the tours on the grounds that it would be superficial. But somehow M'hamid's down-at-heel and indifferent ambience had convinced me that anything we might find here would be more authentic.

The waiter pointed to a small building further down the street when we asked him if he knew where we could organize an excursion. We had passed it earlier but there was nothing to indicate that it was a place of business. But as we approached it again I could see a small sign on the window indicating that this was the office of 'the best guide in the Sahara,' a claim that seemed wildly incongruous given the modest piece of cardboard it was written on.

As we became accustomed to the poor light inside it was clear that whoever presided over this place had a Spartan disregard for ornamentation. There was a table and three plastic chairs, and bearing the only hint of what was on offer, a frayed picture of sand dunes and camels. Cathy was ready to leave but I was curious as to what the best guide in the Sahara looked like. I pointed out that maybe he preferred to invest in perfecting the experience for potential clients rather than wasting money on advertising and show. It was the desert we wanted to see, not some fancy air-conditioned building.

Eventually, from behind a partition at the back of the room a figure appeared, swatting away the flies that were buzzing around him. Dressed in blue robes with a black scarf around his head he looked much more striking than his surroundings. He shook our hands, invited us to sit down on his plastic chairs and introduced himself as Ahmed, the proprietor of the establishment.

As if well aware of our initial impression he added that we should not be fooled by the meagre state of his office. His customers, he claimed, included many famous people and from the pocket of his robes he produced some crumpled pieces of paper, references he had accumulated from grateful patrons. 'No one pays to sit in here,' he said, echoing my sentiment. 'What they want to see is out there.'

Accepting his invitation to drink some tea he

then went through the various tours he was able to provide. 'I can take you for two weeks if you want, even longer. Last month I had a group from France who wanted to go to Mauritania. I have their letter somewhere if you want to read it.'

Somewhat apologetically I replied that we were looking for something much less adventurous. Unfortunately, we only had a few days at our disposal before we had to return to Marrakesh. Could he do an evening and a couple of days?

He seemed disappointed and asked us what we expected to see in such a short period of time. I explained that all we wanted was a brief tour, something that would give us a flavour of the landscape I had relished in Algeria and Sudan. Some sand dunes, an open horizon, a few palm trees and no one for miles around would be just fine.

After I had finished he said there was a small oasis not far from M'hamid where he occasionally took clients who were short of time. It was accessible in our own vehicle. 'Come back in an hour or so,' he concluded after we had agreed a price. 'My cousin will come with us. He will be our cook but I need to go and find him.'

It was mid-afternoon by the time we reached the oasis. In front of us a range of dunes blocked any further progress. At the foot of one was an area of lush greenery watered by a small stream that lost itself in the sand a short distance beyond.

We had a couple of hours to explore the area,

Ahmed said, but warned us not to stray too far. Night fell quickly in the desert and there were no defining landmarks to orient us if we got lost. While we were instructed to enjoy the scenery he and his cousin, a young man who had said little from the time we had been introduced, would pitch a tent, set up base for the night and find some wood to light a fire and cook our supper. In fact, supper had featured prominently in the conversation we had had on the drive there. While I was interested to hear about the geography and history of the area, Ahmed seemed much more inclined to enthuse about the culinary delights that would be conjured up by his cousin later that evening.

Back at the car at the appointed time we found a pitched tent, some blankets for us to sit on and a pot of tea with some glasses beside it. Neither of our two companions was in sight. 'They must still be looking for wood,' I said to Cathy, something of an undertaking in an area largely devoid of trees. 'They'll be back soon enough, I expect.'

But an hour later with the sun disappeared, the first stars emerging and no sign of the fire we had been promised, we were still on our own and wondering if our guide had failed to follow his own advice and managed to get himself lost. Remembering my past experience when we had rescued the French couple in southern Algeria I switched on the car headlights and sounded the horn in case our companions needed something to orientate themselves by. But apart from Cathy's increasingly exasperated sighs and comments only silence ensued.

Another hour passed and our irritation had transformed into genuine concern. 'I've read about bad things happening to foreigners in the desert,' Cathy said, echoing my current thinking. I had promised Youssef after my experience on the beach near Rabat never to place myself in a similar situation, yet here I was on the edge of the Sahara with no one around that could help us if something went wrong. 'What if Ahmed and his cousin are not what they seem to be?' Cathy continued. 'We should have asked for some kind of identification. This is a perfect place to commit a robbery.'

'But why leave us? If they wanted to take our belongings, they could have done that hours ago when we were off exploring the dunes. And if it's our car they wanted, well, Ahmed has the keys since I left them with him so he could offload our supplies. I'm sure there's a good reason why they're not here,' I concluded, trying to sound more upbeat than what I felt.

It was Cathy who spotted the fire a short while later, flickering on top of one of the dunes and against which we could make out the silhouettes of two figures. 'I told you so,' she said, in considerable consternation. 'They're sitting there plotting what to do to us. Why else would they have left us here on our own?'

I could find no plausible explanation other than

confirming Cathy's suspicions. 'We'll sit in the car and lock all the doors. At least that will offer us some protection.'

When the figures eventually detached themselves from the fire I switched on the car headlights to help track their progress. They did not even attempt to conceal their approach and seemed quite open and brazen as they walked towards us. 'They know there is nowhere for us to escape to,' Cathy said. 'Promise me not to open the doors, no matter what they say. Just hand them what they want through the window.'

By the time they reached us I already had my words prepared. Where was the desert hospitality that was such a strong feature of local tradition? Wasn't it part of nomadic culture to offer help even to one's enemies? The soldiers who had checked our papers outside M'hamid were aware of our whereabouts. If we didn't show up in the next day or so they would send out a search party. Then there was the waiter who had directed us to Ahmed's office. If anything happened to us he would testify as to exactly where he had sent us.

But it was Ahmed who spoke first before I had a chance to say anything, stopping just outside the car door and motioning me to wind down the window. 'I told you my cousin is an excellent cook,' he said and, signalling him to step forward, he presented with a flourish a large tray on which several steaming plates of food were visible. Through the window came the mouth-watering aroma of roast meat, vegetables and, strongest of all, the smell of fresh bread. Was there a bakery nearby?, I wondered.

I tried to look as nonchalant as possible. 'But why didn't you light the fire down here as you had said?'

'Desert bread is best baked where the sand is cleanest,' he replied, pointing in the direction they had just come from. 'That's up there on the edge of the dunes. In any case the food is getting cold. Let's eat.'

As we walked back up the hill to where the fire was burning, Ahmed said that something was puzzling him. Why had we been sitting in the car all this time? They had watched us while they were preparing our food and could come to no agreement as to our reasons. Hadn't I mentioned that the traffic of Rabat, Casablanca and Marrakesh was driving me crazy and that I wanted to be away from all that noise and pollution? Why not sit outside and enjoy the space and openness of the desert that I had earlier enthused about?

'Because we wanted to listen to some music on the radio,' Cathy answered blithely. 'It adds to the atmosphere.'

Sometime later, well fed, we had to admit that Ahmed's cousin fully merited his reputation. We were effusive in our praise, which seemed to please them immensely. As Ahmed began to prepare the last part of our meal, green tea flavoured with mint that concluded all such occasions, I bent towards him and asked if he had some kind of identification he could show me.

'Sure,' he replied, reaching into his robes and producing a smart looking card with his name, address, telephone number and occupation. 'But why now? Why didn't you ask for it back in M'hamid?'

Again Cathy was more prepared as I mentally stumbled for some kind of excuse that would not offend him. 'We have some friends coming here in a few weeks' time. They need a good, reliable guide. Now we have found one we need to know how they can contact you.'

'Well don't forget to tell them about my cousin too,' he replied, handing us his credentials. 'Don't you agree that he is the best cook in southern Morocco?'

CHAPTER 6

IN BETWEEN

During my first six months in Morocco I would sometimes pause and tell myself that my status was about to change and that I would soon become a father. Kwadzi would send me regular updates on her condition, the trials, tribulations and milestones that come with every pregnancy. But despite these reminders the telephone call received from her brother in the small hours of the morning took me aback. He was phoning to tell me that she had been taken into hospital the previous evening and that the baby was due soon.

'So, shall I come immediately,' I asked, 'or wait for further news?'

'Kwadzi said wait for now. Sometimes there are false alarms. Here is the telephone number of the hospital. You can ring at any time to get an update.'

A few hours later I managed to get through to a nurse on the maternity ward, who communicated an air of impatience as if she had more important things to deal with than my enquiries. 'I'm phoning about a Mrs Nyanungo. She was taken to your hospital last night. I just wanted to find out about her condition.'

'Why don't you come and see for yourself? Visiting hours start in about thirty minutes.'

'Because I'm not actually in the country at the moment. I'm phoning from Morocco.'

'We don't give information out to just anybody. What relationship do you have with the person you are enquiring about?'

'I'm the husband. It's my wife who was brought in last night.'

There was a significant pause at the end of the line. When the voice resumed it was not what I expected. 'Oh, so you're like our Zimbabwean men who are never around when their wives have babies. We thought that foreign husbands were different.'

I was getting irritated. 'Look, I didn't phone to get a lecture on our marital status. Can you just tell me if my wife is okay and when the baby is expected so I can organize my journey?'

'You don't have to get so upset. Wait a minute and I'll find out.'

Some five minutes later there was another voice on the line that at first I did not recognize. I shouted down the phone. 'Excuse me. I only want to find out if my wife is all right. It can't be too difficult to get me that simple information.'

'You fool. It's me, Kwadzi. Jesus, why did you have to make such a fuss and tell them I had to come to the phone. I was in the delivery room since the baby is due. Get a ticket and come as soon as you can. And for God's sake, don't worry.'

The phone went dead before I had a chance to apologise and explain that I hadn't asked for her to come to the phone at all. I promised myself that when I arrived in Harare I would go to the hospital, find out the name of the nurse I had spoken to and make a formal complaint.

That same evening I was on a flight to Zimbabwe, having been informed by Kwadzi's brother in the interim that the baby had arrived, that mother and son were doing well and that I should relax, everything had turned out as expected. But I was jittery on the flight and apprehensive too, not because I doubted the accuracy of what I had been told. For the first time it had dawned on me that things were not the same, that now I had new and other responsibilities, that parenthood was no longer an abstract concept but something real, concrete and present.

How would I manage? What would I do when I was asked to hold the baby? What would I say to all the relatives who would gather round and congratulate me on being a father? I regretted that I had not been around for the past six months. Not because I felt guilty at having left Kwadzi, since we had both agreed that I needed to pursue my career. But from a distance I had had no time to prepare myself for my new role and had missed out on the period of apprenticeship that sharing a pregnancy would have brought with it.

At the airport when I arrived I noticed a large group of people at one end of the building. 'They must be waiting for some Government dignitary,' I said to the man beside me whom I had befriended on the flight. But I wondered why Kwadzi's brother was standing among them and why he did not detach himself when he noticed me coming towards him.

It turned out that the large group was a family entourage come to greet me. As the women began to ululate, clap their hands and dance as I approached, the airport around me seemed to come to a temporary halt. Embarrassed by all the attention and the bemused stares of the other passengers I sheepishly accepted all the hugs, the handshakes, the slaps on the back and the reassurances of everyone that the baby looked just like me.

I had been used to being addressed as 'Mukwasha' by Kwadzi's relatives, the Shona word for 'son-in-law'. But now I had acquired a new title, a name I would be addressed by forever after as the phrase that defined me in their eyes. 'Baba Mhiko' was what I would be called, 'the father of Mhiko.' I was taken aback as we had never discussed what we would call our son or daughter. I had expected that decision to take place after I arrived.

'You know my sister well enough by now,' her brother said as we made our way towards the exit and I asked him why I had not been consulted. 'Once she makes up her mind then that's how it's going to be. She took one look at the baby and said that it was a Mhiko and that if others couldn't see that name written across his forehead then that was their problem.'

'But what does it mean?' I asked, aware that many Shona names signified something in English. 'Accident', 'Chance' and 'Unfortunate' were ones I had come across among my circle of friends and acquaintances.

'I have no idea. But look. It's easy enough to say. No one is going to stutter over the pronunciation. I'd accept it if I were you and be thankful she didn't call him something you would really want to object to.'

Although she had given birth the previous day Kwadzi was at home, resting in one of the bedrooms, surrounded by a group of excited women. 'So, there you are,' she said when I entered, as if I had stepped out of the house only a few minutes previously instead of the six or so months since we had last seen each other.

'And there he is,' she added, handing me a small shape wrapped in a bundle of shawls and blankets, repeating what I had been told in the airport and the drive home about the family resemblance that was obvious to everyone. But all I could see was a small squashed face, a scrunched-up nose and a pair of curious eyes. The moment these fixed on my own face he commenced a small explosion of coughing, spluttering and tears that only abated when I returned him to his mother.

Washington, Kwadzi's brother who had children of his own, had warned me. 'For the first year babies belong to their mother. Don't worry about the feeling of exclusion. It's normal.'

Over the next few days a bewildering number of relatives, friends, neighbours and what at times seemed curious onlookers came round to see the baby. A large part of the conversation revolved around the shape of his nose, the colour of his eyes, and his various facial expressions in an attempt to decipher which one of his parents he actually looked like. Everyone seemed keen to reassure me about his parentage as if I was harbouring some doubts as to whether I was the actual father. Kwadzi laughed when I asked why everyone seemed so fixated on spotting the family likeness and echoed what her brother had told me. 'Don't worry. It's only a way of making you feel less left out. It's what we say to all fathers on the birth of their first child, even if there is no resemblance at all.'

Kwadzi's extended family had always been friendly and hospitable and had made me feel welcome at family gatherings. But I noticed over these few days a change in attitude, as if my status had altered and I had been accepted into a different fraternity. Nothing was said. Nothing was explained. But sitting one evening on the porch of our house, half listening to a conversation that the men were conducting around me, Washington interrupted my reverie to tell me that my opinion was also wanted.

'Sorry, about what exactly? I can barely follow what is being said.'

It was to do with the behaviour of one of Kwadzi's cousins, involving some dispute between him and his wife. I had never met him, had never been asked for my views before and was reluctant to express an ill-informed opinion in a cultural context that was frequently unclear to me. But Washington was insistent, claiming that my opinion was as important as everyone else's and that my views on such matters were now expected. It seemed that having presented a son to the clan entitled me to a say on important family issues, no matter how inappropriate and misconceived.

I managed to offer a tentative judgement while the men around me respectfully nodded their heads. They raised their bottles of beer towards me after I had finished as if I had delivered some pearls of wisdom that none of them had thought of before. Then they returned to their argument as to the best course of action to follow. Whether they had taken account of anything I had actually said was unclear to me as they continued, but I couldn't help feeling worthier and more important.

'You look very pleased with yourself,' Kwadzi remarked later that evening after everyone had departed. 'I'm glad you don't seem to mind all the relatives coming round. To be honest I worried that you might be fed up with all the family attention.'

We returned to that subject a few weeks later when I reminded her one morning that I only had a few days left before I was scheduled to return to Morocco. The constant visitors, the family get-togethers, the baby being the centre of attention meant we had had little private time. I missed the intimacy we had enjoyed before.

Although I avoided saying the words, I was conscious of the feeling of distance that had grown over the six months. Watching Kwadzi now with the baby, surrounded by her relatives, interacting with her friends, looking more complete in many ways than I remembered, that feeling of separation was only heightened. While I had gained another kind of membership within her extended family, my immediate one seemed to be drifting away. The fact that I was about to leave again, that it would be another six months before we would see each other, made it even more important that we had some time to reconnect.

As we sat together, watching the baby asleep, part of me was hoping that she would say, 'Don't go back to Morocco. The family is more important than your career.' But I knew that Kwadzi was not the kind of woman to ever make such a statement, not just because it would signal a weakness that she would be reluctant ever to admit, but because she knew as well as I that this appeal would come back to haunt our relationship in later years.

If these words were to be said, then they would have to come from me. But as time elapsed and the moment to say them disappeared, I also realised that they would not be spoken. Part of this was about pride, the fact that I too would not want to acknowledge a weakness and admit that I could not cope on my own. Part of it was a practical consideration about earning a decent wage and being able to support a new family with a relatively comfortable standard of living. Every year thousands of Zimbabwean men left their villages and towns to work in the farms, mines and factories of South Africa. In that sense I was no different, just another economic migrant trying to support a wife and child back home.

But even as these justifications for not opening my mouth circled around in my head, I knew that the reason why I would not hand in my notice was something else entirely. The fact was that the nomadic lifestyle I had taken up again was what I wanted most. The thrill of living and working in different places, that mixture of trepidation, fear and excitement of being constantly on the move was as strong now as it had been when I had embarked on my overseas adventure a decade previously.

Stronger than my temptation to build a home was my fear of standing still, of becoming settled, of waking up each morning to the same ceiling above me, the same walls around me and the same routines stretching into the distant future in an unbroken line. So whether it was Kwadzi or I who spoke out and encouraged a decision not to leave, I knew that in a month's time, maybe a year or even a decade from now, there would be a feeling of regret that I had broken my journey and not continued to the road's end, wherever that may be.

'You'll come back when you're ready,' were Kwadzi's final words a few days later as I packed my bags and prepared for the flight back to Casablanca. As we said our goodbyes I wondered whether that moment might ever come at all.

Once back in Morocco the pressure of work soon pushed personal issues into the background. There were regular visits to be conducted to different parts of the country to monitor the quality of our projects for children. There were endless rounds of meetings with local and national officials to assure them that we had no agenda that conflicted with their own priorities. Meanwhile the business of going through our finances, checking our expenditures and producing reports and updates for our head office, donors and the Government Ministries we interacted with, also managed to consume a significant portion of my time. With my beach now out of bounds and little else to do at weekends and evenings, I brought work home from the office, occasionally venturing outdoors to my local café or a meeting with Youssef to break the routine.

Several months after my return, our secretary entered my office to announce that there was a young woman who wanted to see me. 'Does she have an appointment?' I asked, mindful that I was already behind with several urgent deadlines.

'No she doesn't but she says that she can wait.'

'Okay, ask her to come in. But after five minutes come and remind me that I have a meeting to attend. I have too many things to do today.'

A few seconds later our visitor entered my room. Apologetic about the intrusion, she came over to shake my hand, introduced herself as Yasmine and said that she was here to ask me a few questions for her newspaper about our disability programme in Khemisset. 'I have all the facts and figures. I know how many children you help. I know how much you spend and I know how long your organization has been in Morocco. Your colleague in Khemisset told me. But I need something more than dry statistics to keep our readers interested.'

As she sat down on the chair opposite with her pen in hand, waiting for me to deliver something 'quotable', I could see that her words were matched by the same confidence in her bright, alert expression. Her stare was something I was not used to either. It was not hostile or unfriendly. But it was a stare nevertheless and something I had not encountered among the women I had interacted with in Morocco who dropped their gaze whenever I talked to them in deference to the decorum expected in their society. Should I stare back? Should I look elsewhere? In the end I fidgeted with some items on my desk but with time enough to register a face of considerable beauty centred on her disconcerting eyes and the look of amusement and curiosity that hovered around them.

'I'm not sure if I have anything more to contribute than what you already have,' I replied, conscious of how limp that sounded while desperately trying to think of something interesting I could offer her. Najia, whom she had already spoken to, had much more detailed knowledge than I, not only about our programme in Khemisset but about the challenges and problems faced by the families we helped.

There was a brief pause, the same stare and then the same direct manner when she resumed. 'Well, let me be more specific then. How do the lives of people with disabilities in your part of the world compare to the lives of people with disabilities in my country?'

For a few seconds I fidgeted some more. If I was honest and confessed my ignorance, there could be an article in a national newspaper complaining that a foreign director of an international organization working in Morocco knew nothing about the subject matter of his programme. If I pretended more than I knew then I ran the risk of being exposed. But I had already decided that Yasmine's was not an ungenerous or insensitive face and I did not have the sense of someone who was out to trip me. Despite my caution when dealing with members of the press when presenting our work, I shrugged my shoulders and admitted that I knew too little about the lives of people with disabilities in both countries to be able to offer a useful opinion. 'But this is something I mean to address. The circumstances of the people we assist can and should be better understood.'

Her notebook was closed and her pen put away. Without any gesture of irritation or disappointment she said that it was refreshing to hear someone confess that they did not know something when asked a question by a member of her profession. 'More often than not they make it up or say something that they think people would like to hear, even if it's not true. Don't worry. The article will be written and it will be a positive appreciation of your work. It just won't be so interesting without a few quotes from the country director, that's all.'

Just then and on cue my secretary knocked on the door, entered the room and announced that my next meeting was about to start and I needed to make a move. As I thanked her for the reminder, I regretted having told her to interrupt us. Despite the unproductive encounter and my own awkwardness in terms of responding to Yasmine's questions, I was intrigued too by the person in front of me. Would I find another opportunity to meet her? What excuse could I make to see her again?

As she rose to leave I apologised for my shallow response to the interview and said that once I had more useful information to share I hoped I might be able to contact her again if she was interested in writing another article.

149

'Here's my card then,' she replied, 'with all my details. You can ring me at my office if you have anything more you want to add about your programme.'

For several weeks, her card propped up on my desk, I would pick up the phone, dial most of the number she had given me and then replace the receiver before I completed the call. What, after all, could I say? A few weeks was not enough to claim that I had had a sudden illumination, that I could now pretend knowledge I did not have such a short while go. And in any case what could I expect and where would it lead if my principal motive for getting in touch with her had nothing to do with work and everything to do with pursuing a fleeting attraction prompted by a beautiful face and her beguiling manner. 'She is probably married in any case,' I said to myself, remembering a friends's observation that beautiful women in Morocco were married off early. As I held back from making the call that curiosity was pushing me towards, I reminded myself that there was the small matter of my own marriage too.

In the end it was Yasmine who contacted me. At first I did not recognize the voice on the other end of the line. 'Oh, so you've forgotten me already,' she said, when I asked who I was speaking to.

'No, of course not,' I protested. 'It's just that you sound a bit different, that's all. I've been meaning to ring you actually.'

'So, why didn't you?' she asked. I made up an

excuse about being too busy and not having the information I promised I would find for her. As I stumbled around for a decent reason I was grateful that she was not in my office to see my red face and the unsettling effect her call had had on me. Several weeks of wanting to contact her and not having the courage to do so had made me nervous.

'I have a proposition for you,' she announced, after I had composed myself and exchanged some pleasantries about the weather, her work and my own recent visit to Khemisset to see our programme.

'What's that?' I replied.

'I belong to a women's group in Rabat. We hold meetings every month and this week we have a prominent activist from the disability movement giving a talk. You mentioned that you wanted to find out more about the lives of people you are helping. I thought you might want to come along.'

We established that men were not only accepted but welcomed to such gatherings. The flaws in our character could never be rectified unless we heard what was wrong with us. The talk would probably be delivered in French but, if it was in Arabic, Yasmine offered to translate.

I remarked, when she told me the location and the time, that it seemed to be late in the evening to be holding a meeting. According to Yasmine this was now standard throughout Morocco for one simple and somewhat superficial reason. On Mondays, Tuesdays and Thursdays the nation was held in thrall from eight to nine o'clock every week by a Brazilian soap opera that had captured national attention. No one dared to organize meetings, conferences, lectures or even coffee with their friends during that time for fear that they would be the only person to turn up.

'It's a fantasy,' Yasmine replied when I asked why it was so popular, 'and maybe that explains the attraction. Three times a week for sixty minutes we are allowed to contemplate a different world from the one we inhabit. Some feminists say it is good for our women to see that there is a different way of interacting between the sexes. Others claim that it only reinforces national stereotypes since most of the women in the story are miserable and unhappy. Our men watch too and they say to their wives, "Look, that's what would happen to you if you lived over there."'

At the venue when I arrived later that week I felt something of a lone and isolated representative despite Yasmine having reassured me that men were welcome. 'I never said that they actually turned up,' she replied, when I complained that I could see no fellow males to keep me company. The thirty or forty women gathered in the hall smiled benignly towards me as I took my seat but I could not help thinking that their occasional glances in my direction were in astonishment that I had dared to turn up.

A few minutes later, accompanied by a round of applause, the speaker for the evening entered the hall. The noise thankfully concealed my gasp of surprise. Almost half my size, her body was doubled up and twisted into what seemed an almost impossible configuration. With considerable difficulty she dragged herself on a pair of crutches to the podium, excused herself for having to sit down because standing for long periods of time was so painful and then, from behind a pair of thick spectacles, scrutinized the audience in front of her as if searching for something.

'People with disabilities are great readers of faces,' she began, 'and what I see in yours is pretty much what I have seen for the past thirty years in the faces of most people when I first meet them. Pity. Confusion. Embarrassment. And most surprisingly of all I see fear. I have often asked myself why. I think it's because disability is not too far away from all of you. Whether you have an accident or illness or simply arrive at old age, sooner or later something similar may happen to you.'

As I tried hard not to avert my gaze or look uncomfortable Selma went on to say that like a lot of children in Morocco she had contracted polio at an early age that left her without the use of her legs and dependent on all sorts of aids and appliances. Her case, as we could see, had been particularly severe.

What saved her, she continued, from the emotions and reactions of the people around her was the strength and determination of her father. It was clear from the way she spoke about him that he had been a major influence and support in her life. 'He repeatedly told me not to feel sorry for myself. That was the worst thing I could succumb to, he said, because it would make me helpless, dependent and imprisoned in the perceptions that other people had of me.'

So Selma, despite her wish to be closeted at home, was forced to play with other children in the neighbourhood, to participate in their games as best she could, to endure the ridicule and condescension that frequently came her way. 'At times I felt like giving up but my father told me that all of this was a preparation for the tougher battles I would have to face later.'

As Selma related her story it was clear that her recurring theme was not the challenges and obstacles she faced because of her limited mobility or the physical pain that accompanied her several operations. What she talked about was the behaviour of others. Teachers at school, family relatives, her college lecturers, prospective employers, and her boss in the first medical practice where she had worked after graduation manifested the same emotions and attitudes she had highlighted earlier. They were not supportive in terms of helping her to realise the kind of person she wanted to become.

'Look, I don't blame them,' she said, referring to her fellow students at the college where she had studied. 'Most of them had never seen a disabled person up close before. So when they stared at me I stared back. When they ignored me I reminded them I was there. And what I have experienced is that attitudes can change. When I came top of my class some of them began to ask me if I could help them with their homework. In my own way I believe I educated them to see me as a person, not as someone almost like them but not quite.'

The words that most struck home during the thirty minutes she spoke related to her observations on the institutions that had been set up to help people with disabilities in Morocco. She acknowledged that children who were paralysed would need wheelchairs and crutches. People who were blind would need white sticks and those who were deaf would need hearing aids. But Government departments, local charities and international organizations lacked a genuine commitment to support people with disabilities to speak out on their own behalf and to challenge the public misperceptions that were the biggest obstacles they faced.

'I described earlier the stereotypes that people have of us, that we are seen as victims meriting pity rather than individuals with rights, entitlements and a contribution to make to our societies. That will never change if we continue to be spoken about rather than having the opportunity to speak for ourselves. My work has allowed me to travel throughout our country and to meet with many disabled people and one thing we all complain about is our invisibility. Unless people with disabilities are at the forefront of telling you what we need you will continue to make mistakes.'

As the applause died down and the audience began to filter out of the hall, Yasmine asked me if I would like to meet the speaker. Probably noticing my look of apprehension she reassured me that despite Selma's strong opinions she would not be hostile. 'I think she will be able to help you. And in any case isn't it important to have your assumptions challenged now and again?'

'Oh, so you're the director of Save the Children in Morocco,' Selma said when I shook her hand as Yasmine introduced us. 'I have a bone to pick with you.'

It turned out that several years previously she had visited our offices. She had complained then about the fact that our premises were inaccessible. There was no ramp for wheelchair users. The lift to our floor was too narrow and there were no railings to help people climb our stairs. Had anything been done about this?

I replied that it hadn't and remembered Youssef making similar complaints about exactly the same thing. But the cost of renovations was high and I had a dilemma too about making such an investment. Wasn't it better to spend our money on actual projects? An overhead like office repairs was a diversion of scarce resources from our core business.

'To be honest,' I continued as politely as I could, 'it's not a priority for us. We have so many other things to spend our money on. I appreciate that it may be inconvenient but we hardly have any

156

visitors with disabilities, you see. The expense would not be worth it.'

That same stare that Selma had directed towards the audience when she first spoke was now firmly fixed towards me. I tried hard not to look away, conscious too of Yasmine beside me and wondering if this conversation was being recorded for replication in an article later. 'Excuse me, young man,' Selma said, 'but have you ever considered that so few people with disabilities bother to visit you precisely because you have such an unwelcoming environment? And the fact that we can't even enter your offices deprives you of the opportunity to hear something useful. This is the kind of thing I would have expected to hear from an ignorant employer, not the head of a supposedly enlightened organization working on our behalf.'

For a moment I thought of repeating what I had said about the need to spend our money on projects and that it was not our responsibility to convert the building, but something told me it was better not to say anything. I had never been entirely comfortable with the arguments I had presented to Youssef when he complained and perhaps the cursory manner in which I had closed any further debate on the subject was because part of me was not convinced either.

'It's not only about discouraging people like myself from visiting you,' Selma continued, 'but about the message you project by not investing in these things. How can you pressure the Government and other institutions to be more sensitive to our needs if you don't practise that philosophy yourself?'

Our exchange was interrupted by another group of women seeking an audience. As I muttered a somewhat embarrassed goodbye Selma extended her hand again and in a kindlier tone said that she was appreciative of the fact that I had bothered to turn up that evening to listen to her. 'And you're the only man in the room too. So that's two counts in your favour,' she concluded before turning away.

One week later I summoned up the courage I had lacked before and phoned Yasmine in her office. 'Can we have a coffee together?' I asked. 'There's something I want to discuss with you.'

There was silence at the other end of the line. Had I made an indelicate request? Was inviting a woman out for coffee inappropriate in Moroccan society? Once again my face turned red as I stumbled around for an apology for probably having blundered against some local tradition. 'I'm not familiar with how things are done here. Where I come from men and women having coffee in public together is no big deal.'

But Yasmine was amused rather than shocked or offended. 'Don't be silly,' she said. 'You haven't done anything wrong. I was just checking my calendar to find a suitable time, that's all. What about the day after tomorrow? I know a good place beside your office.'

At the café when we met I told her that I wanted to thank her for having invited me to her meeting. I had thought long and hard about what Selma had said. She had been right. We had a programme that inadequately consulted people with disabilities as well as activities that were not geared to challenging public misconceptions and prejudice. So I had discussed with Cathy and others in my team the idea of a book, a collection of voices from people with disabilities in Morocco so that in their own words they could tell their stories and present themselves to a national audience. My boss had agreed upon my request to allocate resources and allow me the time to put this publication together.

'What a fantastic idea,' Yasmine enthused with some feeling. 'I didn't think that a casual invitation on my part would have led to such dramatic consequences. Would you keep me informed as to how this develops? I'm sure my newspaper would be interested in giving you some publicity.'

'But I didn't just ask you here to inform you about an idea,' I continued. 'You're a writer. You know the subject. We need to interview people and edit what they say into a story that is accessible, interesting and compelling. I want you to play a part in this too.'

I could see from her face that she was flattered. There was interest too. But she had concerns around the fact that she was employed full-time by her newspaper, that she would be unable to dedicate herself sufficiently to an undertaking that would be time-consuming and demanding. But all of this, I replied, could be negotiated. This would be a long-term endeavour where her involvement could be fitted in. 'I'm not asking you to jump ship completely and hand in your notice. We can work something out that respects your commitments.'

'Look, I'll ring you in a day or so with my decision,' she replied after I had finished my attempts at persuasion. 'There are a few things I need to think about before I could agree to your proposition.'

I nodded my head and said that was fine, trying to conceal my disappointment that I had not been able to procure an immediate agreement. I was convinced that she would be perfect for what the publication needed. And there was the pleasurable anticipation too of working closely together and enjoying more of her company.

Perhaps she noticed the slight deflation on my part since she added that it was considered bad form in her country to agree immediately to important decisions. Again there was that same hint of amusement and mischievous humour that had struck me so forcibly during our previous encounters. 'We have a saying in Morocco that husbands don't appreciate wives who accept their offer of marriage the first time round. If we value ourselves properly we need to be asked three times. So be patient,' she concluded. 'Phone me tomorrow and the day after and you'll probably get the answer you're looking for.'

'So why are you going to Safi?' Youssef asked me a few months later. 'It's a long drive to see nothing much unless you like factories and fish.' My guide-book had said the same thing, namely that pottery and sardines were the principal attractions it had to offer and little else of interest besides. But I had been put in touch with someone whom we should interview for our book. Widad was well known within the disability movement for cham-pioning the cause of people with hearing impairments. When I phoned her office her assist-ant told me that she would be more than happy to meet me and so an appointment had been set for the following week.

'Are you driving on your own?' Youssef asked. 'It's a long way without company.'

'Oh, don't worry,' I replied, as casually as I could. 'Yasmine will be travelling with me. She will help with the discussion.'

Over the past few months I had worked with her on identifying, conducting and editing the inter-views that would form the core material for our publication. Her work schedule with her news-paper meant that much of this had been done in the evenings in our office. Youssef and Cathy would frequently join us as we scrutinized the texts, identified what was still needed and argued about how far we wanted to go in terms of upsetting some influential people in Morocco. Despite such long periods of time in Yasmine's company no opportunity had opened up to discuss anything other than the project. Now we would be together with no one else around. Would there be space to have a different conversation or would convention and propriety limit us to the professional exchanges we had traded so far?

Past Casablanca on a road that tracked the wild coastline further south I asked her the question that had been circling around in my head for some time. Was a boyfriend she had mentioned on a previous occasion an intended husband or 'something else'? When she turned towards me and in that same humorous tone asked me what 'something else' might mean, I was embarrassed and said that casual relations were common in my part of the world but maybe not in hers.

'You're right. Generally, we don't have casual relationships in Morocco,' she replied, but without any irritation to signal that I had intruded into forbidden territory. 'If a man and woman are seeing each other then ninety-nine times out of a hundred they will end up as husband and wife. For the small percentage for whom that doesn't work out, well, there are consequences. Women in failed relationships acquire a reputation. Prospective future husbands will wonder what is wrong with a woman who had a chance at marriage but failed to take it. And of course they will want to know all the minute details of what happened before. You know in my culture jealousy is regarded differently, a sign that a man wants to protect his honour. So yes, in answer to your question, I think one day we will probably get married.'

'Does he make you happy?' I continued, conscious that if I was probing too far and had strayed from an etiquette that was acceptable Yasmine would be firm enough to tell me so.

'That's a difficult question to answer,' she replied. 'Unlike you we don't have a chance to find out much about our partners before we get married. We sit around with our families. We meet in a public place for coffee. Occasionally we get a small amount of time on our own to exchange a few words beyond the usual pleasantries. What we have to do is to make our best guess about what the future will bring with another person. It's a leap in the dark and in hope that it will turn out right.'

She added that our respective definitions of happiness were probably different too and wondered if this was something I had noticed in my interactions with people in some of the other countries where I had worked. 'From our point of view we sometimes think that when people from your part of the world talk about happiness they are referring to something that is much more private, individual and perhaps selfish than what we mean in our society. At the same time we don't judge our lives after marriage by the same measure we use beforehand. I'm not saying I agree with this entirely but in my society individual happiness is sacrificed in marriage for things like duty, the happiness of our children, family and community expectations of our role. Maybe that makes women here more docile. Or maybe that makes us more resilient.'

When I remarked that she was still quite young to make such an important decision she went on to say that pressure on her to marry was exacerbated by the fact that her father had died some time ago. Although her memories were vague she recalled a parent who had been keen for her to have a good education and supportive of an early assertiveness on her part that had grated with other members of her family. 'As for my mother, well, she just wants grandchildren. She keeps on saying that at twenty-four I'm turning into an old woman, that men will no longer look at me and that in a few years' time it will be too late.'

I wondered if Yasmine was keen to change the topic of our discussion when she remarked on the view that was spread before us of rolling hills, small picturesque villages and, occasionally breaking through, a windswept ocean crashing on the rocks and beaches of the coastline below us. But several hours short of our destination and after we had stopped at a roadside café for lunch, she turned towards me. Exchanging confidences was supposed to be done by both parties, she said, and it was now my turn to share something of myself.

'Such as?' I replied, trying not to sound as nervous as I felt.

'Well you mentioned a wife and a recent child. Where are they?"

'Nine thousand, five hundred and fifty kilometres away,' I answered, attempting some jocularity. I added that I needed to pursue my career and that opportunities had been scarce in Zimbabwe. So I had found work here. Since my wife had an important post in the civil service and since her family was there too we thought that the best thing would be to live apart for a while until circumstances allowed us to be together again.

Having seen her at work I knew that Yasmine would pursue this further. 'Are you happy with that arrangement? Don't you get lonely?'

Having been asked that question before, I had an answer. 'Of course it's not easy. There's a lot that I miss. But other families do it. There are probably more men working outside Zimbabwe and separated from their wives for a few years than those living with their families inside the country. You learn how to cope.'

'Of course we have that here too,' Yasmine responded, adding that migration was common in Morocco and that there were consequences for family life that happened as a result. 'Thousands of our men are working in France and Spain. Some for most of their lives. Although it is not openly spoken about everyone knows that over there they have temporary wives and girlfriends. They pay for sex too. When I spoke to some women here about this they said that such a thing was normal and what else could their men be expected to do? So long as their husbands sent money every month, gave them four children and returned once a year with gifts for the family then their duties had been fulfilled. Girlfriends or prostitutes, they said, were not serious rivals.'

'So are you asking me if I have a secret girlfriend somewhere in Morocco or pay for sex?' I replied, feigning indignation. For the first time since we had met, Yasmine's confident manner was exchanged for something more uncertain as she stammered an apology and said that she had never meant to insinuate such a thing. It was my turn to laugh and assure her that I had taken no offence. I was teasing, that was all. But as we moved to the safer topic of commenting on the landscape we were passing through, the reflections that her questions had prompted continued to circle around in my head. Did I feel lonely? Yes. How did I cope with it? I couldn't tell her that one of the reasons I enjoyed being with her was precisely because I wanted the company of someone I was attracted to. I knew that this was a conservative Muslim society. I knew that casual relationships were not accepted. I knew that she had a boyfriend she would probably marry and that I had a wife and child back home. But when I was with her I could imagine for a while that reality was different and that my circumstances had changed, that a moment would present itself where I could hold her hand, lean over and kiss her without the shock and consternation that would be the likeliest outcome in the world we inhabited.

My thoughts were interrupted when Yasmine pointed to a sign on the road announcing that Safi was only thirty kilometres away. 'Have you thought about how we will actually interact with Widad?' she asked, her practical question bringing me back to the present and the principal reason we had made this journey. I confessed a certain nervousness. The few hearing-impaired children in our programme in Khemisset communicated through an elaborate series of hand signals with which I had no familiarity. Even Cathy, who had many more years' experience than I, could only manage short, summary conversations. Despite having heard that Widad was perfectly able to talk I wondered how someone who had lost their hearing at an early age could have acquired language skills at all.

In the small city of several hundred thousand people, and as many smoking chimneys as inhabitants it seemed, we were directed to the address I had been given. It was a school for children with disabilities and at the office when we arrived, we were greeted by a young woman who welcomed us to the centre, enquired about our journey and asked if we would like some tea or coffee.

'This must be the assistant I spoke to on the

phone,' I whispered to Yasmine, adding that I hoped she would be present at the interview. Her warm, personable manner and her familiarity with her boss would help with a discussion that I feared might be problematic. But when she escorted us into another room, invited us to sit down and adjust our positions so she could read our lips more clearly I realised that this was the person we had come all the way to see.

Remembering Selma's observation about people with disabilities being excellent readers of faces I offered an apology about the mistaken identity. Her youthfulness had surprised me too and for someone who had the reputation of being a well-known activist I confessed that I had expected her to be considerably older. 'You see. I have discriminated against you already and we haven't even started our conversation.'

Widad laughed and said that unlike people with obvious physical disabilities there was often little to differentiate those with hearing impairments from the general population. 'But in some ways that is part of our problem,' she added. 'I have had people get angry with me when I found it difficult to understand what they are saying as if there are no allowances made for our differences.'

Her French was perfect although the words were spoken without much intonation and tone, but her animated face made up for the lack of expression in her voice, accompanied by the use of her hands whenever she wanted to emphasize a particular point. As we proceeded I became aware that my own speech pattern had altered. This was not only because of my concern to make allowances for the fact that she could not hear a word of what was said but my awkwardness at being under such intense scrutiny whenever I spoke. 'Don't worry, Mr Chris,' Widad reassured me, probably noticing my somewhat hesitant manner. 'Speaking with a deaf person is something you have to get used to. Most men I speak to who don't know I'm deaf, think I am staring at them because of their incredible good looks. When I tell them the real reason they always seem rather disappointed.'

Not for the first time in our conversations with people with disabilities, families featured prominently in the way they either confronted or avoided the world. 'In my own case,' Widad explained, 'there was none of what happens in other families where children with disabilities are hidden away as if they are an embarrassment. When I got into a fight with some of the other children in our neighbourhood who were making fun of me and other parents came round to complain, my father told them that his daughter had every right to defend herself. It was a great loss to me when he died a few years ago. I felt I had lost my biggest fan.'

Widad, like Selma, had also struggled against the reaction of most people when they found out she was deaf. Pity reinforced inability amongst those it was directed towards. Her own upbringing never allowed that to happen to her but she acknowledged she was lucky in that regard and privileged because of her family's attitudes. Most people with disabilities in Morocco, she claimed, succumbed to that reaction and in turn reinforced the stereotypes that were widespread in her society.

'I have trouble with other people who are deaf, although I understand where their passivity, their resignation and lack of ambition come from. I remember when I put myself forward for an acting role in a play that was being staged in Safi. Some of my friends who were deaf too told me I must be crazy. They said I would make a fool of myself and that it was better for me to accept who I was. That only made me more determined. I got the part. The play won a national prize and we even performed in another country. I often think of all the things we have never tried because of other people's attitudes and the limited expectations they have of us.'

She smiled when Yasmine asked her whether her disability meant a barrier to relationships with Moroccan men and an impediment to marriage. 'Of course you know it is impolite to raise this subject with a woman in our conservative society. Most people are curious but are too concerned about whether I will get indignant or upset to ask the question.'

She said that she was not married but this was

out of choice rather than because of anything arising from her disability. 'It's not my being deaf that is the issue but the fact that I'm strong-willed and argumentative. Moroccan men are intimated by that,' a remark which prompted vigorous agreement from Yasmine. 'They want a docile wife, someone to give them children and have their dinner waiting on the table as soon as they come home. I'm afraid these are roles I don't fit into.'

She added that there was another dynamic she had observed. Women with disabilities were subject to considerable prejudice so when men proposed marriage they regarded it as a favour conferred on someone who should be grateful. This led to abusive relationships. 'When women with disabilities complain to their families about how they are treated, they are frequently told that they are lucky to have a husband at all and so should accept whatever comes their way.'

These kinds of norms and social pressures meant that some women, particularly those with physical disabilities, did everything they could to conceal their condition. This included, when they could afford it, expensive, cosmetic operations that frequently did more harm than good.

'For them disability is an embarrassment, something that prevents them from aspiring to the life that women are taught to dream about in most societies. It's no different here than in your part of the world where there is this model of physical perfection and beauty, where a flaw or blemish is perceived as something that disadvantages you and puts you in an inferior position to your competitors. I know one woman here who is young, beautiful and intelligent. She spent her money on an operation that has now left her in considerably more pain than what she had before. But she considers herself happier because men would not notice her slight limp and the fact that one leg was a few centimetres shorter than the other.'

It was difficult to describe to those who were not deaf what it was like, she concluded, when I asked my final question. For her what was most problematic was a sense of isolation and frustration at not being able to hear what was going on in the world around her. She had seen people's faces light up when listening to music, for example, and had realised that there was a dimension of experience she was missing.

She was thankful however that compared to others she had been fortunate. The encouragement and support she had been given meant that at least she had a language to permit interaction with other people. 'But I sometimes think that words do not have the same meaning for me as they do for you because they cannot really convey the emotions I feel. That is why I wave my arms around a lot and get animated when I am talking. At times I have the impression that I am not getting through, that I cannot really present the person I am. Being deaf at times is like being in a prison where you can't shout out to others to let them know you are there.'

Under the watchful eyes of four waiters, who had nothing else to do but stare since we were the only customers in the hotel restaurant, I had dinner that evening with Yasmine. As I avoided straying into any discussions of a personal nature, I reflected on Widad's comment about the prison she said she was in, how lack of hearing and inadequate control of language meant an inability to communicate what she was feeling. But that was also true of people who had no such disadvantages. Wasn't that the situation I was in now, sitting across the table from the person I most wanted to be with, yet unable to share anything more meaningful or relevant than some bland observations about the city we were visiting and the quality of the food that had been placed in front of us.

'Are you worried about something?' Yasmine asked at one point.

'No nothing. Just tired after our journey,' was all I was able to reply, not having the courage to open a conversation that might be more in line with what I wanted to say but would be fraught with awkwardness and risk at the same time.

At the top of the stairs on the second floor where our paths diverged we said goodnight. Our rooms were on opposite ends of a long corridor, courtesy of the hotel receptionist who on establishing that we were not married had placed us as far away from each other as possible. But as Yasmine turned to move away I leaned forward and kissed her on the cheek. 'That's long enough,' I had time to think to myself as I prolonged the contact, aware that what I was doing was more than what would be considered acceptable between 'just friends' in my own society, let alone in Morocco where even married couples would never attempt such a gesture in public.

She said nothing when I finally disengaged, apart from repeating another 'good night'. As I sat on my bed later I reflected that this was a strong enough signal to back off, to accept that this attraction on my part would never go anywhere and that I should not risk a valuable friendship by causing offence with inappropriate and unacceptable behaviour.

Breakfast was cordial enough, the same four waiters apparently not having moved from the same position they had occupied the previous evening. When Yasmine asked me if I had slept well I nodded my head, not wanting to disclose that I had tossed and turned for most of the night, occasionally waking up in disbelief at what I had done. As I paid the bill, tipped the doorman and started the car, Yasmine remarked on the ugliness of a city with so many chimneys, and I breathed a sigh of relief that seemingly no harm had dented our relationship. Whatever move I had attempted the previous night had probably been consigned to a file marked 'temporary foolishness' and so we could go on as we had done before.

But some distance from Safi and between villages on a road that had become routine and boring Yasmine pointed to a sign ahead that indicated a detour to the coastline we were following. There was no one else at the small car park that fronted a large area of beach, the waves crashing and rolling on the sand in front of us as we sat contemplating the view.

'What are your feelings towards me?' Yasmine asked, finally breaking the silence.

'I think I'm in love with you,' I replied, realizing that what I had done the previous evening had indeed pushed us into a place where I would have to be more honest than I had been before.

'What does that mean?' she responded, in a tone of voice that was not dismissive or irritated but curious, as if genuinely puzzled by what I had just confessed.

'I'm not sure,' I continued, wondering how you explained to someone the feelings evoked by that word and the strange, irrational things it some-times prompted you to do. 'All I know is that when I'm with you there is nowhere else I would rather be and when I'm not I feel an emptiness, a need to be in your company.'

Again there was that same expression I had seen on her face before when she was conducting inter-views, when she was pursuing something that needed an explanation in order to present it clearly to the readers of her articles. Was the word 'love', I wondered, such an alien concept in her vocabulary that it needed an effort to understand it? I had time to reflect too, with some disappointment, that this must be because it was in no way reciprocated, that it found no echo in her own emotions that it prompted this reaction. 'And this feeling you have for me,' she said after a while. 'Where do you want it to go? Where do you want it to end up?'

For a moment these blunt, practical questions forced me to think what it must be like for her; hearing my words, receiving my confession, being on the receiving end of my clumsy kiss the previous evening. The puzzlement I had heard in her voice was now my own since what indeed could I be proposing when I said I loved her that was at all of any consequence. How far was I prepared to go to translate this emotion into anything practical and real? In the silence that followed I could only shrug my shoulders and look blank.

As if determined to explore what I would not, she continued. Would I be prepared to divorce my wife? Could I offer her stability? Would I abandon the lifestyle I was used to, this moving around with no attachments, living in different cultures, having the freedom to explore my dreams? Would I have the courage to stand up in front of hundreds of people in her local mosque and proclaim that I had now embraced her religion, a precondition for marriage in her society?

How much of my past would I be prepared to give up to secure our future together?

My continued silence was answer enough and when I turned towards her again after staring for some time at the ocean I was shocked to see tears in her eyes. Her normal, confident, self-assured expression had been exchanged for the face of a young girl, vulnerable and fragile. For the first time in our exchange on this subject I heard blame and condemnation as she saw my expression of surprise, my bewilderment that I had provoked this reaction. 'Are you so blind,' she said. 'that you can't see that I have feelings too? Are you so insensitive?'

But unlike me she had kept her emotions to herself, being smart enough to realise that only regret would come if we tried to action what was best left alone. I felt ashamed, having thought all along that I was the one who was more mature in these matters, that someone younger and with less experience and cultural familiarity could see more clearly than I the dead end where this was headed.

A few minutes later there was firmness again in her voice, her dark eyes determinedly focused ahead. 'Both you and I know that we can't have an affair. That would not only be bad for me but for you as well. So, we will continue as friends. I would really like that. But we will get on with our lives and what might have happened between us will be a matter only for our imaginations. On the subject of our feelings towards each other this is the last we will speak of it.'

One year later in the same café where we had first discussed her potential involvement in our project, Yasmine showed me the inside page of a national newspaper that was reflecting on our recently published book. The article was positive about the fact that people with disabilities had been given a chance to express their opinions but there was defensiveness in some of the comments too. A Government official had remarked that disabled people should be more appreciative of the charity they were given and claimed that complaining too much could dry up the good will they were dependent on.

That response did not surprise me. I reminded Yasmine of what Selma had previously said. Many people who had been engaged in disability work for many years were not used to hearing anything more than 'thank you'. It came as a shock to them that there was another conversation to be had than expressions of constant gratitude. 'But I don't want to sound too judgemental either,' I added. 'A year ago their prejudices were my own. It's only through my involvement in this project that I have had the opportunity to see things differently.'

As we sipped our tea and reflected on the fact that provoking a reaction was part of what we had intended I found some space to tell Yasmine that I would shortly be leaving the country. My boss had phoned me a few weeks previously to tell me that a decision had been made to wind down our Morocco programme. Our work was almost over. Much of what we had established had been handed on to local organizations. At the end of our call she had added that a Country Director post for the Caribbean was now vacant. 'I think you should apply.'

'I bet you're excited,' Yasmine remarked, when I told her that my application had been successful. 'Three years in any one place is probably long enough for you. Tell me more about your new job.'

At the interview I had been informed that the post would involve a lot of travel. Most of our projects were spread across Cuba, Haiti and Jamaica and it was expected that I would spend equal amounts of time in each of these islands. I would not have a fixed base that I could call home. That spread of geography was appealing as well as the fact that I would be expected to commence new programmes of work in these locations as opposed to what I had been doing for the past few years in Morocco, winding down what had already been established.

'Can I ask you a personal question?' Yasmine continued, after I had communicated my enthusiasm for the new direction my life would be taking and the fact that yet again I was moving to another part of the world I knew nothing about.

'Sure, go ahead,' I replied. Since our conversation

we had continued as friends and, true to her word, nothing more had ever been spoken of what had transpired between us. I was sure that nothing on that matter would surface again.

'At the moment you are at the other end of Africa from your wife and child. Next month you will be at the other end of the world. Doesn't that bother you?'

I shrugged my shoulders. 'You know my story well enough by now. As for distance, well there's not much difference being twenty thousand miles away than ten thousand.'

That remark brought a frown, not of irritation but concern. 'I see your nomadic inclinations as a kind of addiction. It's fine for a while but not forever. You need family around you to have a sense of belonging, to provide you with stability. I worry about where you will end up in a few years' time.'

Perhaps Yasmine noticed my edginess in pursuing this discussion any further. What could I say? That I would have appreciated being with someone who was prepared to share my travels, my sense of adventure, someone perhaps like her? 'Since we are exchanging confidences about our futures,' she interjected before I could respond, 'there is something I want to tell you too.'

'What's that?'

'I'm getting married in a few months. Looks as if you'll miss the wedding.'

'That's wonderful news,' I responded, trying

to sound more positive and congratulatory than I felt. Even as I said the words I could feel a similar unease about the direction her life would be taking that she had just expressed about mine. Much of this was no doubt mixed up with emotions I still felt towards her, but part of it was about whether the person she had chosen was right for her, whether there would be happiness later.

Several months after we had returned from Safi she had asked me to meet him. I had hesitated at first but she had said that it was important to her and that he had asked to meet me too. She had spoken to him on many occasions of our work together and how important our project was for her professional development. He had asked to be introduced so that he could thank me for the opportunity she had been given. I accepted and over the dinner that Yasmine had cooked I was genial and friendly.

'He's a good man,' I had said later when she asked me for my opinion. I could see that what I said was important to her. 'You'll be happy with him. He's responsible and will give you a good home and family.' I did not say that I was concerned whether in time he might try to control her and limit her aspirations and dreams.

Shortly before leaving Morocco I phoned again. There were only a few days left before my departure. Could we have a farewell coffee?

This time the pause at the other end of the line

was not about consulting her diary. 'I don't think so, Chris,' she said. 'Not this time.'

'Why?' I asked. 'Doesn't our friendship merit a final goodbye?'

But even as I asked the question I knew the answer. It was the same for myself. We would both be unhappy at the prospect of never seeing each other again. And everything that could be said between us had already been spoken.

'I'll write you,' she said, before I hung up. 'I promise.'

But I knew, even as I responded with a similar commitment, that neither of us ever would.

CHAPTER 7

THE PEARL OF THE ANTILLES

At a check-in desk in Miami airport a US customs officials looked at my passport, asked me if I was carrying any drugs or weapons and, handing me back my documents, advised me not to travel to Haiti. He proceeded to tell me that his cousin was in the armed forces and had had a tour of duty there. Then he recited a list of what he deemed I had to look forward to: mosquitoes, dirty water, open sewers, a sweltering climate, government corruption and hostile people. 'I don't know why anybody would want to go there voluntarily. What's your reason?'

I told him that I worked for an aid agency, that I had lived in other 'difficult' places and that I was sure that like every other country in the world Haiti had positives as well as negatives. But his conviction that I was about to travel to 'the poorest, most desperate country in the Western hemisphere' would not be shaken.

'So you're one of those missionary types who want to change the world,' he continued. 'I admire that. But my cousin told me that the people in Haiti have their own way of doing things, and despite what we have been trying to teach them for the last few hundred years nothing has worked. I think you'll be wasting your time.'

Tempted to correct his misconception that an aid worker was a synonym for a missionary I realised that any further attempt at clarification would fall on deaf ears. I collected my passport, thanked the official for his advice and proceeded towards the departure lounge where another official informed us that our flight to Port Au Prince had been delayed because of a strike by airport workers. 'Don't worry,' a priest beside me said. He was returning home after many years away from the island. 'There is nothing permanent in my country, including bad news.'

Three hours after our scheduled departure there was another announcement that the dispute with the workers was over and that we would be taking off as soon as possible. The voice was distinctly brusque and we were hurriedly ushered on to the aircraft in a matter of minutes. The priest I had befriended explained the sudden rush to leave as concern on the part of the airline that if we delayed too long another strike would have commenced by the time we arrived.

Father Luc was in his early fifties and had the open, jovial and confident demeanour of someone at ease in his vocation. When tempers became frayed among some passengers over the long delay, he intervened between them and an airline representative to calm everyone down. He told me he had been in the priesthood since his early twenties and that it was common for boys from lower income families like his own to end up in one of the few opportunities for employment on the island. 'It was either soldier, policeman, thief or man of the cloth,' he joked, 'and the latter seemed the safest option at the time.'

He responded to my curiosity about his country during the long hours we had at our disposal by providing me with a colourful and in his own words 'personalized' description of its culture and people. He also talked at some length about the fraught relationship Haiti continued to have with its powerful northern neighbour. This despite the fact that many of his countrymen spent much of their lives there. Of the ten million or so estimated Haitians he reckoned that fully a quarter were resident in the United States, many of them illegally.

'But you know, of all the Caribbean people who are here I believe it is Haitians who are most nationalistic, conscious of our culture and identity and attached to our original homeland. Of course once we get back on Haitian soil we complain about the climate, the potholes, the mosquitoes, the poverty, the crowds of people jostling us at the markets and the complicated politics that no one understands. It's a love – hate relationship, and nowhere is love more evident than in exile and nowhere is dislike more evident than when we are back home.'

I had read about the strong sense of national identity that characterized many Haitian communities in the United States, where suburbs of New York and Miami had place names from the island and where French Creole, the local language, was more common than English. What explained that sense of allegiance, I asked, among a population many of whom had fled their home either out of economic necessity or physical persecution?

Father Luc turned out to be something of an historian, claiming that no understanding of contemporary Haiti was possible without referring to its earlier, troubled history. 'I suppose that's true for most places but in our case I think it's particularly important. Haiti was the first country in this part of the world to get rid of slavery and in many ways we are still paying the price for that up till now.'

Haiti, he continued to explain, was the original Indian name for the island and meant 'place of mountains.' When they occupied it in 1492 in the wake of Columbus' discovery of the Americas, its Spanish settlers gave it the title of Hispaniola, which encompassed at that time not only current day Haiti but the entire eastern part of the island now known as the Dominican Republic. For several decades, the indigenous inhabitants, an estimated one million Arawak Indians, laboured on the farms and gold mines of the colonialists. But within that period of time they disappeared.

'They were quite literally worked to death,'

Father Luc said with some feeling, 'and combined with the fact that they had no resistance to the diseases the Spanish brought with them they were erased from history as if they had never existed. But the colony had to go on and so when they died out the trade in African slaves began, a pattern as you know that was repeated throughout the Caribbean and much of the Americas.'

As a result of infighting among the European powers and their scramble for overseas colonies, the French also established a foothold on the western part of Hispaniola where they began to grow crops such as cotton, cocoa and indigo. Gradually their presence became so substantial that the Spanish in a treaty towards the latter part of the seventeenth century agreed to transfer one third of the island to them. This part was renamed Saint Domingue.

The elevation of the French coincided with a radical transformation in the production of sugar which until then had been somewhat inefficiently extracted from beets grown in northern Europe. This was now replaced by sugar cane and such was the scale of demand that entire islands in the Caribbean were converted into plantations.

The soil and climate of Saint Domingue were ideal for its production, yet to realise this potential it required many more slaves. 'That's when the ruthlessness of our own colonialists also played its part since it was reckoned that of a bad bunch they were probably the worst.'

When I asked Father Luc how many slaves it was estimated had ended up in Haiti he replied that it was impossible to know the exact number because many of the records were sketchy and much of that history had deliberately been concealed by later generations.

'But keeping in mind that an average slave only lasted six or seven years before they died it's likely to have been hundreds of thousands. For much of the eighteenth century Saint Dominique was the biggest producer of sugar and coffee in the world and they say that the houses of the plantation owners were grander and more lavish than anything you could have found in Paris. That's when Haiti became known as "the Pearl of the Antilles," although if you visit the island today you would be hard pressed to understand how it could ever have merited such a title.'

For the governance of its overseas territories in the Caribbean the French developed something called 'the Code Noire.' According to Father Luc this was a book of rules that stipulated the ways in which black people in their colonies had to be treated. It demanded that every slave should be baptized and instructed in Catholicism. All other religious beliefs were forbidden, a prohibition aimed particularly at the cultural practices that most Africans brought with them from their home continent. It even offered guidance on how many lashes of the whip someone should receive if they did not show enough enthusiasm for their new religion.

Father Luc was open enough to admit that the Catholic Church had played a significant part in the history of slavery on the island. The Vatican had endorsed the trade in Africans to the Americas as part of a civilizing mission, where in exchange for hard work and harsh treatment they would be offered salvation.

'It's not an honourable part of our history and it's important that we are honest about these kinds of things. But I also happen to believe that there is a redeeming feature in what occurred, although I am not claiming that this provides any kind of justification.'

Many slaves, he continued, extracted from the body of belief they were exposed to examples of struggle and sacrifice that inspired their own aspirations of freedom. At the same time, they were conscious of the contradictions in what they were being told. 'If the priest who mistreats you as an inferior also tells you that everyone is equal in the eyes of God, then these words don't match the reality of what you see around you. This led many to question their circumstances. In fact, many slave owners urged the church to be less enthusiastic in its efforts at conversion because they could see that it radicalised many of those who worked for them and they were smart enough to know where that might end up.'

The other radicalizing influence that took place towards the end of the eighteenth century was the French revolution, which overthrew the old aristocracy in France and replaced its culture of hierarchy and privilege with an ideology of liberation and equality. One of the first pronouncements of the new Government was the abolition of slavery, although this was ignored by the administrators of its colonies who tried to conceal the extent of what had happened for fear that it would prompt something similar closer to home.

But years of mistreatment and news of what had happened in Europe meant that the revolution the aristocracy of Saint Dominique feared finally took place. In 1792, a group of escaped slaves declared the start of a revolt that would play itself out for over a decade until the island gained its independence and its people their freedom. 'That point in time is embedded in our collective memory. Any Haitian, no matter whether they are politically active or not, no matter whether they have been born on the island or elsewhere, is conscious of the dark shadow of the centuries before that date and the break with slavery that came after it.'

But Father Luc went on to say that independence did not mean positive or cordial relations with the various European powers of the day. Fearful of a similar revolt in their own Caribbean colonies, the British even attempted an invasion of Haiti, the new name for Saint Domingue, in order to reinstate the former plantation owners who had fled. Napoleon also sent an army to return the island to French control but yellow fever, malaria and the unorthodox warfare practised by the islanders in the forests and mountains led to a humiliating defeat.

I was surprised to hear about the conditions that had been imposed in order for Haiti to be left in peace. 'Despite losing their war the French insisted that our independence would only be recognized if we agreed to compensate former landowners and pay a penalty to the French Government for lost revenues. Our leaders agreed because they did not want a protracted conflict. Do you know that this debt took us almost one hundred years to pay off and cost the island millions of dollars that we could not afford?'

Closer to home, the United States only recognized Haiti's independence in 1862, some sixty years after the fact. Much of this opposition had been orchestrated by the southern states of the then Union who were deeply alarmed by what had occurred fearing that it would make their own black populations restless. But Father Luc believed there was another dimension too.

'The unfortunate fact is that we are geographically too close to our powerful northern neighbour for our own good. That's as true for Haiti as it is for Cuba, Jamaica, Nicaragua, Honduras and all the other countries in America's backyard. There is extreme sensitivity to our policies, our ideology, our external relations so anything that is seen as too radical and subversive, a flirtation with ideas that they do not like, means that we are in trouble.'

That 'trouble' included an occupation by American forces for almost thirty years in the early part of the twentieth century. 'Many Haitians took to the streets in protest. Hundreds were shot and killed. Forced labour was reinstated to improve the infrastructure of the island but this only reminded people of their former slavery. Even at the cost of being beaten and imprisoned many refused to participate in these schemes.'

One of the legacies of that occupation and according to Father Luc one of its most damning indictments was the creation of a local army, trained and resourced by its American backers. 'We had no external enemies. Who on earth would have wanted to invade us at that time, with all our poverty and chaos and no valuable resources worth having? Its principal function was to repress and control the people and this is exactly what happened under successive dictatorships.'

The worst of these was the Duvalier family who between father and son ruled Haiti for almost thirty years. Though ignorant of much of what Father Luc had so far related, this was a name I recognized, having watched on television a decade previously the exile of Baby Doc Duvalier to a luxurious villa in the south of France.

'Haitians are not stupid. We know the support the Duvaliers had behind them. The fact that they provided favourable conditions for the establishment of American companies, the fact that they spoke the Cold War rhetoric of anti-Communism, the fact that they guaranteed the docility of the population were enough to ensure that the United States would not intervene, even when repression and killings claimed over thirty thousand lives.'

As the announcement of our impending flight to Port Au Prince was broadcast, Father Luc placed a friendly hand on my shoulder and apologised for relating a somewhat bleak and depressing history. I had told him earlier about the comment of the immigration officer that I was departing to the worst country in the western hemisphere. My new acquaintance was keen to point out that this was not his perspective, that his purpose was not to dissuade me from visiting his island.

'Look, I'm a priest and my first and foremost allegiance is to my church and the ideology of hope and optimism that is carried in the Gospels. But like most Haitians, I have been radicalized not by any theory or philosophy but simply through having been born there. What we have gone through over the last three to four hundred years has turned us, I believe, not into cynics but into people who are more conscious than most of what freedom means. It has also made us angry about how our aspirations have been constantly undermined by the greed of some and the connivance of others. You'll find my countrymen to be opinionated, defensive, angry and prone to losing their temper, but when you begin to understand our past then I hope you'll be generous in your judgements.'

★   ★   ★

Some ten minutes away from our destination the person beside me pointed out Haiti below us. But all that was visible was an ocean stretching to the horizon and the white trail of a few ships to break the monotony. There was no sight of land anywhere and I assumed that I must have misinterpreted what he had said.

'You see that long, brown stain in the water,' he continued, 'where the colour is different from the blue on either side of it? That's Haiti being washed out to sea. Most of the soils of the island are now at the bottom of the ocean. Some say there's more of Haiti there than on dry land.'

I had heard that the country's environmental degradation was one of the most serious in the world. The lush, green, luxuriant vegetation that had attracted its first colonizers had apparently disappeared. My fellow passenger turned out to be an agronomist, contracted by the French Government to assist the Haitian Ministry responsible for reforestation with various tree planting projects. These were designed to halt the soil erosion, but he was disparaging of the results he had seen.

'Much of what we do is a waste of time. We preach to the people not to cut their trees in order to protect the soil and then return a few months later to find out that this is exactly what they have done. I don't blame them. If you don't have electricity, bricks for building or fuel for heating your food, and if wood is your only resource, then of course you'll use it. But I get a good salary. The people are friendly. So I'm not complaining.'

A short while later, rising from the sea like a formidable wall in front of us, the mountains of Haiti came into view. They had wisps of white cloud capping their peaks and were much higher than I had expected. As we got closer, I could see the dark brown stains that gashed many of the hillsides where the trees had been cut and the soil exposed. Clusters of dwellings clung precariously to the slopes, evidence that there was no part of the island that remained unexploited, that did not bear the marks of an overcrowded, economically desperate population.

The passengers had cheered when the announcement was made that we were approaching Port Au Prince. But the mood changed quickly when it was announced that another strike had commenced at the airport, this time among the baggage handlers. We would be able to disembark, get through the formalities of immigration, but when our bags might be offloaded was anyone's guess.

Father Luc had warned me that Haiti would be hot, pointing to the jacket I was wearing in Miami airport and adding that I would not need it again until I returned. But I was not prepared for the blast of hot, humid air that greeted us when we exited the aircraft. Within a minute of walking the considerable distance to where we had been directed, my shirt was soaking wet, my discomfort only tempered by the fact that everyone else around me was similarly struggling.

There was something ironic in having a marimba band welcome us into the airport building. None of us entered with any great enthusiasm since the general prediction was that we would be stranded there for quite a few hours until our bags materialized. 'In other Caribbean islands they have these bands too,' my French acquaintance remarked with some cynicism as we shuffled towards the queue for immigration, 'but that's because you have a relaxing holiday in front of you, something to look forward to later. Here they play music in commiseration.'

The predictions turned out to be correct. Some three hours later we were still waiting, having been directed into one of the airport hangars where we had been told our bags were to be deposited once the strike was over. It was hotter inside than out so many of us chose to lounge around in the shadow of the building under the watchful eye of security guards who shooed us back whenever we strayed too far from our prescribed territory.

Already I could tell the difference between those who had only recently left the island and those who were returning after a long absence. There was calm resignation on the faces of the former, considerable frustration in the expressions of the latter. 'I told you so,' I overheard one woman remonstrating with her husband who was trying to appease a group of disgruntled children as they complained that things were not like this where they had just come from. 'We should never have left home.'

Father Luc continued his job of placating everyone and offered me some words of encouragement too when I bumped into him. 'Most airports never reflect the reality of the countries they are sited in. But in Port Au Prince it doesn't pretend to be any different from what you can expect in the market, at the bus stop or in the Government building on the other side of the road. You have your introduction to our country already.'

Eventually we spotted a tractor towing some trailers in our direction. They contained our bags which were unceremoniously dumped in a large heap in the middle of the hangar. 'Find your own,' was the curt reply offered to one passenger when he asked what was to happen now.

I was surprised at the orderly way in which the people around me then proceeded to sort out the piles of luggage. I had imagined a mad, chaotic scramble after the frustration of the past few hours and had decided to keep myself at a safe distance until mine was the last one remaining. But instead several individuals volunteered to shout out the names on the baggage labels, after which the owner was to come forward, collect their suitcase and move smartly away. 'Our circumstances might not be civilized,' Father Luc said as he shook my hand before leaving with his bag, 'but that doesn't mean that we have to behave badly too.'

* * *

After such a protracted delay due to our late departure from Miami and then the hold-up with our luggage I had presumed that the driver who had been sent to meet me would long since have given up in frustration. But at the gates of the airport when I exited I could see someone holding up a sign with my first name misspelled in the French fashion, 'Christophe,' and my surname that of the American TV detective in his eponymous show 'MacGyver.'

The latter I was used to. MacGyver was the name of a famous television character who could blow up buildings with sugar, washing powder and a plastic bag. Even in remote villages of rural Africa when I gave my name I was immediately surrounded by excited adults and awe-struck children asking if I was related to the only character from American television they had ever been exposed to. I had long since given up trying to explain that 'MacGyver' was a distortion of the Scottish original. 'But have you met him?' was the only thing anyone was interested in knowing.

Like everyone else congregated around the exit, the driver wore a pair of thick, dark sunglasses that gave him a sinister appearance. Tall and thin, he used his considerable height and elbows to force a path through the crowd as we struggled to his car. He seemed slightly irritated when I apologized yet again for having kept him waiting for six hours. The last passenger he had picked up from the airport, he replied, was two days late. Haitians, he added, were a people of infinite patience.

His name was Claude and he worked for one of the organizations whose projects I would be visiting over the next few weeks. They had offered to organize my accommodation and an itinerary, as well as provide me with a vehicle and driver. From what I had been told about traffic in Port Au Prince that meant we would be together for a considerable period of time. I was relieved, therefore, that far from being reserved and diffident he seemed willing not only to answer my questions but to offer his opinions on a range of other topics, even when I hadn't asked for them.

I attributed this forthrightness not only to the national character that Father Luc had described, but also to the fact that I was being driven around by a college graduate. It turned out that my driver had a degree in civil engineering. He explained that since jobs were few and far between in Haiti he had ended up in this current line of work.

Although he aspired to something more in keeping with his qualifications he had resisted the temptation to follow in the footsteps of tens of thousands of unemployed men and women by jumping onto one of the island's fishing boats and attempting an exodus across the intervening ocean to Miami. He was determined not to follow them, even with the prospect of more rewarding employment. 'There are too many important things happening here right now for me to leave. Besides what place would I have in a country like the United Sates that doesn't want me?'

The airport of Port Au Prince was set at sea level on a flat, open plain whose boundaries were marked by some of the squalid looking shanty towns we had flown over earlier. These were kept from encroaching on to the runways by a formidable wire fence with watchtowers set at regular intervals to reinforce the 'Keep Out' signs. As we took the road towards the city, Claude described the airport as the entry point for invading armies and the exit point for fleeing dictators, his explanation as to why it looked more like a fortress than a civilian establishment. He pointed to the several jeeps that were patrolling the perimeter. The men inside them were holding their guns in a much more aggressive fashion than what I had seen elsewhere, where soldiers were a decoration and looked bored and listless as if they wanted to be someplace else.

For the past few years Haiti had been under a de facto military occupation, with the United Nations playing a prominent role in trying to keep the peace. This had been prompted by a coup against the elected President, Jean Bertrand Aristide, who had been forced into exile. Such was the level of international condemnation, however, that a few years later he had been flown back to the island but this time with an American army behind him. The coup leaders had been removed and Aristide had resumed his Presidency under the watchful eye of his protectors.

Claude declared himself a former Aristide supporter. The coup, he claimed, was because the President had dared to challenge the interference of the Haitian military in the country's political affairs. Fearful of losing their privileges and status they had organized his removal, much to the anger of the Haitian population who had voted in large numbers to elect him.

Many now felt that since his return Aristide had changed. Claude concurred, claiming he was no longer the principled, popular leader he had been when first in office. A former man of the cloth he had shocked a deeply religious people by marrying, especially since he was still a priest when he assumed the Presidency. The humble man, who had once lived in the poorest suburb of Port Au Prince handing out bread and clothes and claiming that capitalism was a mortal sin, now resided in a palatial mansion on the outskirts of the city. He was only ever seen in smart limousines and under armed escort, much like the politicians he had previously castigated for being too remote and distant from the populations they were supposed to serve.

'Many of us celebrated when he came back and welcomed the foreign soldiers he brought with him. But now it looks as if we are back to business as usual and we are asking when they will leave.'

In keeping with Claude's assertion that ease of access to the airport was essential for a quick escape out of the country when the situation became too volatile, the road we were driving along was well maintained and nothing like what I had expected. We sped along it for quite some time prompting me to wonder what all the fuss had been about when I had been warned about the traffic.

Then as we progressed further into the downtown part of the city our movement slowed to a crawl. Along potholed roads crammed with cars that looked as if they had been rescued from a previous era, competing with donkey carts and throngs of people who had spilled over from the narrow pavements, I realised that my colleagues had not been exaggerating when they talked about the unique traffic jams of Port Au Prince.

One advantage of the slow pace was that it allowed me a first impression of the city. There were even refreshments on offer. Every few minutes someone would rap on the window to present a variety of canned juices, sandwiches and local fruit I couldn't recognize. Such was the pace of our progress that I was not surprised when Claude informed me that many people consumed their breakfast, lunch and dinner not in the comfort of their homes, but in the discomfort of their vehicles where they spent a large part of their day commuting in and out of work. There were rumours that traffic jams were deliberately orchestrated by the petty traders of the city in order for them to sell their products to hungry and frustrated drivers and their passengers. 'It sounds like a form of wealth distribution,' I remarked, 'a tax on those privileged enough to be driving a vehicle.'

Against the drab, down-at-heel buildings in the part of the city we were passing through, it was the people who provided the colour. Very few were dressed in white, black or grey. Bright T-shirts emblazoned with images of football stars from Manchester United or Barcelona seemed to predominate. Claude informed me that fashions in the poorer parts of town were set by the availability of what was on offer at any one time. A large shipment of T-shirts from Taiwan or China would flood the markets for a number of months until another and different batch arrived to establish the new trend. The only concession to consumer demand was that whatever people wore it had to stand out, the more garish the better.

That same affirmation of colour was visible in the ornate scarves and handkerchiefs that many of the women tied around their heads. Combined with the extravagant sunglasses that were as popular as the T-shirts, it gave me an impression of a people determined to make a gesture in defiance of their circumstances, part of the resilience that Father Luc had talked about.

Much of that resilience seemed to disappear a short while later when the skies opened up, sending people scurrying for whatever cover was available.

I had been warned that Caribbean showers were nothing like the nagging but relatively benign drizzle of northern Scotland. For some time and despite the furious pace of the windscreen wipers we could see nothing in front of us but the tail lights of the next vehicle, which like ours had come to a complete stop.

Where a street had once been there was now a river and Claude did nothing to calm my nerves when he told me that a few weeks previously a bus carrying scores of passengers had been swept off a road into a nearby ravine. He displayed his civil engineering background when he proceeded to give me a detailed and unwelcome update on the ruinous state of the country's drainage system. He reckoned that the infrastructure of Port Au Prince was only capable of handling one tenth of its current population. The water flowing all around us was a clear indication that it could not cope.

'But you don't have to be alarmed,' he added, probably noticing my look of apprehension in the rear-view mirror. 'It's only on the slopes of the mountains you have to be worried if you get caught out in the rain. We're not there yet.'

As abruptly as it had arrived, the storm swept off in thick black clouds to some other part of the city. The traffic began to move and for a few minutes there was a clean, swept quality to the streets we passed through, a freshness in the air that contrasted with the smells of decaying fruit and vegetables and the rotting garbage that had prevailed earlier.

From downtown Port Au Prince, we finally emerged to begin our ascent of a road that wound its way up a steep slope in front of us. We were headed to the hotel where I would be staying and the part of the city where most foreigners resided. As a general rule, Claude explained, the higher up the mountain, the smarter the suburbs. The reason was simple. With every few hundred metres of altitude the temperature dropped and people were prepared to pay good money for that relative climatic luxury. 'From their place in the clouds the rich of Port Au Prince look down on the poor below them and thank their good fortune that they don't have to live among them. Meanwhile these same poor people look upwards as if contemplating a different world and wonder what stroke of good fortune might one day transport them in that direction.'

The streets of Petion Ville where we arrived half an hour later did indeed look as if they belonged to a different city. As we passed fashionable shops selling imported goods from France and Italy, posh restaurants that offered international cuisine and extravagant villas with razor wire on the surrounding walls, Claude told me that the suburb had been named after one of the heroes of their revolution.

Alexander Petion was the third President after Independence and had been renowned for championing the cause of the underprivileged and marginalized. He had presided over a large scale redistribution of land that had given priority to former slaves. While this had aroused the anger of some and had undermined the export economy that had brought the island much of its previous wealth, it had won him the affection of the peasant population who had given him the title 'Papa Bon Coeur' or 'Good Hearted Father.' But now Petion-Ville had become synonymous with privilege, luxury, wealth and status, an irony that Claude lamented as a betrayal of what this popular figure had once stood for.

It was late afternoon by the time we pulled up outside the place where I would be staying. Its spacious car park was full of smart-looking vehicles and I expressed some surprise that at such a troubled time the country could still sustain a tourist industry that filled its hotels. But as we walked towards the reception I was asked to take a closer look at the vehicles. There were hardly any that did not display the logo either of the United Nations or an aid agency, some of which I recognised.

The tourists that used to come to Petion Ville, Claude explained, had now been replaced by an army of aid workers. That was the only growth industry in the country and one that provided better wages than any position in Government or the private sector. It also explained why rents in Petion Ville were now so high and why most

Haitians, even those lucky enough to find work, could not afford to stay there.

According to Claude, anyone who had a decent house in the suburb would only rent it out to foreigners who worked for international charities or the United Nations. 'They can get paid in dollars and can name their price. Some agencies have even taken over entire hotels. There are rumours too that even our prostitutes won't accept local clients any more. Aid has become a big business here and like any other, it has had its unforeseen consequences.'

I thought Claude was joking when he told me that he would pick me up early the next day at five o'clock. 'I didn't realise we would be travelling to another part of the island,' I responded, wondering why such a start was necessary when the schedule I had been sent had only mentioned some visits to other parts of the city. But apparently the morning traffic was worse than we had so far encountered. In order to avoid it, the hour before sunrise was the best time to set off.

He added that first on our itinerary was the office of his organization, after which we would proceed to a place called Cité Soleil. This name had a pleasant enough ring to it and I wondered whether an aid programme for the neediest would be top priority in such a location. But Claude had a few words of caution.

I was to leave my wallet in the hotel. My watch

was best left behind too. I should have a copy of my passport ready to show at the roadblocks we might encounter. If I was asked any questions I was to leave all the talking to him. 'At least you don't have an American accent,' he added, 'so that should make things easier.'

'You make it sound like a war zone,' I responded, thinking he must be exaggerating. I was also tempted to remind him that I was well travelled in parts of Africa and more than capable of handling anything that a Caribbean island could throw up. 'We're only visiting another suburb of the city after all, so why the fuss?'

He replied that the term 'war zone' was probably an accurate description of where we were headed. Cité Soleil was even off-limits to the police unless they had a military escort. A few months previously their station in the settlement had been burned down by an angry mob in the wake of the arrest of one of the local residents.

He then proceeded to recite a list that included kidnapping, gang warfare, armed robberies, drug dealing, rape and murder. Any crime I could possibly think of could be found inside the borders of the worst slum on the island. I should not be fooled by its name since if there was any place in Haiti where sunshine was absent then it was there. As if guessing my previous thoughts, he added that in keeping with its desperation it also had the highest needs. Any assistance we could provide would not be wasted.

The alarming statistics and criminality were further elaborated upon the next day in the office of the organization that was hosting my visit. Office was something of a misnomer. It turned out that the agency was part of a religious order. The room where I was sitting was in an annex to their principal location in Port Au Prince and the people I was to interact with were nuns in blue robes and white headscarves.

Sister Celine introduced herself as the director of the aid programme they had started a number of years previously to help deprived communities in the city. She seemed young to be holding such a prominent position. I guessed she was in her mid-twenties since she had a youthful, sprightly appearance that her garb could not entirely conceal. Unsure of how I should greet her, I was taken aback when she gave me a firm hug. She then apologized for organizing an itinerary that involved me waking up at such an early hour. 'I hope my timetable has not inconvenienced you.'

I was slightly apprehensive that religious enthusiasm might substitute for a clear, practical description and analysis of the charitable work they were asking us to support but it became clear soon enough that Sister Celine had a firm grasp of the detail of the programmes she supervised. She was keen to assure me that while commitment to the principles of her religion provided the motivation for what they were trying to achieve, there were no ideological strings attached to the assistance they provided.

'Even though you haven't asked the question, I'll save you the embarrassment of having to do so later. We don't proselytize on the back of our charity. We don't force our beliefs on anyone. If someone is interested in hearing about the Gospels and finding consolation in our church, then of course we minister to them. But that is not a condition of our assistance. They can be communists for all we care.'

As Claude negotiated the morning traffic, Sister Celine proceeded with a description of what I could expect to find in Cité Soleil. She had spent much of her working life in what she chose to call a separate city. The word 'suburb' implied that it was part of something and the authorities in Port Au Prince, she claimed, had made it clear they wanted nothing to do with it.

While her observations echoed something of what I had heard the previous evening I did not catch the same tone of condemnation. Any frustration she communicated was directed at the circumstances that had forced people to live in such terrible conditions. The abandonment by the government of Cité Soleil and the fact that it had no municipal services of any kind was what had pushed her Order to intervene.

'Three hundred thousand people are crammed together in a space that should only have a fraction of that number. They have no running water, no electricity, no garbage collection, no sewage disposal and no police force to maintain law and order. The only schools and clinics are organized by church groups like my own. But I want to tell you something important you need to remember. The people who live there have a courage and determination that I have not seen anywhere else. Most of us would not last more than a day if we had to endure their conditions yet they have formed a community of sorts. They have not abandoned hope altogether.'

The location around which Cité Soleil had been established, she continued, had once been an up-market coastal resort. That had been in a previous century and in the intervening years the spill-over from expanding urban areas of the city had long since driven the wealthy away from their former holiday homes. In the early 1960s, in the wake of a terrible earthquake that had devastated the southern part of the island, thousands of people who had been displaced had made their way to Port Au Prince. Most had been resettled in an impromptu refugee camp that was called Cité Simone, after the wife of the then President. That name had been subsequently changed to Cité Soleil after her son, who had inherited the Presidency, was later deposed.

Our imminent arrival was announced a short while later by a barrier across the road, an army tank to one side of it and heavily armed soldiers checking the documents of the drivers they had stopped. One of them poked his head inside the car and greeted Sister Celine with some familiarity. He was a member of an Indian contingent of the United Nations forces on the island and, after exchanging pleasantries, he asked her who I was and why I had come to visit. As I handed over a copy of my passport I was tempted to ask him how Cité Soleil compared to the slums of Bombay and Calcutta, but I held back in case he took offence. Quite why the soldiers were there was unclear to me. Sister Celine could not offer an explanation either as we proceeded beyond the checkpoint. As we passed the charred remains of the police station she informed me that when it had happened the soldiers had stood back and watched.

From the elevation and distance of the road, Cité Soleil presented a kind of ordered and unexpected symmetry. I could see that it was crammed and compact, that there were no green areas to indicate any recreational or decorative space, that its numerous dwellings ran right up to the edge of the sea. But its details blurred, it did not look as alarming as I had imagined, an observation that solicited a wry smile from Claude and some words of caution from Sister Celine that it was best to reserve judgement until we got closer.

As we progressed it was the smell I noticed first, a sharp, acrid odour emanating from a canal that tracked the road we were driving along. I was informed that it carried not only the domestic effluent from other suburbs, but that it was also the principal discharge point for several chemical factories further inland. The smell, Sister Celine added, was probably sulphur and the yellowish sheen on top of the water indicated that it had not been treated before being discharged into the stream that ran right through the settlement.

I was shocked to see a group of women in front of us carrying buckets of water they had collected from the same source. Further along I could see a group of noisy children splashing around, seemingly oblivious that they were bathing in a poisonous stew. I asked why people weren't kept away, why there was no fence or even signs to warn the inhabitants against utilizing something that was so clearly harmful to their health.

'You can't stop children from swimming here if they have no other place to go. You can't stop women collecting water if this is the only source. Now and again some aid agencies will organize a water truck to deliver a clean supply that will last a few days. In another part of the settlement they have constructed a tank and some wells. But for most people here life in Cité Soleil is entirely about not having alternatives. Isn't that what poverty in the end is really all about, an absence of choices?'

In the shanty towns I had seen in Khartoum and Casablanca the principal building materials used to construct dwellings were wood and tin sheeting. While not particularly durable, they were at least building materials of a sort that gave the impression of a structure that could still be called a home. But from what I could see as we drove through the cramped, narrow streets that dissected Cité Soleil, a large number of inhabitants did not even have the luxury of these resources. Instead, there was a predominance of flimsy cardboard, plastic sheeting that served as roofing material, bits of scavenged vehicles that functioned as walls and tin cans hammered into a flat surface and nailed together to provide doors and windows. While Sister Celine applauded the ingenuity of the inhabitants in being able to transform whatever they could from the refuse of the city, she acknowledged that their dwellings were a hazard. If one burned down, there was the risk of an entire section going up in flames.

She asked if I would like to inspect one of these residences so that I could gather a better impression of the typical living conditions. Although the woman she spoke to seemed willing enough for me to look inside, I felt like a voyeur intruding on whatever meagre privacy her shelter allowed her. It was impossible to stand upright inside the two rooms the family of five occupied. A stove in one corner emitted a steady stream of smoke from the charcoal it was burning and since there was no chimney or vent to let it escape it had gathered in a thick cloud that left me gasping for breath. Three children and an old grandmother sat to one side and occasionally, as if to keep me company, echoed my own spluttering cough before returning to the preparation of whatever they were cooking.

Such was the pressure of space that some families, like this one, had even built their dwellings right on the edge of the sea. As we entered I had noticed between the cracks in the makeshift floor some brackish water swirling around its foundations. A few months previously during a particularly high tide combined with a strong onshore wind, one section of the street we were on had been swept away. My question as to why the family had rebuilt in the same spot where the likelihood of a similar recurrence was high, was met with the same resigned shrug of the shoulders as when I had asked Sister Celine why people continued to use the contaminated water of the canal. 'There is no alternative. They have no place else to go.'

Occasionally, interspersed between the makeshift structures that comprised most of the settlement, a house would stand out in stark contrast to what there was around it. Made of brick and mortar, with a solid roof and glass windows, sometimes even a garden in front, they looked as if they had been physically transported from a different part of the city. Outside one of them we saw a smart four-wheel drive vehicle being polished to a considerable shine by a group of young boys carrying buckets of water.

I had assumed that anyone with means at their disposal would have done their utmost to flee, not only to escape their surroundings but to avoid the irritation of jealous neighbours who would surely view such places as an affront to their own impoverished circumstances. There were no high walls or fences to protect them either. Wasn't that a risk?

It turned out that most of these houses belonged to the leaders of the thirty or so gangs who between them had divided up the suburb. It was not only fear that protected them but loyalty too. 'It's safer for them to stay where they are,' Sister Celine explained, 'surrounded by their supporters in the neighbourhoods they control rather than in a location where their rivals can get to them.'

Their considerable wealth was generated by a trade in guns, drugs, alcohol and women as well as their involvement in the lucrative smuggling of desperate Haitians out of the island. They even rented out crowds for demonstrations and provided votes to the highest bidder during election time. Not for the first time I heard that the line between criminality and politics was very thin in Haiti, which was why these gangs were more often tolerated than repressed.

At the school in the centre of the settlement which her religious order had established, the energy and commitment of the nuns who ran it had created a small island of order and normality that seemed out of place in its surroundings. There was a clinic nearby that they ran too, with a long line of patients queuing up for treatment. An older, sterner version of Sister Celine presided over a group of nurses attending to them. I was not surprised when she told us that among the common ailments of malaria, diarrheal infections, malnutrition and complications of pregnancy, knife wounds were a recurring feature among boys and young men.

'We patch them up, watch them leave and a few months later they are back with another wound to be treated. Some of them seem to view these marks of conflict as trophies of war, something that will enhance their reputations within the gang culture they inhabit. Of course we try to warn them that the next time their injuries might prove fatal or that it could be a bullet, but they simply reply that unless you fight for the little you have it will be taken away from you.'

In the classrooms I visited the pupils were crammed together on insufficient benches and hunched over a meagre supply of textbooks, but they seemed keen and attentive, focused on what their teachers were telling them. The school operated a system that I had seen often in Africa. There were three shifts on offer; one in the morning, another in the afternoon and the last one in the early evening. Yet even so, such was the scale of demand that only a small percentage of children in Cité Soleil accessed education of any kind. 'Why don't you ask them some questions?' Sister Celine suggested in one room where a group of students were studying a subject called 'School and Society'.

I could think of little else than some standard questions about what they were studying, the subjects they liked best at school and their ambitions for the future. Dutifully and politely they trotted out the answers that they probably thought I wanted to hear. It was only when their teacher invited them to reflect on the problems they faced in their community and what they thought should be done about them that the discussion became more animated.

The children complained about the violence outside and inside their homes. Sharing a cramped space with numerous siblings and no privacy created inevitable tensions and conflicts. There were limited prospects for employment, since the openings in the nearby factories were few and far between. The girls aspired to marry someone who could take them far away, a remark that provoked laughter among the boys that sounded as if it was also tinged with envy. One of the latter confessed that the only opportunity for them was to join one of the gangs, acknowledging too that such a life was fraught with danger. As to a solution to their problems the children were unanimous that unless the country's leaders agreed that Cité Soleil should be assisted rather than ignored, there was little prospect of anything ever getting better.

The last words were spoken by a young girl who stood up as we were about to leave and indicated that she wanted to say something different from her classmates. She seemed nervous at first but gained confidence as she spoke, echoing in her own way what Sister Celine had told me before we had commenced our visit that morning.

'Strangers only see the problems here but they don't see the things we share, the cooperation between us, the things we do for ourselves. When I visit my cousins in another part of the city they turn up their noses when Cité Soleil is mentioned and tell me how terrible it must be that I have to live here. But when they throw away their tins of Coca Cola after they have drunk them, I tell them that our people turn them into all sorts of wonderful things that are useful. Their garbage is full of materials we value and I tell them that they don't appreciate what they have. When their electricity is cut they begin to cry and complain about how bad things are on the island. Then I tell them that my brother has fixed a wire to one of the pylons that supplies a nearby factory and that we have all the electricity we need.'

'I just want to say that it is not all negative,' she continued, adding that their circumstances had taught them some important lessons. 'Some things can and should be better. But when people say that Cité Soleil should be swept into the sea I think that it not just our homes and dwellings that will disappear but a community too, something we have created. Maybe one day someone will ask us a question about what is right about this place, not only about what is wrong.'

CHAPTER 8

THE EARTH IN OUR HANDS

From his grand title as director and founder of one of Haiti's most respected rural development organizations, I had expected Jean Daniel to be formal, officious and constrained for time. But, dressed in a T-shirt and jeans, joking with a member of his staff when I was escorted into his room, he had given me an effusive handshake, asked if I wanted tea or coffee then announced, after I had barely introduced myself, that he could see from my face that we could definitely do business together.

Within a short time I had warmed to him considerably and not just because of the welcome. His gentle, personable manner was clearly backed up by a detailed knowledge of Haiti and its myriad problems. I could sense too, from the way he described the work his organization carried out in remote rural areas, that here was someone who through background and conviction strongly identified with the people he was helping. He explained that he had set up his organization some five years previously because he had become fed up with the way that peasant farmers, the majority of the island's population, were treated by so-called development experts, whether from outside the island or home-grown.

'Agronomists can be worse than doctors who never want to explain to their patients why they are prescribing a particular course of treatment,' he had joked. 'It's the same with our graduates out of agricultural college. They look down on the people they are supposed to be advising as if they are backward, ignorant and incapable of understanding what they're talking about. My grandfather, who supported a family of numerous children through farming on a few hectares of stony soil in the mountains of central Haiti, was more of an expert than any of us. That is what our organization is all about: mutual respect, shared learning and working together at solving problems rather than delivering instructions that do not relate to the reality on the ground.'

Midway through a description of one of his projects, he broke off and asked me what I was doing for the following five days. I had some meetings to attend with other organizations in Port Au Prince. There was a report that was due for head office and a visit to a donor to ask for money. Why had he asked?

'Every month I spend at least a week visiting our projects and seeing for myself the work we are doing. I get bored sitting behind my desk or attending another conference to discuss the plight of the Haitian peasant. It's out there that I find my inspiration and the energy I need to get me through the other three weeks of the month. I'm scheduled to travel tomorrow. Why don't you join me?'

I quickly juggled in my head the possibility of postponing the meetings and sending an excuse to my boss about a delay in the report. The visit to the donor was unlikely to raise funds anyway and could wait a week. And the prospect of a guided tour of rural Haiti in the company of someone who was so familiar with its people and their issues was too great an opportunity to miss.

'Good, that's settled then,' he announced, when I nodded and said I would be delighted to tag along. 'You'll be my guest tonight as well since we start early tomorrow morning and I don't want to have to make a detour to your hotel. Come back late afternoon and we'll drive home together.'

Any concern that I was gate-crashing or intruding was dispelled by the same easy-going manner that pervaded Jean Daniel's family. His wife brushed aside my apology for arriving unannounced and jokingly told me that visitors offered a welcome opportunity to converse over supper about something other than the price of cotton in the local market or the latest low-cost technology her husband had read about in one of his numerous journals.

The two children were polite without being diffident and the eldest asked me if I could spare a few minutes to read through an English essay he had to present to his teacher the following morning. The youngest, a bright, precocious girl who was still at primary school, insisted on sitting with us to approve my corrections. At the dinner table a short while later she presented the various dishes that had been prepared and pointed out the ones she was sure I would not like. 'That one comes from the area where my father was born. It tastes like grass,' she said to everyone's amusement, 'but my father likes to remind himself of where he came from.'

I had been intrigued by Jean Daniel's earlier remark about his grandfather and seized the opportunity to ask him about where his family had originated and how he had ended up as one of the country's most prominent agricultural experts now based in the capital.

'Maybe that's a conversation for the car tomorrow,' he replied. 'My family has heard the story about my childhood many times before and I don't want my children to fall asleep before they finish their homework.'

'But our homework is finished and we don't mind hearing your story again,' the youngest protested, nudging her brother to signal his assent. Whether out of genuine interest or because he wanted to delay completing his English essay, he backed her up.

'My father was a "restavec",' his sister continued. 'Do you know what that is?' When I shook my head she added that there were thousands of 'restavecs' in the country and it was the one thing in the world you would not want to be.

'Now you're exaggerating,' Jean Daniel interjected, 'and there are many things in this world that are worse. But you're right that their lives are not easy and in that sense you can be thankful that you don't have to go through what I did.' Turning towards me he added that the term 'restavec' was simple enough to understand. It was an Haitian word for a domestic servant and that's what he had been, growing up. It seemed he would have to tell his story after all.

Jean Daniel explained that his father, like his own before him, was a peasant farmer in the same part of the island they had lived in for several generations. 'For each generation it got worse. In our system of inheritance, the sons are entitled to a portion of their father's land. That means it gets divided up to a point where it can no longer sustain a family, let alone be divided again to hand over to any of the children.'

His father had realised that for Jean Daniel, his eldest son, there was nothing worthwhile to hand on. The only escape from poverty and limited opportunity was to send him to school, to acquire an education that could offer him a better future. 'The problem was that there were no schools in the area where we lived, even at primary level. All education was centred in the cities and most of it in Port Au Prince. The other problem was that we had no relatives there, hence no one I could stay with while I proceeded with my schooling.'

One day a man had come to the village and announced that he could provide access for children to attend school in the capital. They would be housed with families who in return for some light domestic labour would support their education. He added that he was visiting all the villages in the district and that he would return on a certain day. If anyone was interested, he would collect their children and make sure that they got to their destination. There was no payment involved. He would get his commission from the receiving families where he would leave them.

'My mother was against it. She said that I was too young. They knew nothing about the family I was to stay with. In effect they would be handing over my safety and welfare to a complete stranger. No matter their circumstances, that risk was not worth taking. But my father insisted. The man had seemed genuine enough and if he was touring the district and other families were considering that option, there was no reason why I should be excluded. They had agreed that school was the only way I could ever escape their poverty. That chance would not come again.'

Jean Daniel had never travelled beyond the boundaries of his own village. As he described the journey he had made by bus to Port Au Prince, the sad faces of the other children beside him that mirrored his own, I asked how he had felt leaving the family behind that he was never to see again until many years later.

'I don't blame them now,' he replied. 'Look what I have become and where I am. If it hadn't been for that decision I might still be back there.' But at the time he didn't understand and thought he was being pushed away. It was only later that his mother told him that they didn't want to show him the sorrow they felt about his leaving, that would upset him all the more if he saw it in their faces.

Although Jean Daniel's description of the family he had been deposited with was delivered in a somewhat dry, matter-of-fact manner, I could sense the hurt that was there and the effort it took not to be drawn into condemnation. It was clear that he had been exploited. He described a typical working day: up before the family to light the fire, fetch water, prepare breakfast, tidy up after them, clean the house from top to bottom, go to the market to purchase provisions, wash clothes, help with dinner, scrub the pots and pans and cut the firewood to be used the following day. He ate what the rest of the family discarded and slept on the kitchen floor.

The household was by no means well off. Domestic servitude, it seemed, was not an exclusive privilege reserved for the wealthier classes who could afford to be indulgent. Effectively thousands of urban families, who occupied a position not much above the poverty line, exploited

226

the desperation of their rural counterparts who wanted to send their sons and daughters to school. Probably aware that they themselves were only a step above the people they looked down on, they had done everything they could to emphasize their differences, to highlight the gap between their own children and the ones who carried out their menial chores.

'Foolishly I thought when I first arrived that I might make friends with the other children in the house. But they ridiculed me for being ignorant, for coming from a part of the island that they considered on a different planet. I don't blame them; it was their parents' influence and prejudice. It was as if I had a disease that might be contagious and so anything that smacked of friendship or charity was simply not tolerated.'

As to the education that had been promised, that at first had not materialized. 'They said that they were trying to find a school that would take me and then made all sorts of excuses. It was only when I threatened to go home that they found a place where I could study for a few hours each day, where I could learn to read and write.'

In that sense Jean Daniel had been fortunate since many 'restavecs' never received the schooling that had been the principal reason their parents had sent them away. I was astonished when he added that still today, an estimated quarter of a million Haitian children were in the same situation. Faced with the kind of treatment he had described and deprived of the one thing that would have offered them a way out, I asked him why they simply did not run away and return home. Why had he himself stayed?

'I asked myself that question many times. I can tell you I thought about it every day. I used to say to myself it was because I didn't know anyone in the city, because I was young, because I didn't have any money to pay for a bus back home. But I realized these were not the principal reasons. It was because of the shame. I used to imagine arriving home, picturing the welcome my mother would give me, the smiles of my brothers and sisters as they came to greet me. But every time that image came into my head I could see too the disappointment in my father's eyes, the sorrow he would feel at my not having taken the one chance he had offered me to make more of myself, to escape his circumstances. I have spoken with other children who were in a similar situation to my own and they mentioned the same thing. Fear of failure, fear of disappointing family expectations, and fear of returning empty-handed are the principal reasons why we all endured something that should never have been expected of us.'

In Jean Daniel's case it seemed that the harsher the treatment the more determined he had become to succeed, to make sure that his education would compensate for what in effect was a lost childhood. To his new family's surprise, he successfully completed the exams that would allow him to proceed to secondary level.

'When they said that secondary education was too expensive, I managed to negotiate a few odd jobs in the neighbourhood to earn some money. I worked extra hard at my domestic chores too, to avoid giving them the excuse that I could not manage both. They weren't happy, I could see that, and maybe part of it was resentment at the fact that I did better at school than their own children. But when I began to help with their class homework I think they realized that I was too important an asset to lose. So they let me continue.'

Some way through secondary school Jean Daniel had acquired enough confidence and promises of casual work to enable him to leave the family that had so poorly substituted for his own. He was still only fourteen but as he described the work he had carried out to earn his school fees, the long evenings he had spent attending study groups with boys his own age to catch up on what they had missed during the day, it brought home to me how much 'childhood' was a relative concept. He had effectively been an adult long before attaining that label officially.

When I asked him what he felt he had lost or missed out on during those years, expecting some tone of injury and hurt, I was impressed yet again by his positive outlook, his ability to acquire from such a difficult experience those admirable character traits that even from a brief acquaintance I was able to identify.

'What I remember most from those years is not all the hard work or the long hours of study but the friendships I made with the boys I shared a room with. Most of us were former "restavecs" who had left our ersatz families in Port Au Prince once we had outgrown them and realized that unless we moved out and made our own future we would remain imprisoned in their misperceptions. We helped each other with school fees, with food, with clothes, with books, with preparations for our exams. When someone fell behind we helped him move forward. Most of all, we never allowed each other to feel sorry for ourselves. If it hadn't been for those friends, I don't think I would have had the determination to succeed.'

Jean Daniel's decision to study agronomy after he completed his secondary level education was not just prompted by the availability of scholarships for bright students to study the subject. In the period between school and further studies he had returned home and one of the things that had struck him was that rural families were still practising the tradition of sending their children to Port Au Prince for an education.

It was that same rural poverty that obliged families to expose their children to exploitation and hardship as the only way to get ahead. When his mother had told him about the anguish they had suffered for many years over sending him away, Jean Daniel had realized that separation was as traumatic for parents as it was for the children who left.

'The Government in Haiti is not in a position to build schools in every part of the country. To be honest they don't have the inclination either, even if they had the resources. Politicians are too preoccupied with lining their own pockets. The only possibility of building schools nearer to rural homes is for communities to acquire enough wealth to build them themselves. And for that to happen agriculture needs to be supported and farmers given the skills and capital to extract more from their land. That's the main reason why I ended up where I am, doing work that I love that has become a vocation. It's my contribution to ensuring that what happened to me does not happen to other children in the future.'

'But that doesn't mean that I think children shouldn't work at all,' Jean Daniel concluded, gently nudging his son and daughter who had been listening intently. Jumping up in anticipation of a forthcoming instruction they announced that they would clear the table and wash the dishes. His wife excused herself too adding that while such enthusiasm for domestic chores was commendable it was better carried out under her supervision.

As we sat together on the veranda a short while later looking at the sights of Port Au Prince and enjoying the cool breeze that blew off the mountains behind us, I thanked Jean Daniel not only for the hospitality but for having trusted me enough to relate a story that could not have been an easy one to tell.

I added that a few days previously I had met an official at one of the embassies who was responsible for allocating money to aid projects in Haiti. He had explained that educated Haitians had no interest in remaining in their country but wanted to flee to the United States where they could forget the poverty they had left behind. That was the reason, he had argued, why investing in schools was a waste of time since it only contributed to an exodus from the island.

I had appreciated Jean Daniel's story precisely because it contradicted such a cynical judgement. Even in the short time I had been there I had met numerous educated Haitians who were determined to see their country succeed and had stayed behind to contribute to that vision.

At the same time, as a former teacher in Africa I felt a loyalty to the inherent value of education. This was not a blithe and unquestioning optimism. I had taught an irrelevant curriculum for several years in Sudan and had seen the poor quality of teaching in numerous schools throughout the countries I had worked in. But the sacrifice that Jean Daniel's family had made confirmed something I had witnessed on many other occasions. This was the realization by those deprived of it that no matter how flawed and imperfect it might be, education offered the only possibility for children to progress, to participate in claiming their futures rather than being dependent on the whims of others. Since Jean Daniel's organization had been established to help facilitate such opportunities I had already made up my mind to offer our help.

The distance from Port Au Prince to Fonds des Verettes, our first port of call on our five-day journey, was only fifty kilometres. But by late morning we were still struggling along a stony, potholed track that had left the coast to penetrate the mountains where we were headed.

When I had flown into the country I had seen something of the scarred hills and denuded plains that had been cleared of vegetation, but I was stunned by the sheer scale of destruction around the capital. In an ever expanding circle that pushed further and further from the city, an army of charcoal producers had cut whatever trees they could find.

Charcoal was now the principal export from the rural areas, its value driven higher both by the lack of an alternative for cooking and its increasing scarcity. At the same time, cheap imports of staples that had once been the mainstay of local agriculture meant that there was little incentive for farmers to maintain the long-term productivity of their land. Cutting trees was their most lucrative financial option. But tropical soils were notoriously fragile and once deprived of cover their nutrients leaked away at a rapid pace. During the heavy rains that fell in summer, entire hillsides were washed away into Haiti's seasonal rivers. This explained the long plume of muddy water I had seen from the air, that extended beyond the coastline many kilometres out to sea.

In effect, large parts of a once luscious island whose fertility had been celebrated by its first colonial settlers had been turned into semi-desert. Cactus and shrubs had replaced extensive forest. Jean Daniel explained that it was only because of their isolation and the difficulty of organizing transport to the cities that the more mountainous areas of Haiti had so far been spared. Indeed, as the track ascended towards the clouds more vegetation appeared, as brown changed to green, hinting at what the island must have once looked like before trees became its most valuable commodity. During the earlier part of our drive I had counted some fifty trucks moving in the opposite direction. Apart from a few, they had been loaded with sacks of charcoal to help serve an estimated market of one million consumers in Port Au Prince.

Away from the more established coastal settlements, the communities we encountered were also different. Haiti's rural population was spread over every available hectare of productive land. Villages, therefore, seemed more transitory than fixed, providing a range of goods and services to the people who occasionally passed through them. A few stores sold car parts and more durable goods. There was a police station to remind everyone of the central authority in Port Au Prince, a bus stop with a kiosk to buy tickets, and a market area that opened for business once or twice a week. The more substantial buildings belonged to the churches: Catholic, Protestant, Adventist, Jehovah's Witness and other local offshoots. These competed for the souls of a rural population many of whom still adhered to the beliefs their ancestors had brought from Africa. Over and above their religious function, Jean Daniel explained, churches also provided the principal educational and medical facilities in their communities. The Government collected taxes and ran elections but clinics and schools were largely provided by religious charities.

One other facility I noticed in nearly every village was a small, brick building that held a position of prominence. They stood out because of the queues lined up outside them and the brightly coloured posters plastered on their walls. These depicted smiling individuals or families holding up wads of cash. Jean Daniel had earlier told me that there were no banks in rural Haiti and that peasant farmers generally invested whatever savings they could accumulate in buying more livestock. 'So what are these?' I asked him.

It turned out that they were offices of the national lottery and they had managed to penetrate the remotest corners of the country more effectively than most other institutions. 'Once a week on a Wednesday evening nearly every family in Haiti, rural and urban, gathers in front of their TV sets or radios to hear whether the tickets they bought will win them a million dollars. The lottery runs a slick advertising campaign. Those who win are interviewed on the radio just to remind everyone that it could happen to them.'

'But why don't people spend their money on something more useful?' I responded somewhat censoriously, thinking of the medicines, school fees and agricultural implements that could be purchased more wisely.

Jean Daniel laughed. 'I used to think that and would tell people to stop wasting resources on gambling their way out of poverty. But an old farmer once told me that he was well aware that the possibility of him ever winning anything was little more than wishful thinking. But at least for a few minutes once a week he and his family could indulge in the luxury of imagining an alternative. Since then I have learnt not to be so judgemental.'

On the outskirts of one of the villages we halted in front of a series of buildings that were fenced around and had a guard posted at the entrance. A large sign in French indicated that they specialized in the rearing and distribution of imported pigs. We had just been discussing what had happened to the native pig population as one of the sorrier aspects of the country's recent history.

Clearly Jean Daniel was well known since the guard raised his hand in greeting and opened the gate to let us through without checking our identification. Supported by an international donor it looked as if the entire facility had been transported from a different part of the globe to end up in a setting which could not have been more at odds with its origins.

The pigs looked fat, contented and prolific, judging by the scores of piglets that trotted around after the sows in the specialized pens. Several men in smart overalls and rubber boots were busy hosing down sections of the buildings. Others distributed feed into troughs where the animals queued up in impatient rows for their midday feed. I was impressed by the cleanliness and order and assumed that we were here to visit one of the projects that Jean Daniel's organization supported. But as we walked around inspecting the plump, pink animals he shook his head and told me that this was the kind of project he would not invest in, that what I saw here was an establishment of no use or relevance to the island.

'Pigs are the mainstay of the peasant economy,' he continued. 'They are the farmers' bank. When you need money you sell one. When you save money you buy some more. When there is a village feast or a wedding celebration they are slaughtered and eaten. They don't need much looking after either. You feed them the scraps that other animals won't even look at. And in return several times a year they give you lots of small offspring for free.'

He went on to explain that over a period of several hundred years a local variety, called the Creole pig, had become the predominant species on the island. It was particularly adapted to the climate and vegetation and was immune to many of the diseases that other breeds would succumb to whenever attempts were made to introduce them.

'But that all changed in the late 1970s when African swine fever hit. It started off in the Dominican Republic and then made its way westwards to affect us here. Within a matter of months thousands of pigs had died. Farmers will tell you of a time when animal carcasses floated down our rivers and out to sea. It was one of the worst things that had ever happened to our rural economy.'

A decision was made by the then Duvalier Government to eradicate the entire native pig population. Jean Daniel described the military campaign that had taken place to ensure that no animal was spared. Farmers who lost their pigs were bribed and cajoled to inform on others who were still hiding theirs. During the search-and-destroy operation families were reputed to have buried their animals underground with hollow straws inserted into their nostrils so they could breathe. The American Government agreed to finance a scheme where fifty dollars was paid for every adult pig that was delivered to collection points for slaughter. But the army and police forcibly confiscated a large number of animals and claimed the compensation for themselves. Most farmers received nothing.

Although traumatic for the rural population Jean Daniel claimed that despite its flawed execution the decision to eradicate all the pigs in Haiti was probably the right one. 'African swine fever is extremely contagious. If nothing had been done all of the pigs would probably have perished in any case. We needed to confine the spread of the disease so that it did not contaminate the entire island. In Europe or the United States when such diseases break out it is relatively easy to quarantine an area and fence it off. But here in Haiti that is impossible. The movement of people and animals can simply not be controlled in that way and so more drastic measures have to be taken. I know the figures sound awful. Within a space of almost five years half a million pigs were destroyed but the island was declared free from swine fever a short while thereafter, offering the possibility of recovery.'

But the programme of replacing what had been lost, according to Jean Daniel, turned out to be flawed. Not for the first time in my development career I heard how the native population was never consulted about what they needed or wanted. A foreign donor funded an expensive scheme to replace the indigenous pigs that had been destroyed by importing another breed that turned out to be unsuited to local conditions: the fat, pink but demanding animals we now saw in front of us.

'They require conditions that most rural families never even enjoy themselves. They need fresh water every day, clean pens, vaccinations every few months and a quantity of food that would bankrupt a farmer in a few months. Look at their skin. In the bright sun they burn easily and pigs can get sunstroke just like humans. No one bothered to ask about their colour either. In Haiti pigs are used for all sorts of religious ceremonies. The Voodoo priests that are present in every village require the sacrifice of a pig at certain times of the year to ensure a good harvest and protection against evil spirits. But the animals have to be black so pink is useless to uphold this strong cultural tradition. If the people who had developed this programme had directed some questions to the local population, they could have avoided spending a lot of money on facilities like this one which have rarely been visited by local farmers looking to acquire new animals.'

But according to Jean Daniel there was another way of doing things and on the outskirts of another village we stopped at a collection of wooden huts which he told me hosted one of their projects which he wanted me to see. A family sat in the inner courtyard shelling peanuts when we arrived and from the enthusiasm with which they greeted us I could get a measure of my companion's popularity and the rapport he had with the local population.

The head of the household was an old farmer with sharp, lined features set in a mournful face. Like many of the other men we had seen on the road he wore a large, floppy hat made of straw that shielded him for the sun. It served another function too since every so often he would extract a sheaf of tobacco and some torn newspaper from its wide brim and twist them into a very smoky cigarette. I noticed that the flies that bothered the rest of us while we were talking steered a course well away from him whenever he lit up.

While the Creole he spoke was obscure I could occasionally catch a few words of French to help me through the conversation. Jean Daniel would sometimes translate a sentence too so I could follow a discussion which seemed to revolve around identifying the numerous pitfalls set in front of local farmers just to make their lives more miserable. The weather had conspired against them that year, delaying the rains by several weeks so that the seeds they had purchased could not be planted. Meanwhile the price paid for peanuts on the market was less than what it cost to produce them. The village merchants did everything they could to fleece them. Fertilizer and other inputs were now beyond their means.

'But what about your pigs?' Jean Daniel finally interjected, as the complaints continued. For the first time in the half hour we had been there the face of our host lit up as the semblance of a smile replaced his doleful expression.

'Let's go and see them,' he replied, leading the way, accompanied by a group of noisy children.

I could smell them first before I saw them. There was a ripe odour of decaying food, rotting vegetables and excrement that thickened the air the closer we approached. In an impromptu pen made of bushes and the branches of trees I counted some fifty small pigs wallowing happily in a pool of mud that could not have offered a sharper contrast to the clean, sanitized environment we had recently come from. A bucket of potato peelings, old mango skins and chopped-up leaves was dumped into a pile in front of them which they proceeded to squabble over in noisy excitement.

I had thought at first they might belong to the native species that Jean Daniel had talked about but he confirmed that all of them had indeed been wiped out. Recognizing, however, the flaws of the new variety that had been imported, several organizations had come together to find a better alternative for Haitian farmers. They had identified a species of pig that came from rural China that in their view best fitted local conditions. Although smaller than their pink counterparts they required considerably less maintenance. As I could see they seemed perfectly happy to feed on scraps of food that cost the farmers nothing. Importantly too, they were black, which endeared them to the religious leaders who enthusiastically endorsed their introduction.

Jean Daniel's project involved setting up small satellite installations among local farmers. This was based on recognition that innovation among a generally conservative peasant community was best initiated by their own members rather than by Government or external agencies, regarded with suspicion. Across the district several families, like the one we were now visiting, had been selected to set up these breeding stations. Our host confirmed that this investment had yielded considerable profit. He had more demand for his pigs than he could fulfil and was already constructing another two pens so he could breed more animals.

It was another hour before we departed. For much of that time nothing was said. Jean Daniel and the farmer seemed quite content to simply watch the pigs rooting around in blissful contentment. 'I get quite emotional when I see them,' Jean Daniel confided as we drove off. 'For me these animals also have symbolic value. We have given up on political leaders solving our problems. We have given up on foreign aid bringing us prosperity. Our future depends on such seemingly small things as a few black pigs eating discarded scraps of food. That is where the future lies for my country, not in grandiose schemes that ignore who we are, which do not consider the world we come from.'

★　★　★

The village of Oriani was like many of the others we had passed: a loose collection of homesteads that surrounded a central market where the line that separated the community from the nearby countryside seemed more imaginary than real. We would stay that night in the project 'guesthouse', a small building rented from the local headman to host the team of agricultural advisors that served the district.

That evening as we sat around an open fire preparing our food, a stream of visitors came by to greet Jean Daniel and share their observations about the various projects his organization supported. With no electricity and no phones, since the national network had not yet penetrated these mountains, I was surprised that word had spread so quickly about our arrival. But Thermidor, the district manager of the pig breeding programme, informed me that the noise of our vehicle could be heard from many miles away. There was no competing traffic to contend with. The villagers had known of our arrival as effectively as if we had phoned ahead.

Over and above the subject of local pigs the other topic of animated discussion concerned trees and the various attempts that had been made to reverse their destruction. Earlier that afternoon we had driven through one of the last remaining areas of native forest left on the entire island. Foret des Pins used to extend all the way from the coast to the border with the Dominican Republic, some one hundred kilometres away. Now it was estimated that only ten per cent of that original forest remained.

On several occasions Jean Daniel had pointed to burnt out tree trunks. Fires had been deliberately set by unscrupulous woodcutters so they could claim the affected part of the forest as dead wood. That way they avoided the legislation that prohibited the cutting down of live trees. Only a handful of forest guards patrolled the area and with inadequate resources and lack of transport no one was under any illusion that they could compete against a slick, coordinated and professional operation run by wealthy businessmen in the capital. Jean Daniel's prediction was that Forêt des Pins would disappear completely in less than a decade.

Faced with such massive deforestation many organizations backed by donor money had tried for a number of years to plant trees in an attempt to reverse the heavy soil erosion that was also occurring. But Jean Daniel confirmed what I had heard before. The success rate was minimal. For every hundred trees planted he reckoned that only five per cent survived, a rate that was considerably eclipsed by the percentage destroyed each year.

'In my view many of my colleagues in other organizations have drawn the wrong conclusions from these figures. They see it as evidence of the backwardness of the peasant farmer, and that local people do not understand the importance of trees or that they are prepared to sacrifice their long-term future for short-term gains. So they find money to establish plantations surrounded by wire fences and patrolled by guards. In other words, they assume that tree planting projects can be successful without the support of the local population. That is why they simply ignore them.'

But such an approach was unsustainable. The country did not have the resources to maintain such policing operations. Once the donor funds ran out and the guards disappeared the fencing would inevitably be removed and the trees cut down for firewood or building materials. Since the community had not been included in the planning of such projects they felt no sense of ownership or commitment to supporting them.

According to Jean Daniel the rural population of Haiti made the same kind of rational decisions as anyone else. Their choice of what to support or not to support was based on a simple calculation of financial interest. Would planting trees outweigh the benefits of cutting them down? Since they lived in such proximity to poverty and destitution their time horizons were understandably short. They did not have the luxury of being able to worry about what would happen to their land in ten to twenty years' time.

'That is why we have to be smart and factor in such considerations. For example, many of the trees that are planted in those reforestation schemes have no short-term benefits. They require thirty years to mature and at the end of that time the only thing they provide is firewood. So local people who are desperate for land see a wasted resource. They would prefer to plant maize or beans in the same patch of ground, which can give them a return in three to four months.'

But there were varieties that had other uses. Jean Daniel's organization had introduced fruit trees that could mature in three to four years. At the end of that period their produce could be sold in the local market. When these had been introduced with the targeted population's collaboration, the survival rate had greatly surpassed the reforestation schemes.

Although I represented an organization focused on helping children, I was taken aback later that evening when I was introduced to a group of boys and girls who were members of the tree planting committee established in the village. Their ages ranged from ten to fifteen and their leader was a young girl with long pigtails, an engaging smile and a level of confidence and affability that I had not expected in such surroundings. On several occasions Jean Daniel had lamented the lack of educational facilities in Fonds des Verettes. In many communities, he had stated, the majority of girls had no access to schooling at all.

Martha responded with some irritation to my question as to what role children played in relation to trees. She pointed out that it was not her father or mother who was responsible for collecting firewood. It was she and her sisters. She reckoned that on average they spent two hours every morning simply collecting what they needed for the rest of the day.

'But it takes longer and longer to find what we need. The forest is moving further away. Each year more of it is cleared for agriculture. That makes our lives more difficult. My grandmother told me of a time when the forest came right up to the door of her house, when all she had to do was step outside to collect what she needed.'

It was children's direct experience of facing the consequences of increasing deforestation, she claimed, that made them obvious allies in any programmes established to address the issue. She acknowledged that when she had stood up at a community meeting to identify the members of the tree planting committee and had volunteered, the adults had laughed and told her to sit down. But she had convinced her father to back her selection and persuaded Jean Daniel too that children needed to be included in such schemes, more so than their parents. To initial community scepticism she and several other children were appointed to the committee, a decision that most if not all of the villagers were now convinced had been a good one.

'I think we are able to stand further back from the present and see some things more clearly than our parents. The choices they make now may not affect their own lives but will definitely affect ours.

I remember travelling with my father to Port Au Prince and seeing nothing growing around the capital apart from some shrubs and bushes and a few fenced-off areas with trees. That is not what we want here.'

In recognition of the enthusiasm they had displayed in community discussions around refor-estation Jean Daniel's organization had decided to provide several hundred children in the district with a variety of trees for planting. Each of them had received twenty seedlings and the results had been impressive. The children had watered and tended their seedlings more effectively than the adults and the survival rate had exceeded seventy-five per cent.

In order to provide a further incentive Jean Daniel had also convinced parents that any proceeds from the sale of fruit from these trees should be handed over to their children to dispense with as they wished. That negotiation had not been easy, but Jean Daniel had told them that the same principles that applied to them should be applied to their sons and daughters, namely that a financial benefit should be attached to any tasks carried out.

'I'll spend what I get from the sale of fruit from my trees on school fees,' Martha responded when I asked her what she would do with the money. 'My parents struggle to pay for my uniform and books, so anything I can do to help with my educa-tion will be welcome. I know that a number of people in this village think we will waste our money on stupid things. They have told our parents to keep it themselves. But we are all determined to prove them wrong and to show them that the best thing that ever happened to tree planting in our district was involving children.'

Several weeks later I found myself in the far north of the island visiting another rural project to which Jean Daniel had directed me. Claude, my original driver, was with me and after we had completed our meetings he informed me that we would take a brief detour to see one of the sights of Haiti. The only thing he was prepared to say about where we were going was that it would come as a surprise. The meagre huts of the local farmers, exactly like those we had seen throughout our journey, and the bumpy track we drove along did little to promise anything out of the ordinary. I imagined some natural feature like a waterfall further ahead or perhaps a spectacular view of the mountains that could occasionally be glimpsed above the canopy of trees that lined the road.

But a short while later we lost all vegetation to find something I had never expected. It was the remains of a palace or castle and though much of it had crumbled and fallen there was enough left standing to indicate something that must once have been truly magnificent. It covered a huge area and its novelty was all the more impressive because of the sameness of what had preceded it.

Apart from some goats that ambled along the path that led to the ruins we had the place to ourselves, or so we thought.

At a small wooden hut that presided over an impromptu car park we found a caretaker in a tattered blue suit and red cap fast asleep. We would have left him undisturbed but a sign attached to the door indicated that there was a fee to be paid to enter an area that had recently been declared a World Heritage Site.

He was startled when we woke him either because we had disturbed his nap or, as was more likely, because we were the first visitors he had seen in a considerable time. We had to write our names in a small book and after paying a negligible fee we received two tickets and a faded brochure in French that we were asked to return when we had finished with it. He added that for an extra cost he was available to give us our own private tour and more out of sympathy than expectation we agreed.

The goats turned out to belong to him and a considerable flock of them began to trot after us like a troop of accompanying cavalry. I asked him if it was appropriate to graze his animals in an area where agriculture was prohibited but the caretaker robustly defended their presence, claiming that his animals performed an extremely important function. If it weren't for them the ruins would have reverted to jungle since they ate any shrubs, small trees or other intrusive vegetation that

251

threatened to invade. He had even suggested to his superiors that he be paid for providing this service but it seemed they were as sceptical as I, believing that the harm caused by goats in terms of eating the island's disappearing greenery far outweighed any possible benefits.

The palace of Sans Soucis was almost two hundred years old and had been built by Henri Christophe, one of the leaders of the original revolution that had liberated the island. A few years after that event, however, infighting among those same leaders had split the country and as the head of one of the factions Henri Christophe had declared himself king of the northern part of the territory.

I was surprised to hear that during his short reign he had built nine palaces, fifteen castles and numerous forts. Sans Soucis was his prize achievement and was reputed to have been modelled on the palace of Potsdam in Germany, built by a monarch who shared the same passion for extravagant construction.

From the scale of what remained as well as the obvious care in workmanship that had gone into it I estimated that the palace must have taken several decades to build. There were elaborate gardens and fountains, a barracks to host a sizeable army and a large church with an ornate dome where the king could enjoy his own private service whenever he felt like it. But the caretaker informed us that it had been finished in only three years, started in 1810 and finished in 1813. He added that thousands of artisans and workers had been conscripted to construct it, and that the entire resources of the state that Henri Christophe had ruled over had been diverted into its speedy completion.

The new king, he stated with some pride, was determined to prove to the European Governments who had opposed the liberation, that a black-ruled kingdom could rival their achievements. For several years Sans Soucis had entertained ambassadors and dignitaries from some of these same countries that had once opposed him, acquiring a reputation for opulence and grandeur that was part of its original intention.

To demonstrate his power and the loyalty of his subjects one story had it that Henri Christophe, when questioned by one of his visitors on what his people thought of him, had marched an entire platoon of soldiers off the steep walls of the palace to be dashed onto the rocks below. 'He was a great king,' our guide enthused, 'and what came after has been a terrible disappointment.'

As I had imagined, Claude had a very different view on the matter and as we continued our tour and listened to more evidence of Henri Christophe's achievements, including a spectacular fortress only a few hours' drive away that had been built to repel a French invasion that never materialized, I could see him become more impatient. According to him 'Sans Soucis', which our guide had told us meant 'Carefree' in English, was better translated as 'Couldn't Care Less.' It was a perfect title for an extravagant waste of resources and people, built to flatter the ego of a leader of the revolution who had betrayed its ideals and turned into the same kind of despot his countrymen had overthrown.

'Imagine if all that wealth, creativity and energy had been put into improving the lives of the people who made it all possible. And why did one individual need so many palaces and castles at a time when the people he ruled over were starving? I enjoy coming here not to admire these buildings but to remind myself of the abuse of power. His castles and palaces for me are a bit like the pyramids of Egypt. They may be magnificent and impressive and even arouse admiration but aren't they a bit ridiculous at the same time?'

Despite our guide claiming that Henri Christophe was much loved by his people it seemed that they were more inclined to Claude's opinion. A few years after Sans Soucis was built many of the peasants he had exploited rose in revolt. The king suffered a stroke and, fearful of what might happen to him as his own soldiers began to turn against him, he was reputed to have committed suicide by firing a silver bullet into his head. Several weeks later his heir, the young Henri Christophe, was assassinated and Haiti was once again unified, under the leadership of Jean Pierre Boyer. Many of the palaces were abandoned and their stones removed for other projects. It was only the remoteness of Sans Soucis and its relative inaccessibility that preserved it for later generations to either admire, or as I had seen, argue over.

Towards the end of our tour we were interrupted by the noise of another vehicle approaching. A small minibus emerged from the trees and parked outside the hut where we had purchased our tickets. The caretaker who seemed to have become somewhat irritated at Claude's obvious lack of enthusiasm in hearing about the achievements of the monarch he thought so highly of excused himself to attend to the new arrivals. Visitors to Sans Soucis came infrequently, he said as he left us, and he did not want to offend them by having them wait too long. We did not begrudge him the possibility of another tour fee and in any case he seemed to have exhausted his store of historical background.

A short while later we encountered a group of about ten men and women. Our guide was busy pointing at the various ruins and we could hear him repeating the same phrases we had heard about Henri Christophe and his emulation of the monarchs of Europe. We guessed that the visitors this time were American from their accents, as we brushed past them along a narrow path that wound around the buildings.

One gentleman dressed in a floral shirt, baggy shorts and a floppy hat broke off for a moment to exchange a greeting. 'I didn't realise there were places like this in the Dominican Republic,' he enthused. 'We thought they only had beaches, hotels and bars.'

'What do you mean, the Dominican Republic?' I asked, as surprised as Claude who had also stopped in his tracks. 'This is Haiti.'

'You're wrong there, bud,' the man laughed, clearly bemused at such a preposterous suggestion. 'Haiti is still some kilometres away over the border in another direction. Our driver is very good with his geography. Jesus, I wouldn't go there if they paid me the same amount I spent on this holiday.'

As he walked off to join his companions the guide who had overheard our conversation also stopped to speak to us. In a conspiratorial whisper he told us that there was no reason to reveal exactly where we were. 'You know what people think about our country. If they had been offered a tour across the border do you think they would have come?'

'But what do you tell them when they get here,' Claude asked, mirroring my incredulity at the deception that had been practised on a group of unsuspecting tourists.

The caretaker shrugged his shoulders, as if our sensitivity on this point was misplaced. 'Isn't it true that at one time our two countries were unified?'

Claude nodded.

'The part calling itself the Dominican Republic only came later?'

Again Claude nodded.

'So it would not be wrong to say that at one time the ruler of Haiti was the ruler of the entire island as well? Maybe Henri Christophe was greater than you think.'

Before we had a chance to refute this selective interpretation of history our guide excused himself, said he had urgent business to attend to and trotted off with his group of goats to rejoin the company exploring the ruins ahead of him.

CHAPTER 9

HAVANA

'What were you doing in Cuba?' another immigration officer in the same airport in Miami asked me after checking my passport and noticing the stamp I had acquired when entering that island. I repeated much the same rationale I had provided previously when I had been quizzed about travelling to Haiti. I worked for an aid agency. I visited once every few months as part of my job, and had no other agenda than wanting to help people who were in need of our assistance.

'They only need your assistance because of that dictator, Fidel Castro,' the official responded. 'If it wasn't for him the people would be fine. What do you think of him?'

Much of my work in the Caribbean depended on travelling through Miami to reach the various islands so I decided that any expression of a favourable opinion might lead to difficulties. But I did not want to endorse any prejudices either so instead resorted to stating my ignorance on such matters. My organization, I said, was apolitical and we only wanted to help vulnerable children regardless of the issues and causes that had landed them in their situation. In the end my passport was stamped but not before I received a final admonition that despite my charitable calling I was wasting my time. The only thing that would save Cuba's children, the official insisted, would be if Castro and his cronies disappeared. 'Have a good day in Miami,' he said, before motioning me to pass through.

My first trip had taken place the previous month. Cuba was a relatively new country for my organization to work in and one of my tasks was to identify a programme of work that would build on the modest intervention that had first brought us there. From my base in Jamaica there were two possible options for travel. The first involved a long detour through Miami to Mexico, from where I could catch a flight to Havana. The other option was to fly on a small ten-seater plane that departed Kingston once a week with a handful of passengers to cross the small stretch of water between the two islands. I was not a fan of small aeroplanes but the thought of saving up to twelve hours of time convinced me that the shorter route was preferable.

For such a small country with a population of only ten million people it seemed to occupy a disproportionate place in terms of global interest, news and attention. The American immigration official had expressed a view that was common among its detractors. I had read books and articles that claimed it was little more than a prison camp where a small step out of line led to imprisonment and years of 're-education'. Meanwhile its sympathizers claimed that it was one of the few places on the planet where genuine socialism and equality was practised, where health care, education and social service provision rivalled those of most first world countries. As we bumped our way above the waves on the one-hour flight to Havana I promised myself to listen and observe, and reserve judgement on a place that prompted such strong and divergent opinions.

When Claude, the taxi driver who had picked me up at the airport in Port Au Prince, informed me that he was a graduate in mechanical engineering who had fallen on hard times, I had expressed some surprise at the mismatch of professions. I had imagined too that it would be difficult to rival that discrepancy between what someone had to offer his country and what he had ended up doing. But on my first day in Havana when Sergio had arrived at my hotel and told me that he was my driver for the next week, arranged in advance of my visit by one of our partner organizations, I realised that Cuba boasted even greater contradictions.

Dressed in a smart floral short and matching trousers, his face partly hidden behind a pair of thick sunglasses, it turned out that Sergio was one of the country's few heart surgeons. He still practised surgery since he was a Government employee but in his spare time and whenever he could he drove foreign visitors like me around to supplement his income. 'I can earn more in a week as a driver than I receive in an entire year from practising medicine. My wife needs a new fridge. Now I can buy one.'

As with Claude I could sense no bitterness about his situation when I asked him. Sergio loved practising medicine. He had specialized in cardiology because it had been a passion although his constant smoking worried me about the example he set for his patients. But as he described the circumstances that had forced many Cubans in prestigious professions to engage in more menial work I had a sense that the pleasure derived in coming up with ingenious schemes to make ends meet partly accounted for his good humour and unwillingness to complain.

Over and above being a part-time driver Sergio supplemented his income by swimming off the coast of Havana with a spear gun on occasional weekends to shoot fish and lobsters for sale to the tourist market. His aunt and uncle ran a small restaurant in their home where the same fish and lobsters caught by their nephew were served to foreign visitors fed up with the staple fare offered in Government establishments. Meanwhile one of his cousins had set up an organic vegetable garden on his roof where human waste collected from his neighbours was the principal fertilizer. 'Don't worry,' Sergio added, probably noticing my look of apprehension. 'We don't serve these vegetables at the family restaurant I will take you to later.'

Hard as circumstances were now it seemed that a few years previously they had been even harder. The country and its people were unprepared for the worst economic shock in their history. 'Cuba used to be described as one of the Soviet Union's satellite republics. In a financial sense it probably was. Our economic system was propped up by generous subsidies. They financed our roads, our railways, our industries, our agriculture, our hospitals and schools. Our beaches and hotels were full of Russian tourists. But when the Soviet Union imploded, our principal support was withdrawn overnight. That's when we realised how dependent we really were.'

Sergio went on to describe the rationing that had taken place: bread only once a week, rice every fortnight, meat and fish reserved for only special occasions. Anything that could be exported to earn the foreign exchange that was needed to keep the country running was taken off the shelves. 'Even coffee and sugar became luxuries we could not afford. It all went to South America in exchange for fuel. The only positive thing at that time was that we all lost weight.'

Not everyone had been able to adapt like Sergio and his family to straitened circumstances. The exodus of people out of the country had increased dramatically during those years and I remembered the stories of Cuba's boat people washing up on the shores of Florida in rafts, dinghies and makeshift wooden vessels to considerable international publicity. The speculation back then had been that like other Soviet satellites Cuba would soon collapse, that their controversial leader Fidel Castro would be overthrown, that within a few years its outdated socialist ideology would have changed into the capitalism it had so stridently rejected. So why had Cuba persisted?, I asked Sergio as diplomatically as I could. Why had the radical change seen elsewhere not materialized?

'One of the answers to that question is in front of you,' he replied, asking me to look out of the window at the city we were driving through. We were on the Malecon, a stretch of road that ran along Havana's considerable coastline. My guide-book had explained that when the breeze from the sea blew onshore in the early evening this part of the city became its most popular hangout, patron-ized by street entertainers, vendors, amorous couples and curious onlookers enjoying the company of thousands of others.

As we drove along the city's main artery I could see that some of the apartment blocks we were passing were new, somewhat ugly, box-like affairs that Sergio told me had been built by the Soviets to accommodate Havana's expanding population. But they stood out in this part of town precisely because they were the exception. Old Havana, slightly worn-out and shabby, hot and humid in the intensity of midsummer, exuded considerable history and a sense of identity that its new buildings could not conceal.

Split up to accommodate more family units, its older style houses had been retained, their Greek columns, shuttered wooden windows and decorative metal railings a reminder of the time when Cuba had been a prized colonial possession. There were some renovations going on to the facades of the buildings that fronted the sea and Sergio informed me that a substantial part of the old city had been declared a World Heritage Site, supported by scarce Government funds allocated to its preservation.

He pointed at one stage to another building whose ornate exterior and classical architecture offered a sharp contrast to the somewhat bleak and functional office block beside it. This was the famous Bacardi headquarters, the business centre of a family who had made Cuban rum famous throughout the world. They had fled into exile because of their support for Fulgencia Batista, the dictator whom Castro and his rebel army had overthrown in the 1950s.

'So you see, we are surrounded by these reminders of our history. Throughout Havana and other cities you will find old buildings like these ones. Maybe they have other uses now. Villas for the rich have been converted into housing for the rest of us and former churches are now Government offices. The famous Opera House that was frequented by

Batista and his relatives was not knocked down. Its prices were reduced instead and now it is patronized by thousands of ordinary Cubans. What all this means is that we have never forgotten where it was we came from. Maybe unlike the other countries you mentioned whose ideologies were forced upon them, we are aware that our history is no one else's but our own.'

Sergio went on to say that the revolution and the political system that came after it had seen many flaws, contradictions and problems. But it was like a child that most of the population in his view did not want to disinherit. 'Yes, we needed financial support to prop us up. Yes, we became a pawn in a game between the Americans and Soviets. But when the latter abruptly withdrew its support it did not mean we were ready to abandon what we had created, as if our past had been invented by others. What I think you will find in Cuba is that we are a slightly dysfunctional family with lots of arguments, tensions and competing opinions. But we remain a family whose members retain a deep loyalty to one another.'

I had a sense of what Sergio was alluding to when he took me through the narrow, winding streets of old Havana to the family restaurant he had talked about earlier. It would have been impossible to find without him. It was not situated near any thoroughfare or public space that would have attracted the attention of potential customers. There were no neon lights in front of it when we arrived nor any sign to point the way as we ascended the stairs to the top of a building. But despite its obscure location and lack of publicity, which Sergio told me was one of the conditions set by the Government for allowing such places to function, most of its tables were occupied and judging by the noise of clinking glasses, laughter and animated conversation, it seemed a popular venue.

Sergio had told me that he had delivered a catch of fish and lobsters the previous weekend but when we arrived his aunt and uncle made a huge fuss over him as if it had been months since they had last seen him. I was hugged and embraced too as if I was a long lost friend of the family who had turned up out of the blue. As we sat down at one of the tables with a continuous stream of relatives and friends coming up to greet us I thought of the formal and slightly frosty atmosphere of the hotel restaurant which I had frequented since my arrival. Although I had not yet sampled the food in this new location, from a social point of view it was clear why these family alternatives were becoming more popular.

Sitting down a short while later beside us, Sergio's uncle placed some glasses in front of us and poured a generous measure from an unmarked bottle. I was informed that this was the best rum in the country, reserved exclusively for export, but through a contact a few spare bottles had found their way to the family. I was instructed not to sip it like an expensive liqueur but in Cuban fashion to toss it down my throat in one expansive gulp. My coughing and spluttering were greeted by looks of amusement among the other customers and on the part of Sergio and his uncle an insistence on pouring me another.

As with the drink I was not offered a choice when it came to deciding the food I was to eat. I was to be honoured with the house specialty: fresh lobster and fish baked in tomato sauce, green vegetables and a staple of the Cuban diet that had the intriguing title of 'Moros y Christianos', which was translated as 'Moors and Christians'. They refused to disclose what such an exotic-sounding dish consisted of but when a plate of black beans and white rice was placed in front of me the reason for the title became apparent. Sergio's aunt presented the meal with a flourish and then sat down on the opposite side of the table to watch us eat. She told me that having guests enjoy her food was as important to her as receiving payment at the end of it. This was confirmed by Sergio who added that on occasion she had waived any charges because she felt that customers had not been entirely satisfied with what they had received.

In between appreciative mouthfuls of beans, rice and seafood, the conversation reverted to our earlier subject of change in Cuba. I asked Sergio's uncle how he had come to set up a restaurant in his home and he replied that it was his response to a set of factors that the country had never encountered before. Private enterprise was a concept associated in their society with the world they had escaped from after the revolution. But once the economic crisis had begun it had found its way back into Cuban society. Being an entrepreneur was still not entirely welcomed by the authorities but what had changed was that anyone inclined to an activity geared to realizing personal profit was now no longer automatically arrested.

A few years previously, he claimed, there had been no family restaurants, small businesses or private ownership of companies. Since the State provided everything – food, shelter, education, health care, recreation and even funerals – they were not needed. Self-help was regarded not as a means of becoming more independent but as an attempt to climb on the backs of others and to reintroduce inequality in a society where it had been supposedly eliminated. 'Of course we have not reached the stage where capitalism in Cuba is the same as capitalism in the United States. But space has recently opened up and more and more we are seeing things taking place here that would have been unthinkable not so long ago.'

While Sergio's uncle felt that the pace of change was being appropriately managed, other members of the family had different views. Sergio's cousin, a young man in his early twenties who had been singing Cuban folk songs in a corner of the restaurant when we arrived, was much more impatient and critical. Having been informed before coming to the country that it would be highly unlikely for any Cuban to voice criticism of their Government in front of a foreigner I was surprised at his candour and openness. If I had not been vouched for by Sergio, I doubted that in other circumstances he would have been quite so blunt.

'Our parents talk repeatedly about what it was like before the revolution, how terrible it was. We had this poured down our throats at school too, as if the world only began for us when the previous regime was overthrown. But for younger people like me, appealing to past history as a justification for not confronting the present does not satisfy our desire for change, our growing impatience at what is around us.'

Tomas had graduated from college the previous year and was employed as a teacher in one of Havana's schools. He had managed to avoid being drafted to one of the provinces, which meant that he could help out at his uncle's restaurant and earn more in tips from appreciative customers than he could in his actual profession. What irritated him most, he said, was the patronizing way in which Cubans were treated by their leaders. He asked me if I had seen the billboards on the way from the airport, the huge signs that were the first thing to greet visitors arriving in the country. I replied that I had, although pronouncements such as 'Socialism or Death,' 'Imperialists: We Have No

Fear of You', 'Vigilance is our Watchword' were a lot more colourful and interesting than the standard advertising of hotels, shops and new cars I had encountered in other countries.

'But the problem is that these slogans cannot compete with all the other influences in our lives. You cannot satisfy an educated population by feeding them simplistic statements. Every day we see tourists entering hotels from which we are excluded, drinking beer that we produce but cannot afford, and driving around in air-conditioned buses that do not break down every five minutes because they have no spare parts. There are contradictions everywhere. Repeatedly telling us that virtue is more important than a good meal is an argument that is no longer winning any converts.'

He went on to add that every day the number of 'Jiniteras' was increasing, explaining that the term described the currency dealers who had arisen in recent years as the economic crisis had deepened. Earlier that day Sergio had pointed to a small group of nervous looking young men gathered around a bigger group of tourists who were taking photos of one of the city's landmarks. The literal meaning of 'Jinitero' was 'jockey', but after Tomas's description I decided that 'tout' or 'hustler' were better titles. They were nervous, Sergio had explained, because their activities were legally prohibited although it was generally understood that the police would turn a blind eye to whatever they were doing in return for a decent cut of whatever transaction they were engaged in.

I was surprised when Tomas added that the term had its female equivalent, 'Jinitera', and that this was used to label the increasing number of young women engaged in an activity that I thought had been prohibited after the revolution of 1959. Prostitution had been at the heart of Batista's attempts to lure foreign visitors to the island during the 1940s and 1950s, when Havana was widely recognized as the fleshpot of the Caribbean with more brothels than any other comparable city.

According to my guidebook the new Government had outlawed prostitution on the grounds that socialism replaced the need for women to sell themselves out of economic desperation. But Tomas claimed that it had significantly resurfaced. Although not condoned by the State in the same way that Batista had encouraged the industry, a blind eye was generally turned towards the sale of sex in contemporary Cuba. There was a simple reason for this, he claimed, namely its importance to the country's developing tourist industry, one of its principal foreign currency earners.

'The majority of tourists who come to Cuba are single men,' Tomas continued. 'We all know this. Maybe they are married back home but many of them come here for one thing only and are prepared to pay for it too. Officially it is prohibited for a Cuban woman to spend the night in the hotel room of a foreigner but I have friends in the tourist industry who tell me it happens all the time.'

When I asked Tomas if attitudes towards such women were condemnatory he replied that there was ambivalence in how people felt about them. No family, he said, had been unaffected by the economic crisis. There were shortages of food, medicine, fuel, basic necessities, all the things that Cubans had taken for granted for many years. So everyone understood the pressure to make ends meet, even if it meant resorting to activities that had previously been prohibited.

He went on to add that one of the reasons why the term 'Jinitera' was used, rather than the Spanish equivalent for 'prostitute', partly reflected an understanding of the situation that many women found themselves in as well as the temporary nature of the activity. Tomas had female colleagues at the college where he had studied who entertained foreign tourists on an occasional basis so that they could continue with their studies. They did not consider sex for money as prostitution but an occasional business transaction that helped them on their way to becoming doctors and lawyers.

'But the point I am making is that while all of this goes on, our leaders churn out the same messages about socialism and sacrifice and virtue as if they are enough to keep people satisfied. But people are not satisfied. Just walk around Havana with a new pair of Nikes and you will see envious stares following you down the street.'

As I was to find out over the next few months of our developing friendship, Sergio occupied more middle ground when it came to judging his country. I noticed too that even when Tomas voiced his opinions with considerable emotion and intensity the relaxed, cordial atmosphere was maintained. Sergio would place a friendly arm around his cousin's shoulders whenever his voice became raised, reminding me of his earlier assertion that while opinions in his society diverged this was not at the expense of the tolerance he had talked about.

'Unlike my cousin here,' Sergio interjected after pouring another round of rum, 'I have been to some of the other countries that our young people look up to, including our hostile neighbour to the north where I attended several conferences. So I have seen that the gloss in which they are sometimes painted is thinner than they think. There is extreme poverty in the so called developed countries of the world. I have seen beggars in Manhattan and old men sleeping on bits of cardboard outside the metro stations. Even if you walk all over Havana you will never find anyone sleeping on the streets. Our people would simply not allow that to happen.'

Change had to come in order to confront a world that was very different from the one they had faced for many years. But like his uncle, Sergio believed that it had to be carefully managed so as not to lose what was valuable in their society: the solidarity, the sense of community, the neighbourliness that he felt were absent in societies that were more competitive.

Like others in Cuba, Sergio had relatives who had left, sailing to Miami on flimsy boats to find what they had dreamed about when things were difficult at home. 'But they write and tell me that what they have found is not what they were led to expect after listening to all the propaganda broadcast in our direction from radio stations in Florida promising Cubans a better life over there. Maybe they can afford a new car. Maybe their children go to college. But they ask about here with a kind of nostalgia that at times seems to me like regret. Rather than exile I would prefer to stay and change my country into something better. We never had Soviet socialism here. There is no reason to have American capitalism either.'

Several weeks after my arrival in Havana I began to wonder why the predominant image on posters and billboards throughout the city was the face of Che Guevara, the Argentinean doctor who had fought alongside Castro during the Cuban revolution. Even in Government buildings he had his photograph framed beside that of the President, a shared honour that I had never witnessed in any other country I had visited where heads of state were always keen to maintain their exclusivity.

As a student, I had had a picture of Guevara stuck on my wall. I had a T-shirt too with his face printed on it that I wore to student union meetings. But like many of my contemporaries who shared a similar attachment I could not have recounted in detail what he had actually done. He was a symbol of non-conformity and youthful rebellion, and his early martyrdom in the mountains of Bolivia meant that he had never reneged on his earlier principles. I had read enough to know that he was a pivotal figure in the Cuban revolution and that at various times he had occupied Ministerial posts in the subsequent Government. But I was surprised to see the extent of his popularity almost thirty years after his death, his presence more evident at times than that of his former leader.

That level of attachment was reinforced one day during a visit to a school in one of the suburbs of Havana. I had been in discussions with the Cuban Ministry of Education shortly after my arrival, since they had expressed an interest in receiving support from my organization. Like other services provided by the State, the Cuban education system was creaking under economic difficulties and the Ministry was looking for help with teaching materials and equipment. At my request they had arranged for me to visit some of their schools.

The classroom I attended had around forty boys and girls lined up in neat rows. I had asked for a minimum of fuss attached to my visit but clearly having a foreigner enter one of their establishments was something of a big deal for the Cuban authorities. I was accompanied by several officials from the Ministry, the headmaster of the school and a minder from some branch of State Security that was never fully explained to me. The latter never said a word throughout the time I was there but wrote notes in a small book of everything I said.

Whether it was normal attire or brought out on the occasion of my visit the children wore neat blue uniforms with red kerchiefs tied around their necks. I was slightly concerned when I was asked to walk around the room and inspect them, as if I was a military general making sure the troops were properly presented. The national anthem was sung with considerable gusto and as I stood to attention I noticed that even the person who was taking notes broke his silence to chip in. The headmaster then had several of the pupils recite a history of the island, which consisted of a description of pre- and post-revolutionary Cuba as well as a speech on the effects of the American blockade. A young girl with pigtails spoke with considerable emotion about how the trade embargo imposed by the USA on Cuba since 1962 prevented the country from acquiring vital medical equipment and hugely inflated the costs of imported goods.

After the formalities were over and the children returned to their seats I was then invited to ask some questions. Their responses surprised me. They were bright, confident students who were able to answer without resorting to the slogans and defensive responses I had partly expected after the officious and clearly orchestrated introduction.

'What are some of the problems in your school?' I asked.

The children talked about the shortage of books, the fact that their classrooms were overcrowded and that technical subjects were poorly taught because they had little or no equipment to practise on. In terms of the curriculum they wanted to know more about other countries and cultures and to acquire skills that were more relevant to the changing circumstances the country was facing. When I asked them about their aspirations for the future most of them wanted to be teachers, doctors or pilots but a few expressed an interest in setting up their own businesses. 'We can't just depend on our Government for everything,' one of the pupils bravely ventured. 'It's up to us to contribute something too.'

My questions over, I thanked the children, the headmaster and the Ministry officials for having given me the opportunity to visit their establishment. Expecting a polite acknowledgment in reply so that the children could return to their studies and the officials to their routines I was surprised when another hand was raised to enquire if I was prepared to answer some questions too. 'Sure,' I agreed, 'if you can spare the time.'

Of course I was asked my impressions of Cuba. That question had been asked of me by every person with whom I had had a conversation lasting more than five minutes. I reminded my audience that I had only been in the country for a month or so and any impressions were bound to be superficial. But from what I had seen I could confidently say that Cubans were warm, generous and friendly and that Havana was a beautiful city with lots of historical attractions and, to its credit, a commitment to preserving its identity. Somewhat mindful of the presence of important Ministry officials I added that I was here as a guest in their country and that my role as the representative of an international charity was to help Cuba in its own development rather than to impose my own ideas. For that statement I received a round of applause from the children and a nod of appreciation from the adults.

'So, where are you actually from?' asked the same girl with the pigtails who had earlier talked about the American embargo.

'Scotland,' I replied, wondering if I would have to draw a map on the blackboard to indicate its geographical position somewhere north of London.

'So what do you think of Braveheart?' she continued, adding that she had seen the film four times and would be happy to see it again.

'Well, it's a fine film,' I responded, 'although I

do think that Mel Gibson was somewhat liberal in terms of his interpretation of Scottish history. How many of you have seen it?'

All the hands in the classroom shot up and even the headmaster nodded his head to signal his appreciation of what was clearly a popular film in Cuba.

'Are you still having problems with the English?' the young girl persisted.

'Well, generally we get on, but like all families we have our occasional squabbles too.'

Not satisfied with that answer her hand shot up again. 'What about independence? Don't you think that Scotland should have its freedom, just like Cuba?'

I hoped my Ministry companions might intrude and spare me the embarrassment of getting further into this politically fraught subject. But they had the same attentive looks as all the children in the classroom. Maybe they enjoyed the distraction of not being interrogated about their own country. I managed a reply about how occasional differences did not mean separation, in the same way that arguments over dinner did not mean that a husband and wife should divorce. But I could see that 'pigtails' was on a roll and from the way she fixed her glasses firmly on her face I knew she was determined not to accept my counter-revolutionary statements.

'Our great hero, Che Guevara, supported liberation struggles in many parts of the globe,' she resumed. 'First he went to Congo. Then he went to South America where he was shot and killed by soldiers loyal to the dictator of Bolivia. He told us that our own revolution was not complete if people in other parts of the world were still oppressed. Why don't the people of Scotland ask the Cuban Government to help in their struggle? I am sure they would listen.'

In the silence that followed this intervention I knew I was expected to make a reply. For a moment I had a vision of newspaper headlines back home reporting that the Scottish representative of a UK charity had gone to Cuba to seek help to overthrow an elected Government. The note-taker paused to register my response but I fancied I could see a look of amusement on his face when I stuttered my appreciation for the offer of assistance but repeated my argument that a family squabble was rarely resolved by bringing in outsiders. With that I thanked my audience again and indicated that I had another pressing meeting to attend.

At the Museum of the Revolution in Havana a teacher called Pedro tried to explain to me why 'El Commandante', the title by which Che Guevara was known in Cuba, was still revered in his country. We were seated in front of a life-size, plaster replica of their hero. Dressed in battle fatigues, a trademark cigar in his mouth, Guevara was accompanied by another famous comrade in arms whom he had fought alongside for several years in the Sierra Madre Mountains of western Cuba.

There were scores of children, some of them Pedro's pupils, gathered around the memorabilia: a gun that Che had used, a uniform he had worn, photographs of him on horseback and donkey, a large painting of the triumphal march of the revolutionary army into Havana with Castro and Che leading the procession. There were photographs too of the makeshift grave in Bolivia where he had been buried after his execution. Located only ten years later his remains were dug up and removed, and now he lay in state in a huge mausoleum in the centre of Cuba's capital city, specifically erected to celebrate his memory.

Pedro and I had found ourselves on the same bench and after exchanging pleasantries we had engaged in a conversation about his country and the challenges it was facing. He laughed when I told him about my recent school visit, adding that the pupils had probably been briefed in advance and the questions prepared beforehand. He was open and friendly and I felt comfortable enough to share with him an impression that the museum we were in resembled something of a religious shrine where devotees came to pay homage and have their beliefs confirmed. I added that I had lived and worked in several countries in Africa where national politics had left me suspicious of the kinds of reverence and displays of loyalty demanded for their heroes. 'I am sure Cuba is different, "I continued, 'but every day I drive through Havana and see these huge billboards urging emulation of your leaders. Is this an attempt to convince people that such figures are beyond reproach, that they are not accountable to those they are meant to serve?'

Pedro listened intently as I spoke and then said when I had finished that in his view one of the reasons why Che was so popular in Cuba was precisely because he promoted a more human face of the revolution. 'He wasn't a saint. He reminded us the whole time that he was just an ordinary man. We were aware of his flaws, the fact that he sometimes made poor political decisions, that he wasn't faithful to his several wives, that he had children outside marriage. But despite his imperfections he committed himself on behalf of a greater cause. Many of us identify more with him than other leaders of the revolution, including Fidel whom we admire but who comes across as more remote, intellectual and detached. In Cuba we say that Castro was the head of the revolution and Guevara its emotional heart.'

Recent economic difficulties in Cuba had also helped to re-establish the significance of Guevara for ordinary people. Once again I was reminded of the shortages of goods and services, the pressure on families to make ends meet, the shock to their society that had come with the withdrawal of their principal financial backer. But everyone knew, Pedro added, that others had endured much greater hardships, including Che who had had every opportunity to lead a comfortable, easy life, firstly as a doctor after qualifying in Argentina and secondly after the revolution when he could have had a sinecure and enjoyed his fame and popularity.

'But that was not enough for him. It doesn't matter whether you think his actions were naïve. Trying to start a revolution in Bolivia was probably flawed to start with. But it's the example of someone who could have had more but made do with very little that inspires us, that and the fact that he gave up his life to help people who were less privileged than him. So whenever we feel like complaining about shortages of electricity or the fact that our coffee is now flavoured with chicory these billboards you talk about remind us that someone made a greater sacrifice, that compared to what Che and others went through our inconveniences are minor.'

My statement to the school children that as the representative of a foreign aid agency I was a guest in their country here to help rather than impose, was one that not only I had made but I'd heard repeatedly on several occasion. As part of the protocol of being allowed to work in Cuba I had been instructed to meet a representative of the Ministry of Foreign Affairs on a frequent basis in order to seek approval for any work we proposed to do as well as to receive direction in terms of our priorities. Sonia was my point of contact and from our first meeting I was left in little doubt as to who was in charge.

She was tall, imposing and pretty in an austere kind of way, a severity partly reinforced by the Soviet accent she had picked up from studying English in Moscow. The first thing she told me was that her Ministry had agonized over agreeing to the presence of aid agencies from countries that had been hostile to her own for quite some time. Aid, she added, was frequently only a cover for other objectives and they were aware that Governments had been undermined by charities pretending to be benefactors. 'Every agency that has come to work in Cuba has been carefully screened to make sure we have the right kinds of organization to help us with what we need. You are welcome but always remember that the permission we gave you to be here can just as easily be taken away.'

Worried that I had irritated her in some way I was relieved to hear from my colleagues in other organizations who had been given similar permission to operate in Cuba that this introduction was routine and had been repeated more or less verbatim by their own points of contact in the same Ministry. The other speech that was standard was the apportionment of blame as to why the country was in need of our assistance in the first place. American aggression, the trade embargo, the dislike of socialism by capitalist countries explained Cuba's isolation and was the reason why help was necessary. If that hostility was removed, then the country would be self-reliant and agencies like our own would not have been welcome.

The principal intervention that had brought us into Cuba was the result of a donation from the European Union of medical supplies and equipment to help the country's ailing health system. Several agencies had been selected to work with the Cuban authorities in terms of delivering these supplies to hospitals and clinics. We had been allocated the remote province of Holguin in the east of Cuba as our area of operations. Maintaining her slightly frosty manner, Sonia told me that one of the province's most popular attractions was a donkey that could take a bottle of beer, extract the top with its teeth and gulp the contents in only a few seconds. 'If you have a few spare moments in between your hard work you should take the opportunity to see it. It is highly amusing.'

'Are there other things that we can help with?' I asked her several months later, after we had met on several occasions and she had expressed her satisfaction with how we were performing.

'Such as?'

'Well what about education? My organization has a lot of experience of working in schools.'

'Like providing equipment, building classrooms, printing books? That kind of thing?' she asked.

'That and maybe help with the curriculum. We are very good at training teachers on active learning and classroom participation.'

'You mean you want to show us how we should teach our children?'

'Well no, not exactly,' I gamely continued. 'I know that Cuba is already doing very well in that area. But there are experiences from other countries that might be of interest. We can share that with you if you like.'

None of the countries I listed were acceptable. All of them had 'reactionary' regimes and an education system geared to promoting an ideology that was the opposite of Cuba's. Providing desks and chairs was fine. Printing more text books was also welcome, as was the provision of paper, rulers, pencils and blackboards. But I should steer clear of what could be classified as interference. The content of what children learned in school was clearly a sensitive topic.

'What about the unforeseen consequences of tourism?' I ventured on another occasion. 'Children can be adversely affected.'

'What do you mean?'

'In Thailand and other countries in Asia we have programmes that work with local communities and the authorities to prevent children from ending up in the sex trade.'

'So what does that have to do with my country?'

I related what I had heard about the number of single men coming to Cuba and having relationships with young women, many of whom were likely to be under the age of eighteen and therefore internationally recognized as minors. 'I know that your country is developing its tourism and I am sure that is a very positive thing. But there are often negative consequences for societies arising from this industry. Is this an area we can help you with?'

Although Sonia's response was unequivocal I did find on this occasion that her tone was less strident, almost as if she partly doubted the official line that she knew she was expected to repeat. It was natural for people, women included, to be friendly to tourists otherwise they wouldn't come, she said. Maybe that friendliness had been misinterpreted by outsiders. At the same time there were strict laws in Cuba about sexual relations with foreigners and it was highly unlikely that these were infringed, especially when it came to girls. The programme I had described in Thailand seemed like an excellent intervention, but once again the context was different and this was an area that they could manage on their own.

A few weeks after this conversation I was sitting in my hotel room in Miramar, a relatively up-market suburb of Havana, watching the evening news broadcast on national television. This had become something of a routine. Not only did it offer me an opportunity to familiarize myself further with the heavily accentuated Spanish that was spoken on the island but also to keep abreast of the official line on key topics of the day. At the end of the half hour broadcast a young, invariably pretty female forecaster would pronounce the weather for the following day. I was amused at how frequently phrases that had nothing to do with the climate appeared in the text, as in statements like 'tomorrow we can expect low pressure to drift south from our hostile and belligerent neighbour to the north that will bring rain and showers to our threatened island'.

This time the weather lady pointed to a map with dark, black clouds on the horizon. We were in the middle of hurricane season and one was brewing not so far off the northern coast with predictions that it would reach land within two days. It was always difficult to track the path of such storms with any accuracy, she added, but their best estimates were that it would hit Havana and then Pinar del Rio in the west before heading north towards the American mainland. The President had announced a full scale alert. Everyone was to be prepared.

'Yes, maybe that is something that you can help with,' Sonia replied, when I phoned her the next day and asked if my organization could assist in any way if the damage turned out to be substantial. 'Cuba is usually well prepared for these events. You will see for yourself the level of our professionalism. But the weather is always unpredictable and who knows what might happen. At least this is something we cannot blame on the Americans,' she joked, providing me for the first time with a glimpse of someone else hiding behind that formal, frosty exterior.

The next evening I was sitting with Sergio in a café on the Malecon, sipping a cold beer and enjoying a glorious sunset in my favourite location. The sea was remarkably calm and there were no thunderclouds piling up in the distance. Maybe the hurricane had veered off in a different direction but Sergio informed me that the prelude to these storms was often clear blue skies and glorious weather. In a few hours, he added, huge waves would soon be crashing over the sea wall and the café where we enjoyed our evening chats would be boarded up and closed for business.

Driving back to the hotel a short while later I could see the preparations the city was making. The army was out in force turning back traffic that was headed for the coast and helping fasten wooden boards to the windows of homes and offices facing the sea. Instead of her usual five-minute slot on evening television the woman who announced the weather interrupted the other programmes every half hour to indicate the path of the storm which was now headed west of Havana. But the edge of it was still expected to catch the city and deposit huge amounts of rain in the process. Fidel appeared too in front of the camera. He did not say anything but stood over a large map with several advisors, occasionally pointing a finger at some feature that would provoke a flurry of commands to subordinates hovering in the background.

'Should I be concerned?' I had asked the hotel receptionist when I had taken my key.

'Of course not,' she replied. 'Fidel is in charge.'

Despite the advice I had received about keeping away from the windows, even if they were shuttered, I couldn't resist the temptation in the small hours of the morning to take a look outside. It was the noise of the wind that had woken me, much more ferocious than I had been used to growing up as a boy in the north of Scotland where we had our fair share of Atlantic gales. It sounded like a person moaning, occasionally rising to a high-pitched scream when a particularly severe gust occurred.

Against the light of the street lamps I could see the solid curtain of rain the forecaster had predicted. But it was the sight of the palm trees along the road outside that most alarmed me. They were inclined at such a crazy angle that it looked as if they must be uprooted at any moment. I reminded myself of what Sergio had told me earlier that day. Palm trees were predominant throughout the Caribbean not just because of the climate but because they were more able than any other tree to withstand the frequent storms that hit the region. It was their pliancy and the fact that they did not try to resist the wind that explained their survivability, he had asserted.

I fell asleep after the noise had abated and when I woke up some hours later and switched on the radio it turned out that the hurricane had left Cuba and veered north towards the Florida coast. Along the Malecon later that morning I watched with Sergio as the army, the police and local residents cleared away the debris that the storm had deposited. Large boulders had been thrown up by the sea over the defensive coastal wall and now littered the road we usually drove along. The trees that had been uprooted, very few of them palms Sergio pointed out, were being sawn into manageable pieces and then dragged away. There were no signs of panic or alarm. In one part of Havana where the local river had burst its banks and flooded the streets some enterprising residents had hired out their canoes for transporting goods and people around the neighbourhood.

I detected a slight hint of smug satisfaction when Sonia phoned me a few days later. There had been no casualties. A few hundred houses had been damaged in Pinar del Rio but the displaced residents were now in a Government hotel while the army carried out the necessary repairs to their homes. Their hurricane alert system had functioned as expected, she added, unlike in Florida where several people had died after ignoring warnings not to venture outdoors and expose themselves to falling debris. 'Maybe the system we have designed here can benefit other countries,' she concluded, after thanking me again for my original offer of assistance. 'Is there anything that you think Cuba can offer to help the families affected in Miami?'

CHAPTER 10

CARRETERA CENTRAL

The central highway that ran east to west along the spine of Cuba for almost four hundred miles could have rivalled many major roads in wealthier countries but the sparse traffic and the occasional horse and ox carts that plodded along it were a clear indication of harsh economic times. One year after my arriving in Cuba the fuel queues had worsened and as buses and trains exhausted their supply of spare parts more people resorted to bicycles in towns and cities and four-legged animals outside it. If they didn't have access to their own transport they stood in long, patient lines on the side of the road with thumbs extended to catch a lift. Inconvenient for them, it meant I had as much company as I wanted on the long drive from Havana to Guantanamo in the far east of the country.

I had informed Sonia about my proposed journey, since she was supposed to keep track of my movements. 'I have a week free and I've heard that Guantanamo, Santiago and Baracoa are all worth visiting. Apart from Havana and a few days in

Holguin I've seen nothing of your beautiful country in the time that I've been here.'

'Where will you stay?' she asked.

'I am sure there are hotels along the way.'

'Do you need me to phone ahead and organize something for you?' she asked, with a solicitous attention that had become more prevalent the longer we were acquainted. A few months previously we had delivered a shipment of children's clothes donated by well-wishers in the UK. I was in her good books since the quality of what had been sent was considerably better than her frequently sceptical Ministry had expected.

Prior to agreeing the deal, she had told me of a donation of condoms gifted by China that had turned out to be impractical and something of an embarrassment to all concerned.

'Why?' I had asked.

"Well, Cuban men and Chinese men are different,' she had replied and when I still hadn't understood she pointed in the direction of my private parts to explain what she had meant. 'Many of the condoms burst and we had complaints from Cuban families that the Government was trying to promote population growth under the guise of supporting birth control. It was a disaster.'

Our own donation had been much more appropriate and since then our relationship had become less formal and officious. But while I had little doubt that her offer of assisting me in my forthcoming journey around Cuba was well intentioned,

I was keen to explore the country on my own and not be bound to any sort of official timetable. 'I'll phone you when I get to Guantanamo,' I reassured her, promising at the same time that if anything 'unexpected' occurred she would be the first to hear from me.

Sergio had drawn an elaborate map so I could exit Havana, but with limited driving experience and having relied on him on so many occasions to ferry me around I soon got lost in an industrial suburb of the city full of factory buildings and smoking chimneys. 'Don't ask anyone for directions,' had been his advice, 'since even if people don't know they'll point you somewhere in any case. If you get lost, find someone who needs a lift to where you are going and get them to navigate.'

'Is anyone here travelling to Cienfuegos?' I shouted towards a line of people along the side of the road. A young man pushed himself forward and announced that he was going to Santa Clara which was in the same direction.

'How much?' he asked, as I motioned him to get in.

'Nothing,' I replied. 'I need a guide to get out of the city. You need a lift. We can help each other.'

Enrique was in his early twenties and was returning to Santa Clara for the weekend to see his family. I had not caught full sight of him before he had entered the car but when he did so I could barely conceal a gasp of surprise. His face was lightly powdered and there were dark shadows painted under his eyes. The T-shirt he wore had some gothic face printed upon it that mirrored his own. For the first time in Cuba I saw someone with a tattoo on his arm that did not proclaim undying loyalty to the revolution but to someone who looked like Jimi Hendrix. The uniform was completed by a pair of leather pants and black boots to match.

Occasionally around town I had heard of a growing number of young people who had abandoned the salsa and rumba of their parents and had discovered rock music instead. The more enthusiastic followers, it was said, had also begun to emulate a similar lifestyle of sex, drugs and raucous parties to that of their counterparts in Europe and the United States several decades previously. This had led to considerable irritation among the Cuban authorities for what was considered to be unpatriotic behaviour, and there was talk of arrests, imprisonment and attempts to rehabilitate the worst offenders.

'Yes, I am a Rockero,' Enrique replied, when I asked him. 'But I suppose that's not too difficult to guess,' he added, as he directed me out of the maze of streets in his suburb and on to the Carratera Central which would take us towards Cienfuegos about one hundred kilometres away.

The fact that I was a Jimi Hendrix fan and could hum a few bars of 'All Along the Watchtower' impressed him immensely and we spent much of the next half hour swapping the names of various bands that had populated my youth and whose music had been miraculously resurrected in Cuba some thirty years later. But Enrique, who had been a student at a college in Havana before dropping out due to failed exams and limited job opportunities, even if he had graduated, clearly had a much more thought-out philosophy than attachment to a few songs rescued from the historical archives.

Once again the billboards along the side of the road and the revolutionary slogans painted on whatever surface could accommodate them prompted a reflection. 'If these were just adverts,' he said, 'promoting shoes, clothes and package holidays then we could choose to ignore them. But in Cuba, sacrifice for the greater good and loyalty to the State penetrates every aspect of our lives. We hear it in kindergarten, in school, in college, in places of entertainment, even in our homes. It is suffocating. So, when I first heard rock music it was like finding an alternative, a space that the Government of my country could not own and control.'

The large sign we were approaching as he talked, depicted a group of young girls and boys dressed in neat uniforms. They were saluting the Cuban flag and proclaiming their faith in the guidance of Jose Marti, another national hero who had helped Cuba to independence from Spain in the late 1800s and had been martyred in the process. I knew that there were competing claims to his ideas since 'Radio Marti' was the name of the radio station in Miami that beamed out messages against the Cuban state on behalf of the exiles who had fled the country.

Once past the billboard I pointed to Enrique's T-shirt and the spiked hair that stood out on his head. 'But aren't you just swapping one uniform for another?' I asked him, hoping he wouldn't take offence. 'I'm sorry to tell you but where I come from rock music today is becoming more a sign of conformity than rebellion. There's nothing revolutionary about its ageing stars sitting on huge piles of cash and enjoying comfortable lifestyles. In my country our billboards now advertise their concerts.'

I added that one of the things I found attractive about Cuba was that it seemed to have resisted the imposition of Western popular culture: the clothes, music, fashion and attitudes that, in many countries I had visited, were becoming more prevalent among young people than the traditions of their parents. 'I am not advocating the preservation of other cultures in a kind of historical museum so that nothing changes, so that modernity passes you by. But in a world that's becoming depressingly similar your sense of identity stands out. I don't think that anyone could come here and imagine this is any other place than Cuba.'

I was glad to see that Enrique's sense of commitment was tempered with a liberal dose of openness to other opinions. He laughed when I told him that some of the rock icons who had thumbed their noses at the establishment when I was growing up were now receiving recognition from politicians who would once have clapped them behind bars. His response was thoughtful too as he reminded me that any new cultural expression sooner or later became fashionable and mainstream and in the process lost something of its original identity and value too.

'Rock music in Cuba today is probably like what it was in your county twenty or thirty years ago. Part of the reason why some of us identify with the movement is precisely because it's not well accepted in our society. If it had the blessing of the authorities, then we would probably return to Salsa or find some other form of expression they didn't approve of.'

As for Cuban cultural independence, he responded that preservation of national identity should come from people having a free choice between alternatives, not because a small group of leaders chose to shelter the population from external influences. Despite the rhetoric of the revolution referring to the sanctity of the people he felt that there was deep mistrust in his Government towards ordinary citizens, as if Cubans needed to be protected from themselves. 'I don't think we will sell our identity if we have Coca Cola and a McDonalds in Havana. And in any case the fact that we see capitalism every day paraded in front of us through tourists in our country, through the windows of dollar stores we can't get into and expensive restaurants that we can't afford, makes it seem more attractive than it probably is.'

One of the other rumours I had picked up in Havana concerning the group that Enrique hung out with was that a number of them had deliberately injected themselves with infected blood that carried the HIV virus. I was aware that on several occasions Cuba had conducted a mass screening of its population to test for the disease and that anyone who was found to be HIV positive was removed from their families and communities and placed in special sanitaria where contact with the outside world was restricted.

On a previous occasion I had asked Sonia whether there was something my organization could do to help the people that were in them. As with my former offer to assist her Ministry to develop a 'responsible' tourism strategy, she indicated that there was too much controversy surrounding the issue to merit external involvement. She had not been totally dismissive however and added that there was a review taking place and that once their deliberations had been concluded she might get back to me with a proposal. Meanwhile the country was stuck in the middle of an international uproar concerning its policy, between those who argued that incarceration no matter how benign was an infringement of the rights of infected people, and those on the other side who pointed out that Cuba's practice of mass screening and quarantine had meant that it had the lowest rates of HIV infection in the western hemisphere.

Although Enrique had not directly come across any fellow rock aficionados who had injected themselves with the virus he was aware that some had done so. The more altruistic interpretation was that out of sympathy with those who had been quarantined and as a protest against Government control and its programme of forced conformity, some few dozen Rockeros had injected themselves. The other more sceptical judgement was that since it was well known that conditions in the sanitaria were relatively pleasant with good food, free accommodation, no pressure to work and as much music as you wanted to listen to, the prime motive was self-interest rather than political solidarity.

'I can't honestly say which is more likely,' Enrique added, 'probably a mixture of both. But what I can say is that ever since it happened we have been inundated with messages about the risks of HIV and how we can avoid catching it.'

Condoms, he continued, were now liberally distributed at their gatherings. Most of them were blown up into decorative balloons. The bands that played at their concerts were instructed to punctuate their performances with messages about safe sex. Leaflets were handed out at these same venues with quotes from Western rock stars about the dangers of contracting HIV and the risks associated with taking drugs, a message that was in stark contrast to the lyrics they belted out in their music.

'It's something of an irony, though,' Enrique added. 'Everyone knows that most of the people in the sanitaria are former soldiers who served in Angola or people involved in the tourist industry who had relationships with foreigners. And if you go to a salsa concert you'll hear much more provocative and sexually explicit music than what you'll hear at a heavy metal venue. To be honest a lot of Rockeros are either too drunk or too stoned to be able to have any sex at all. We're probably the safest group in the country.'

In a small town where I was to turn south and Enrique was to continue the short distance east to Santa Clara we stopped at a petrol station to refuel the car. There was a café attached to one end of it and I invited him to join me for some refreshment before we continued our separate journeys.

I noticed the stares he elicited as we got out of the vehicle, more amusement than any hostility, and the glances thrown in his direction by the waitresses when we entered their café. At different times they all came up to confirm our order and to take the opportunity to check what they were seeing from a closer distance. 'I get that all the time,' Enrique replied when I asked him if he minded the attention. 'Mostly it's all good-humoured and pleasant enough but occasionally someone will tell me to change my clothes, sort out my hair and be more patriotic. I remind them that by their definition Che Guevara would probably have been one of the world's first hippies and that usually shuts them up for a while.'

Midway through our coffee Enrique excused himself to go to the bathroom. I wondered if he had contracted food poisoning or if he was unwell since it was quite some time before he returned. The surprise I had registered when I first caught sight of him repeated itself when he sat down. There had been a complete transformation. His T-shirt had been swapped for a more conservative, short-sleeved alternative. The black pants and heavy boots had been changed for cotton trousers and brown shoes. His makeup had been washed off and his spiky hair was now respectfully flattened over his head. He shrugged his shoulders as I stared at him with my mouth open.

'Look, there's no point in needlessly irritating my parents, is there? I can't be bothered with the hassle of explaining my identity to a family who wouldn't understand.' He went on to say that he was attending a large family gathering to commemorate the passing of their grandfather who had died the previous year. As he had been a stalwart of the revolution and a keen party member Enrique's arrival in his 'outfit' would only have been seen as provocative and disrespectful of his memory. Nodding my appreciation and understanding of his sense of propriety I offered the example of some well-known rock stars who had cut their hair and changed their clothes whenever they visited their mums.

Ignoring the giggles of the waitresses as we passed them Enrique shook my hand and thanked me as we exited the café. 'I didn't tell you that I waited for several hours this morning before you came along to give me a lift. At least in these clothes I'll get picked up in five minutes.'

The potholed road I found myself on later had branched off from Cienfuegos towards the place where I was headed. I worried for a while that I had taken a wrong direction since one of Cuba's most famous landmarks should surely merit a better means of getting there. But the signs were clear enough. Playa Giron was somewhere in front of me and as the billboards proclaiming this location as the site where the revolution had been defeated 'in martyrs' blood' became more frequent, I guessed that it could not be too far away.

It wasn't only potholes, however, that slowed me down. Part of the route skirted a reedy, water-logged area of land known as Zapata swamp. Apparently I had arrived in the middle of the animal migration season. Thousands of crabs were scuttling across the road forcing me to reduce my speed to a leisurely crawl.

A few miles back I had picked up an old man in a straw hat and ragged clothes waving a piece of cardboard with 'Playa Giron' painted upon it.

I hoped he could give me a history of his area and some reassurance that I was definitely on the right road. I barely understood a word of the garbled Spanish that he fired at me but I was left in little doubt that he failed to appreciate my delicate manoeuvring.

'Vamos, vamos!' he shouted, pointing to the accelerator and urging me to commit carnage among the crabs. He was exasperated when I failed to do so and then demanded that I drop him off some distance from our destination. As he planted himself on the road in front of my vehicle he proceeded to wave his sign at some following traffic. Judging by the speed and the marks on their sides the drivers behind me shared his same dismissive attitude towards the local wildlife. To my amusement they did not stop to pick him up and just to irritate him even more I sped off at the same brisk pace, having first checked that the road was clear in front of me.

'Playa Giron' was the 'Bay of Pigs'. I had read about its significance in Cuban history before but there was no shortage of reminders in the country as to what had happened there. In the Museum of the Revolution back in Havana a whole section had been reserved to commemorate what had occurred. In one school that I had visited some of the students could recite the names of the over one hundred Cuban soldiers and civilians who had died in the invasion. Although interpretations of what had taken place had been disputed between the principal contestants, distance in time had reduced some of the emotions and subjectivity and many of the facts were now agreed and accepted.

In the early 1960s, alarmed by the rhetoric coming from Castro after he had overthrown one of their key allies in the Caribbean, the US Government had adopted a policy of destabilizing the island. This included covert support to Cubans who had fled the revolution and who had set up camp in Miami to create an opposition movement to the new regime. This group had come up with a plan to invade Cuba, promising the CIA that their compatriots back home were ready to over-throw Castro once a small spark had been ignited to mobilize them.

Provided with weapons and transport and trained by US army officers, a force of some two thousand men was deposited by ship and aeroplane on the southern coast of Cuba on the 17th of April, 1961. Playa Giron was selected because its sandy beaches made for an easy landing and its relatively short distance to Havana meant an invading force could reach it in a couple of days. But there were early setbacks that indicated the kind of cavalier attitude that must have prevailed at the time as well as lack of foresight and planning. A large section of the soldiers deposited on the beaches that morning was rendered ineffective because most of their equipment was lost at sea. A parachute brigade that was meant to secure the main road north was deposited in the middle of Zapata swamp from which they emerged a few days later, long after the conclusive battle was over.

Perhaps the biggest blunder was underestimating the size and professionalism of the forces ranged against them as well as the popular support that Castro widely enjoyed during the first heady years of his revolution. He had taken personal control of his troops and, backed up by airpower and superior artillery, he had forced the invaders to surrender in less than three days. Some of them escaped back to their base in Miami courtesy of the US ships anchored off the southern coast. The majority were either killed or captured, with many of the latter paraded in front of the international media to confirm the Government's claim that they were little more than American stooges.

It was later revealed that many of the prisoners captured in the Bay of Pigs invasion were ransomed by the Cuban Government to their American counterpart in order to permit their return to their families in Florida. The asking price had been several hundred tractors which ironically had helped the country the subsequent year to register one of its largest sugar harvests on record.

No doubt irritated at having been outsmarted and humiliated in front of an international audience, the US Government had continued its policy of aggressive opposition. In late 1961 they announced a punitive embargo that prohibited everything bar essential medical equipment from being traded with the island. Rumours circulated too of various extravagant plots to get rid of Castro, including the invention of an exploding cigar to be inserted in his collection.

'It doesn't matter whether this is fact or fiction,' Sergio had once told me. 'What is fact is that our northern neighbour has a policy of open hostility towards our leaders. But don't they understand that this unifies us even more? We don't like being bullied. It means that Castro has been turned into a hero for standing up to them. Remove that opposition and it would diminish his reputation. The excuse he can always make is that it's someone else behind our problems, an external opposition that requires us to spend as much on security and our armed forces as on health and education. Many of us can't understand why a country like the United States with such a sophisticated infrastructure and economy can be so naïve when it comes to foreign policy.'

Because of all the patriotic noise that surrounded it I had conjured up an image in my mind of a place littered with the relics of war and public reminders of its significance in Cuban revolutionary history. But when I finally arrived at the Bay of Pigs I found a resort not geared to preserving memories of what had occurred thirty years previously but to offering recreational pleasures associated with its prime location. There were gift shops, restaurants, cafés and a disco on the main street. Several kiosks announced fishing, scuba diving and water sports. On the beach where I had expected to find rusting tanks and perhaps a grave-yard for the fallen there were numerous 'Cabanas' for foreign visitors to change into their bathing costumes before plunging into the clear blue waters of the Caribbean.

'That way to the museum,' a young man in shorts and a floral short replied when I asked him where I could find the place that commemorated the invasion, mentioned in my guidebook as worth a visit. But he seemed surprised that I had enquired. 'Hey, mister, I can take you fishing for a very good price. That shop over there belongs to my uncle. He has a good boat. Fifty dollars only,' adding as I moved away that he was prepared to throw in some female company for no extra charge if I was interested.

Maria was the caretaker of the museum where I pitched up a short while later. The buildings had been easy to find not because of the cursory directions I had received but because of the huge artillery piece and the military aircraft that stood guard outside it. She jumped to attention when I entered and, judging by the warm handshake I received, I guessed that her establishment compared somewhat unfavourably with all the other recrea-tional facilities available in town. She also turned out to be the guide for the day and, for a price considerably less than I had been offered for a reclining chair on the beach, she suggested that she show me around.

Perhaps because I was the only person there and because it had not featured prominently in Playa Giron's self-promotion, I had assumed a few meagre exhibitions and photographs of a victorious Castro presiding over his troops. But the museum boasted several sections that were well resourced and maintained, offering a wider insight into the lives of its inhabitants than what had occurred over a few days in 1961.

The pre-revolutionary section included ageing photographs of the 'Zapatistas', the population of the area who had derived their livelihoods from production of charcoal and trade in crocodile skins. The swamp where they lived was the largest area of wetland on the island with mangroves that stretched for miles along the southern coast. The faces that stared back from the early part of the century were all hard and unsmiling, echoing the grim descriptions of the captions below them. Illiteracy stood at almost one hundred per cent. The nearest medical facility was some one hundred kilometres away. There were no schools. Housing consisted of wooden huts in clearings carved out from the forest where mosquitoes and other hostile insects made life even more unpleasant.

Not entirely unexpectedly, there was a certain triumphalism in the section of the museum devoted to post-revolutionary life in Cienaga de Zapata. The wooden huts had been replaced, courtesy of a visit from Fidel who, when he had seen where the 'carabaneros', the charcoal producers, had been living, had instructed his army to build them proper houses. There were photographs of the road I had driven along, looking considerably more pristine after its initial construction and free of potholes and migrating crabs. A successful literacy campaign had allowed its inhabitants 'to join the rest of the country', and there were pictures of smiling children outside the several schools, clinics and community centres that serviced the population.

Maria, who had told me that her grandfather came from this area and had derived a living similar to that depicted in the earlier section of the museum, admitted that there was some exaggeration in the way that contemporary life was portrayed. The clinics were short of medicines. The schools were short of books. The community centres only functioned sporadically because of frequent electricity cuts. 'But at least they are there,' she added.

'When my grandfather has drunk too much he will start talking about the freedom of his former life in the forest, the fact that there was no one to tell them what he had to do, that there were no bosses. But when he is sober he will tell you how terrible it was, how they were dependent on middle men for selling what they produced and how badly they were exploited. He lost several children because they had no hospital. The rest migrated because there was no work. In the last thirty years this place has become unrecognizable from what it once was.'

The largest section of the museum was devoted to the battle itself and there were numerous maps depicting the hourly movement of troops, the initial gains of the opposition forces, the arrival of Castro and his army, the red stars marking battle sites where the invaders had been repulsed. Whether out of historical interest of just because it was part of her job Maria explained each of them with military precision. 'That is where their soldiers landed . . . Here is where we pushed them back . . . A tank was destroyed in that location . . . This is the place where the last of the invaders surrendered.'

Interspersed among the charts and papier mâché models of the conflict was military hardware captured from the enemy: machine guns, rifles, bullets and helmets. The aeroplane outside had been shot down. The artillery piece had been abandoned by retreating troops. They even had several boats on display which had been used to ferry soldiers from the American ships that had brought them to Cuba. But for a moment Maria's polished and clinical presentation melted when we came to a wall where the photographs and names of the Cubans who had been killed in the conflict were displayed. She seemed genuinely moved as she recited the stories of some of them, young men from neighbouring towns who had heeded the call to arms to defend the country, the personal letters that Castro had written to each of their families to acknowledge their sacrifice.

As we sipped coffee at her desk a short while later, the tour completed, I gestured towards the rooms we had just visited and the silence that hung about them in the absence of any other visitors. 'Who comes here? How many people actually see all this?'

Maria shrugged. This was not the best time of year. In August at the peak of the tourist season the numbers would pick up. Of course there were the inevitable and more frequent school trips when children from Havana and other cities came to visit the museum as part of their vacation. 'The boys like the tank and the aeroplane. The girls get a bit more emotional when they see the photographs and hear some of the stories. But after a short while I can see them getting bored, wondering when they will be released so they can get on with the real business of visiting the beach and enjoying their holiday. My own children are like that. The living only have so much time for the dead, I suppose.'

But when I pressed her Maria was adamant that the museum served an important function, that places like this one dotted around the country to commemorate similar events had a definite place and should not be neglected. 'It's about preserving memories, isn't it? Not just out of historical interest or curiosity, not just because important things happened here. The key message of all our military museums is not to glorify conflict. It's about reminding people to be careful that it doesn't happen again, that the stories of these young men now stuck on that wall should never be repeated.'

CHAPTER 11

GUANTANAMO

In the cafés in Havana where groups of Cuban musicians serenaded foreign visitors, and on the radio whenever I switched it on, 'Guantanamera' invariably featured as the predominant offering. I had heard the Pete Seeger version some years before so the song was familiar but I had never bothered to find out what the title actually referred to. This was to change the day after I had visited Playa Giron when Elisa stepped into my vehicle. Some distance beyond a small town called Sancti Spiritus where I had stopped to give her a lift she had announced, when I asked her where she was from, that she was indeed a 'Guantanamera' and began to sing some lines of the melody that was more popular in Cuba than the national anthem.

'Don't tell me you don't know what it means,' she laughed, my puzzled face giving me away. The song, she explained, had several versions and something of a disputed history. But what was not in doubt was that it had been prompted by the impression that a young woman from the countryside around Guantanamo had made on the composer.

'We are supposed to be very beautiful,' she had joked, and ever the gallant gentleman I had nodded my head and said that was undoubtedly true. In the case of Elisa with waist-length black hair, dark brown eyes and an engaging smile, that conclusion was not a difficult one to come to.

The town I had just passed before picking her up had a secondary school where Elisa taught physical education and mathematics to boys and girls who were more interested in the former than the latter. 'I don't blame them,' she said. 'There's more of a future playing basketball or competing in the Olympics than there is in learning algebra or calculus.'

She had been there for a number of years but was hoping to be transferred nearer to her family whom she could rarely visit because of the distance. Previously she had travelled by train but that had now become so unreliable in terms of delays that it was easier, if less comfortable, to stand by the side of the road waiting for a lift. In the short time I had taken to drive through Sancti Spiritus I had seen a church, a few Government buildings and stores and not much else. Elisa confirmed that it was 'quiet', not like the towns of eastern Cuba where she came from. But teachers who completed several years in what were unofficially called 'hardship' locations had more of a say in their next posting.

When I had stopped the vehicle on the side of the road to offer her a lift I was surprised that anyone was there. The only feature that stood out against the forested hills and the brown plains of the open countryside around us was a distant factory belching clouds of white smoke into the sky. There were no other houses or buildings nearby.

Elisa told me we were beside a large sugar estate and that there would be many more on the road east to where we were headed. Hadn't I noticed the smell that hung in the air, she asked, winding down the window. The fragrance I picked up was not like the refined sweetness of commercial sugar but was something much earthier, rich and pungent. We were in the middle of harvesting season. As we drove further along she pointed to the ox carts loaded with cane, the men and women in straw hats being ferried by trucks to the next field to be cut, the freight cars on the railway that tracked the road waiting to be loaded with produce from factories like the one we had passed earlier.

'So, were you visiting friends or relatives back there?' I asked, wondering how she had come to be in the place where I had found her.

'No,' she replied, 'I was working. A few days ago you would have found me in one of these fields with a straw hat on my head and a knife in my hand and hoping that the day would soon be over.' Once a year she and some colleagues from the school where she taught volunteered themselves for a few weeks to help cut sugar cane. It sounded like extremely hard work and on top of the busy school year she had previously described I wondered where she found the energy and commitment to make a contribution. Was it a free choice or had they been 'encouraged'?

'No, none of us were forced to make the effort. We volunteered for different reasons. In my own case it's something of a debt I want to repay, in recognition of what my country has done for me.'

I was intrigued and, with her easy-going, open manner, I felt that further probing on my part would not be taken amiss. 'What do you mean?' I asked, managing a quick glance to make sure that I had not provoked any irritation.

'Don't worry, I can confide a few secrets,' she had laughed, probably noticing my hesitation. 'For several generations my family were simple famers in the east of the country. I'm sure you've read some Cuban history in the time you've been here so you'll know that before the revolution most of the land was owned by a few wealthy individuals. The peasants were exploited. They were little more than slaves. But all that changed when Fidel took over. The land was nationalized. The previous owners fled the country and for the first time people like my father could hope for a better life for his children. I suppose you can call me a daughter of the revolution. If it hadn't happened I would probably be working on some farm near Guantanamo with six children of my own, a drunken husband who would beat me and no future but the same past my family came from.

That's why once a year I exchange my teacher's clothes for an old jacket and patched-up trousers and join a brigade to help cut sugar.'

Elisa went on to explain that these brigades were present throughout the country, that people from all sections of society: teachers, doctors, students, academics, Government functionaries and even housewives, volunteered their time for a few weeks to help out. They even had occasional foreigners offer their services and, though she had not come across them herself, considerable national publicity had attached itself to a 'Yankee' brigade comprising American students who wanted to show some solidarity with a country ostracized by their own. Although I was aware of its importance I had not realised that sugar accounted for over three quarters of Cuba's exports. Without it they would have no oil from Latin America, no machinery from the former Soviet Union and nothing to sweeten the cheap coffee they imported from elsewhere.

I asked about the economic hardships that Cubans were facing and whether that compromised the willingness of people to volunteer their time either because they were too busy with their own welfare or because irritation at what was happening had undermined their previous solidarity. Yes, the numbers had declined in recent years, Elisa replied, although she was more inclined to attribute this to competing priorities for economic survival than any disillusionment.

But as she went on to describe the daily routine

of getting up every morning at five o'clock, the slashing and cutting that they conducted until late afternoon with only a short break for lunch, the camaraderie of sharing hard physical labour with others and the restful sleep that came from being thoroughly exhausted, it seemed clear to me that these few weeks meant more to her than a simple contribution to a struggling economy. For Elisa it seemed to offer a chance to reconnect to some deeper national identity. Sugar had defined the country's culture and economy for most of its existence and taking part in the harvest brought her back in touch with that history and the people she came from.

'What about you?' she asked. 'Did you ever do something like that? Are there work brigades in your country?'

The nearest that came to it in my own experience was picking potatoes as a teenager during the summer holidays on farms in northern Scotland. But I had to confess that the only motive for doing so was desire on my part to earn enough money to buy Led Zeppelin or Pink Floyd records. Solidarity had nothing to do with it, nor altruism, nor payment for an historical debt in terms of what my country had done for me. Perhaps I sounded slightly rueful since Elisa went on to say that if I ever wanted to spend some time in such an endeavour she could direct me to a labour office where they would be more than happy to have my services.

★　　★　　★

At the town of Camaguey half way to Guantanamo and over a sandwich in a small café where we had stopped for some refreshments, my plans for the rest of my excursion around Cuba took a more definite direction.

'So, why are you travelling to my hometown?' Elisa asked.

'Because it's at the end of this road,' I had replied, adding that what was important for me was the journey to get there and my desire to see the country and experience its people in a more engaged way than my fleeting and somewhat superficial acquaintanceship so far.

'So, what will you do once you arrive?' she continued.

I shrugged my shoulders since I had nothing definite worked out. I had the address of the main hotel in Guantanamo and some recommendations gleaned from my guidebook as to what was worth seeing: the beach at Baracoa on the eastern tip of the island, a glimpse of the American military base simply so I could say that I had been there, a trip to Santiago further south which predated Havana in terms of its history and was reputed to have the best traditional music venues in the country.

'But that won't get you any closer to the people you want to interact with, will it?' she replied. 'So, why don't you stay with me and my family for a few days? You'll eat the same food. You'll sleep on a mattress on the floor like the rest of us. We have a small farm in the mountains where I always go when I return home. It's the time of year to pick coffee so, if you don't mind some physical work, you can come along too. And all this,' she added with a smile that made me feel as welcome as her words, 'for no cost whatsoever, out of nothing more than Cuban hospitality.'

'But won't your family mind?' I said, despite my eagerness to accept her offer. 'They're not expecting me and maybe I'll get in the way. They only see you once a year and I'm sure they'll want you all to themselves.'

She laughed. 'Of course not. You'll be most welcome. And as I said you'll do your bit to contribute too. It's not every day they have the offer of free labour.'

She could see I was still hesitant, something circling at the back of my mind. 'If you're concerned about what they will think about my turning up with a strange man, well that's my business. I've had male friends visit before. And don't worry. I don't have a boyfriend who will get jealous and want to beat you up. Really there's no problem. But of course if you'd rather not, I understand. It's up to you.'

'I'd love to,' I said, reassured that my turning up unannounced would not be taken amiss or cause an extra burden. 'But really I'd like to make some financial contribution. I know how difficult it is for families in Cuba at present and I'm an extra mouth to feed.'

Elisa was adamant that no payment was to be

exchanged. That, she said, would be a transaction that would compromise her offer of friendship and undermine the dynamics of the experience she hoped I would have. She relented, however, when I insisted that I buy some gifts for her family. At a nearby dollar store I purchased some bottles of rum, coffee and cigars, all of which were produced locally but were beyond the pockets of most Cubans unless they had access to foreign currency.

It was well past midnight by the time we arrived in Guantanamo and, apart from a few ambulatory policemen and some stray dogs, the streets were deserted. I had offered to pay for rooms at the hotel so as not to disturb anyone at such a late hour but Elisa was insistent that no time was inconvenient for us to pitch up.

The suburb where she directed me seemed to accommodate a large section of her extended family. A house to the left belonged to an aunt. Another one further down was her cousin's. Outside a two-storey building next door to her uncle's she told me to stop the vehicle. We had reached our destination, the place where her parents, some brothers and sisters and grandmother resided.

I expressed some concern when she banged on the door to announce our arrival, but Elisa pointed out that the noise of our car in the narrow streets would have woken up everyone in any case. She was right. The darkened windows in the houses around us all lit up a short while later with people framed against them checking out the commotion. Then the doors opened but instead of complaints and arguments about having their sleep disturbed they gathered round in welcome. Home for Elisa, it seemed, comprised most of the community rather than just the house we were parked outside.

Still unsure about my reception and with no advance warning of my arrival, I extended a nervous hand to Elisa's mother and father when she introduced me to them. Ignoring my formality, they both embraced me as if I was the one returning after a long absence.

Nor did we lose the neighbours, friends and relatives who had appeared, when we entered the house. I had been told before that Cubans needed little excuse to have a party but I had not expected such an impromptu and widespread celebration in the middle of the night only shortly after everyone had been fast asleep. The rum was opened, the cigars were distributed and I spent the next hour shaking hands, explaining who I was and what I was doing in Guantanamo and accepting invitations for breakfast, lunch and dinner over the next few days in what seemed like every residence in the neighbourhood.

Despite Elisa's promise and my pleas that I wanted no special treatment, her parents would have none of it. Some bleary-eyed children who were instructed to greet me were vacated from one of the rooms and I was pointed to a bed and told that this would be my place for the duration of my stay. Elisa offered a resigned smile when I said to her that this was not part of the deal, that I was clear that I did not want special treatment. 'My father told me that if anyone in the neighbourhood finds out that a foreign visitor to their home had slept on the floor in a room with the rest of the family he would be too ashamed to show his face in public again. Don't worry,' she concluded, as she said goodnight. 'You can help with the dishes tomorrow.'

The early start I had committed to in order to assist with family chores was similarly shelved as I slept well into the morning. I was woken by the door to my room being opened and, expecting to find Elisa announcing that it was time to get up, I turned to acknowledge that I was ready to begin the day.

But it was not Elisa or anyone else I could recall from the previous evening who stood in the doorway. An old woman with glasses, a white shawl draped around her shoulders, and greying hair tied up into a tight bun, was inspecting me. Despite my stating who I was and what I was doing in the house I had the impression that it was not my words being listened to but something else that was being scrutinized.

For some time she said nothing. Then, assisted by a walking stick, she moved towards the bed, pulled up a chair, sat down and finally, like royalty condescending to greet a subject, she proffered a hand for me to shake. By that stage I had guessed this might be Elisa's grandmother. 'You'll meet her later,' she had said shortly after we had arrived, since she was the only person not to have woken up to greet us. 'She's quite a character and sees herself as the queen of the family to whom we all have to pay homage. Most of us do. You'll see what I mean.'

Should I stay where I was? Should I get up? In the end I did nothing but look uncomfortable until, finally breaking the silence, the old woman thumped on the floor with her stick and, shouting through the open door behind her, demanded that I should be brought some coffee. To my relief Elisa appeared a few moments later.

'I see you've met my grandmother,' she said, depositing a tray of breakfast in front of me, a further breach of the routines we had agreed when she had invited me. 'She seems to like you.'

'But we haven't exchanged a word in about thirty minutes,' I responded, wondering how she had come to that conclusion.

'My grandmother says that language does more to conceal a person than to show who they are. She says that a face is more honest than the words that come out of our mouths.'

But awkward though the silence had been, it was preferable to our first conversation.

'So what are you doing in Guantanamo?' her grandmother began, as I sat in bed nervously eating my breakfast.

I explained the work I did in Cuba, my desire

to see the country, my meeting with her grand-daughter and my acceptance of her kind invitation to spend some time with her family.

'Are you married?' she continued, ignoring Elisa's interjection that it was none of her business.

I answered that I was but that my wife and son lived in southern Africa.

'When did you last see them?'

'Some months ago.'

'Why so long?'

'Because of the nature of my work and the distance. It's not so easy to fly back to Zimbabwe more frequently.'

'So why is she not here with you?'

'Because she is working and her family live there too. We agreed that this would be the best arrangement for a while.'

'Do you have a girlfriend in Cuba?'

I shook my head and partly hid my face behind the mug of coffee as she fixed me with her uncomfortable stare. Somewhere in the background Elisa shrugged her shoulders as if to say that once her grandmother was determined on something there was no stopping her. It was best just to endure the interrogation until it was over.

'When my husband was sent to work in another part of the island I always went with him. I made sure he was never far away. Men don't like living on their own without a woman nearby and if it isn't their wives then it will be someone else.' This statement brought another embarrassed smile as

I wondered if it was just a general observation on human nature or something specifically directed at my own circumstances.

When she gestured to Elisa that she was ready to leave, I tried hard not to look relieved. But there was one last observation she wanted to share.

'I can see unhappiness in your face, something that is troubling you. Is that correct?'

I shook my head indicating that I was content in my work, that my family life was fine despite the distance, that anything she might have seen was purely due to tiredness and the long drive we had made the previous day. Conscious of what Elisa had said about her grandmother's skill in reading faces I put on the bravest smile I could.

'There is nothing worse in this life than regret, young man,' she concluded, before turning on her heels and hobbling out of the door. Her exit was accompanied by Elisa's apologetic smile as I tried to pretend enthusiasm at my strange and unexpected breakfast.

'You mentioned that you wanted to see the American military base,' Elisa said later that day as we sat in her uncle's house, drinking coffee while he showed me how to play a Cuban version of dominoes. Earlier we had done a brief tour of her city and I had remarked on the number of soldiers I had seen, more than in other locations of the country where men and women in uniform were always present.

Elisa had told me that the US base was only fifteen kilometres away, which explained the somewhat garrison atmosphere of Guantanamo where the Cuban army housed some of its forces. Having also mentioned that it was on my itinerary of places to see, she had added that permission was necessary to get anywhere near it, that generally the process took weeks to complete but that her uncle, who had served in the military for a number of years, might be able to make it happen sooner.

If Playa Giron functioned in the national psyche as the location where the enemy had once been defeated, then Guantanamo served as a reminder that their struggle with the 'gringos' was not yet over. Sonia's uncle elaborated on the history I was partly familiar with.

At the beginning of the twentieth century and after the Americans had fought the Spanish over control of the island, they had handed independence to the Cubans on several conditions. One of these was that they would maintain a military presence for some years to come, ostensibly to help with the country's defence against the defeated Spanish but in reality because they coveted a deep water harbour in the middle of the Caribbean and Guantanamo was the ideal location.

An enclave of some thirty square kilometres had been leased to the Americans on a temporary basis. In 1934 the lease was extended indefinitely. Thereafter, and in keeping with its value established by the two parties at the time, the US

Government would send an annual cheque to their Cuban counterpart.

Not surprisingly Castro had claimed that the agreement was illegal, that it had been established through coercion and that he would not recognize American sovereignty over the area. Every year in front of a national television audience he would display the cheque that had been received, open a desk in the drawer in front of him and stuff it unceremoniously among the pile of other cheques that had built up since he took over. Only one had ever been cashed during his rule and that was done by mistake, he claimed, the money never spent.

According to Elisa's uncle the Cubans were not prepared to go to war over the disputed territory. Despite the fact that the base could be overrun in less than a day, given the size of forces they had at their disposal, they did not want to provoke the Americans into further sanctions and more destabilization.

But more importantly, he added with some candour, it suited Castro to have Guantanamo as a constant reminder of foreign occupation, a symbol that helped to unify the population behind him. Not for the first time in Cuba I heard the view expressed that US hostility helped to promote both the system and its leaders that they opposed. A more benign and cordial relationship would remove some of the excuses for maintaining the status quo that otherwise might have changed.

'So, why all the troops?' I asked, 'and if there is

no intention on either side to have a conflict then what do they do all day?'

The Cuban army was there for two reasons, he replied. If they were not present in significant numbers, then the symbolic value of Guantanamo would lose its potency. Being seen to stand up to the Americans with a sizeable force was necessary to rally people behind the call for national vigilance and solidarity.

At the same time since the base was effectively an extension of American territory it served as a potential magnet for disaffected Cubans seeking asylum. Instead of having to sail across the straits of Florida in flimsy boats and wooden rafts, a hazardous journey that dissuaded many from the attempt, if the borders with Guantanamo were unguarded they could simply walk across with no inconvenience whatsoever.

He added that this was a situation that the US Government did not want either: thousands of Cubans crossing the border and having to be shipped to Miami to process their applications. As a result, both sides had established a sizeable military zone around the base, full of soldiers, hardware, fences and surveillance equipment. Some resolute individuals did try to swim across Guantanamo bay from the Cuban side to the American but numerous guards, navy patrols and sharks provided considerable dissuasion. He reckoned that no more than thirty to forty a year attempted this route to exile. A significant percentage of that number, though never publicly admitted, were either caught or drowned.

As to what the soldiers did all day he claimed that boredom was the predominant concern of army generals on both sides of the dividing line. Routines were therefore established that in his view had little value apart from keeping their forces occupied. This included frequent military exercises, numerous patrols along the fence, a lot of staring at each other through binoculars and recording their observations, and the construction of facilities such as underground bunkers whose necessity was dubious.

The US army, he added with some amusement, seemed more prone to boredom. Their soldiers would dress up to impersonate Castro, sporting long beards and smoking cigars, and then walk up and down in front of the Cuban observation posts to provoke a reaction. On several occasions they would line up along the fence, turn their backs on the soldiers on the other side and then drop their pants. 'That kind of stuff never bothered us, to be honest. Most of us found it funny.' But he added that in the small museum on the edge of the city that commemorated the history of Guantanamo and its occupation there was a section entitled 'Enemy Provocation and Immaturity' where photographs of marines without their trousers had pride of place.

When Elisa informed him of my interest in seeing the base but added that I had no permission to do so he was doubtful that I would receive the necessary clearance. He promised to make a few calls but given the sensitivity of the area and the fact that potential visitors were supposed to be screened before they arrived he put my chances at slim.

This was confirmed the following day. The only person who could have made such a decision was on leave for a few weeks. Even though he also knew the deputy in charge, that person was reluctant to take the risk of offending his superior when he returned.

'That's how it is in Cuba,' Sonia's uncle concluded with a resigned shrug. 'My friend has the authority to sign that piece of paper. But if he did so it would raise questions as to what role his manager plays if the person below him can sign the same document in his absence. That's a rule that explains a large part of the bureaucracy in our country. If anyone steps in to do someone else's work, then what would be the point of employing that other person in the first place? It has a logic but not one related to efficiency.'

Elisa had warned me beforehand that the steep, four-hour climb to their farm on the outskirts of Baracoa would test me. Reasonably fit, I had joked that she would probably be the one unable to keep up. But as we struggled through the undergrowth on the lower slopes of the mountain where we were headed it was she and her cousin who had to wait for me, constantly offering a hand to pull me through the jungle or having to direct my footsteps across the numerous streams that dissected the area we were passing through.

The heat too at these levels was intense and soon I had stripped to the waist, irritated that I had ignored earlier advice to wear shorts rather than trousers. Despite my somewhat tokenistic protestations, Elisa's cousin, a young man who infuriatingly flitted up and down the track we were on like a nimble mountain goat, took my bag and added it to his own.

Meanwhile the spray I had brought with me all the way from Scotland and that promised to repel the nastiest tropical insects was useless against the hordes of mosquitoes and other biting flies that plagued our progress. Elisa had then produced some foul-smelling cream made by her grandmother and liberally smeared some on my face, back and arms. 'Don't ask what it's made from,' she had replied when I had protested about the smell. 'Only complain if it doesn't work.' As we moved forward I could see the same wall of insects almost a metre away but amazingly none of them ventured any closer through the invisible fog that kept them at bay.

Over and above the help from her cousin and her words of encouragement the other thing that motivated me was the prospect of what lay ahead of us at the end of our trek. Occasionally through a break in the forest I could see the upper slopes of the mountain where bits of cloud promised a cooler breeze and where the trees had thinned to a Cuban version of the British countryside. The temperature would be half of what it was where we were now. A light wind would keep the insects away. Elisa had enthused about the magnificent view that was waiting for us, the food that her aunt would have prepared, and the fire that we would sit around later that evening, drinking rum and coffee and joking about the long, arduous hike we had made to get there.

Earlier I had asked her about the status of her family farm. I knew that private ownership of land in Cuba was prohibited, that agriculture was controlled by the State and that quotas for production and prices for foodstuffs were set by the Government each year and rigidly enforced. She confirmed that there were limits on the size of holdings, that these were not owned as such but that farmers were only given rights of use. This meant that land could not be traded on the market in the way that property was sold in my own part of the world.

While she felt that this avoided the concentration of wealth in the hands of a few individuals that prevailed before the revolution, she was more critical of the agricultural policy of her Government and the fact that Cuba was now a major importer of food. Previously it had supplied neighbouring Caribbean countries and parts of Latin America with a variety of products. Now it was only sugar that was exported and cigars made from local tobacco.

'There used to be a time when there were more cows than people in Cuba. Today you need a special permit just to kill one because they are like an endangered species. The prices offered to farmers on the local market are so low that there is no incentive to produce anything more than what they need for themselves.'

Perhaps 'farm' was the wrong title for the few hectares of land where Elisa and her family chilled out on occasional weekends and long vacations. The goats, chickens and pigs that rooted around the main house looking for scraps seemed more like long-standing residents than potential supper. The large garden that stretched in front of the communal veranda was full of flowers and decorative plants with only a small patch of vegetables to one side. Meanwhile the coffee plantation that Elisa had talked about when she had first invited me to spend time with her family in the mountains, and where I had presumed I would be gainfully occupied for several hours each day, picking beans, turned out to be nothing more than a few dozen bushes in another part of the property.

'So, how am I supposed to contribute to my upkeep?' I had asked when we had completed the tour. 'This looks more like a recreational facility than a business enterprise. The only work I can see myself doing is lifting my fork and knife when your aunt places dinner in front of me, just like she did a few hours ago when we first arrived.'

As with the family home in Guantanamo city, the line that separated one household from the next seemed much more fluid and permeable than in other places I was familiar with. It wasn't that privacy was unavailable but just that people seemed to be much more comfortable in each other's company. There was no time of the day or night when a constant stream of visitors from the surrounding area was not present. No one knocked on any doors. No one needed to invite anyone to come in. Neighbours would simply walk up to the veranda or the living room or the kitchen, sit themselves in a chair and begin a conversation as if they were continuing from where they had left off only a few minutes previously.

There were family sleep-overs too. This was largely to do with the fact that evening visits were accompanied by a liberal consumption of rum that left the male heads of households unable to stagger the short distance home to their own houses. It was simpler to provide mattresses and blankets. The children went to bed first. The mothers followed them to another room. Then the fathers would consume the last dregs of whatever it was that was circulating until they fell asleep on the floor, to be woken the next morning by the women who had surfaced earlier to make breakfast.

Originally we had agreed that we would stay three days until Elisa had to return to prepare for her trip back to Sancti Spiritus and the start of the school term. My own itinerary was more flexible with only a visit to Santiago de Cuba that remained from the itinerary I had abandoned. But as our departure approached I began to wish that our stay could be prolonged, that another few days could be found from somewhere that would delay our descent down the mountain.

It wasn't just the morning walks, the fresh air and the magnificent views I had begun to enjoy, or the leisurely afternoon routine of visiting neighbours and conversing for long hours with members of a household who had made me feel at home. Elisa had promised to open a window for me on family life in a community that was not my own and by and large that experience had been delivered. In the process, however, my feelings towards her had changed too, not surprisingly perhaps given her beauty and warm personality but also because my own situation seemed to be nudging me in that direction.

During the evenings in front of the communal fire that was routinely lit near the veranda, I would notice the open displays of affection between husbands and wives and imagine a situation where my life would be different, where I would not be someone looking in. Watching Elisa, I would think of the words her grandmother had said, about not waiting for happiness until it had passed, until it was replaced by regret that a moment had not been seized. But imagination often runs stronger where the likelihood of something happening is less probable, and as much as I would speculate on what a relationship with her might look like I would remember at the same time the fact of my marriage and the family I had in Zimbabwe. So, despite my growing feelings of affection, I maintained the easy familiarity that seemed to prevail between men and women in the community I was in, but respected the division that was there too, the line that should not be crossed unless another set of consequences was prepared to be faced.

'But another few days with her would be most welcome,' I would catch myself thinking as our departure loomed. 'Who knows what might happen during that time?'

On the morning of our scheduled descent, with our bags packed, our farewells said to the neighbours that would remain, the insect repellant smeared on whatever exposed parts of our bodies would be accessible further down the mountain, Elisa's cousin knocked on the door of the room where I was changing to announce that there were some men who wanted to see me.

'What men?'

'Some policemen. They heard you were here and just want to check your papers.'

'Why?'

He seemed confused by the question. It was normal in Cuba for policemen to check documents. It was routine, that was all.

But, as I approached the gate where two officers in uniform were conversing with Sonia and some other members of the family, I was conscious of the fact that I had not brought my papers with me. 'Always keep your passport in a safe and secure location,' was the advice in my country director's handbook. Trekking around the mountains of a foreign country had seemed like one of those occasions where it was wiser to leave it behind. Which was exactly what I had done.

The policemen were firm but not officious or unfriendly. One of them had offered a hand to greet me when I had drawn up beside them. Maybe they would be content with my answers to their questions and not ask for anything else. They wanted to know where I was from. What was I doing in the mountains? How long had I been there? What was the nature of my work in Cuba? When would I return to Havana?

But when they asked to see my passport and I said that I did not have it with me, that it was sitting in the drawer of a cupboard in a house in Guantanamo, I could see them stiffen, their faces harden, and I guessed that this meant trouble. The same surprise was registered on the faces of Elisa and her cousin. 'What does he mean, he doesn't have his papers with him?' was what they seemed to be thinking.

'Everyone has papers in Cuba, Senhor,' one of the officers said. 'Even foreigners. Weren't you told to have your documents with you when you travel around?'

I remembered the conversation I had had with Sonia in the Ministry of Foreign Affairs when I had first arrived in the country, her 'briefing' she had called it on some local rules. Cuba was a nervous country, she had said. It had every reason to be. It had experienced years of subversion from foreign powers and that explained why everyone was cautious and the authorities more officious than in other places I might have frequented. 'This stamp in your passport,' she had said, pointing to the one that had been granted by her Ministry to representatives of aid agencies like myself, 'is designed to protect you. Just show it to anyone who asks and they will leave you alone.'

'I thought I might lose it,' was the excuse I offered as the two policemen waited for me to answer. 'That's why I left it behind. But I can take it to the police station in Guantanamo when I get back. Won't that work?'

For a moment I thought the look they exchanged between them might mean a reprieve, a realization that I was who I said I was, a recognition that the hassle of taking this further was not worth the inconvenience for all of us. But I must have misinterpreted the signal. One of the officers took out a walkie-talkie from the bag on his back, walked around for a few minutes to find a signal and then proceeded to converse with someone at the other end of it. I heard the words 'foreigner', 'passport' and then the phrase 'nothing, sir' repeated several times, accompanied by a shrug of the shoulders that suggested the other person on the line was as incredulous as everyone else.

While he was talking, I managed to whisper an apology to Elisa and tried to explain what had prompted me to leave my passport behind. There was a reason after all. It wasn't just forgetfulness. 'And what is all the fuss about in any case? It's not as if we are near any sensitive military building or Government facility that is top secret. We're in the Cuban mountains among chickens, goats and pigs, in a place with no strategic value for anyone trying to subvert the country. Can't I just say I'm sorry, that it won't happen again and we can all move on?'

'Chris, this is Cuba not Scotland,' she managed to reply, while the officers conversed further with their colleague on the radio. 'Without papers you could be anyone. You cannot prove who you are. They will ask us too why we invited someone here that we do not know. And without a document to confirm your identity, they will say that we were negligent, that it is not just you but us who are at fault.'

Maybe noticing my look of alarm and concern that this was going to go further than I had feared, and not just for myself but for her and her family, she added that maybe they would let us off with a warning, an admonition that it should not happen again.

'Do you really think so?' I asked.

'Yes, maybe that's what will happen,' she replied, but from her face and the grim look of her cousin I guessed that this was not an option that had much hope of materializing.

Our descent down the mountain was unpleasant and not just because of the heat, the insects and the same difficult terrain we had negotiated a few days earlier. This time there was no prospect of anything better at the end of it to compensate for the discomfort.

'You will have to come with us to the police station in Baracoa,' one of the officers had said after concluding their conversation on the radio. 'Your business will be dealt with there.'

Elisa and her cousin were instructed to come too. We were given five minutes to conclude our preparations. One of the policemen marched in front. The other took up a position at the rear. At the bottom of the mountain several hours later there was a long, heated conversation over the radio between the policemen and the person they had called. It turned out that there were no vehicles available to pick us up. 'We'll have to travel in your car, Senhor,' one of them said, apologetically adding that he hoped I didn't mind.

What seemed to irritate them the most was that they would have to come with us. One complained that there was a family event in his village in the mountains that he would now miss. Fortunately, from the conversation that ensued between them and Sonia as we drove the thirty kilometres to Baracoa, it was not us who were being blamed for the inconvenience. 'How can we do our jobs if we are not given the resources to do so?' they asked.

'Cuba y Cuba,' Elisa replied, a phrase that provoked considerable amusement among everyone else in the vehicle as the conversation turned to the numerous afflictions that plagued the country and the lack of resources that meant people could not do their work effectively.

At the station when we arrived several officers gathered round as we were asked to fill out forms that were placed in front of us. The atmosphere was not unfriendly and as each of them repeated the same question, 'Why do you not have any documents?' the same look was there that I had seen on the face of every other person when I had answered the question. My 'excuse' was so incredible that I had the impression they actually believed it. Anyone with a subversive agenda would have come up with a much better story. Stupid I may have been but not malevolent or ill intentioned.

In a small room where I was ushered later by a plain-clothes officer, who seemed to command considerable authority judging by the deferential salutes that greeted his arrival, I was asked to relate my history in Cuba, the reasons for my excursion in the mountains and the same explanation about my missing documents. At the end of the narrative he asked if there was anyone in authority I knew in Cuba who could confirm my story.

The person who came most readily to mind was Sonia but, since it was a weekend and the office would be closed, I doubted if he would be able to reach her. There was no harm in trying, he said. He then departed for some time, returning later to confirm my fears that despite their best efforts they had been unable to get through. That meant that it might only be the day after tomorrow when Government offices opened that they would be able to establish contact. He nodded his head when I asked him if that meant I would have to remain in the police station until that happened.

As with his colleagues earlier there was an almost apologetic manner that characterized his interaction with me. I had fallen foul not of some criminal code but a set of bureaucratic procedures prompted by my naïvety. These procedures were ones which, once set in motion, he had as little control over as I.

'Yes, unfortunately, they will have to remain here too,' he replied, when I asked him if the same constraints applied to Elisa and her cousin, whose only fault had been their hospitality. 'I am sure your story will be confirmed,' he added when I expressed a sigh of frustration, 'but rules have to be respected. At this moment we do not have proof of who you are or any independent confirmation of why you spent so much time in the mountains near Baracoa. As soon as that happens we can all go home.'

I politely repeated the same questions I had asked Elisa. Why the sensitivity? Why the nervousness? I was nowhere near any military facility that I was aware of or any part of the country where for security reasons I shouldn't have been. If I was a spy, for example, what on earth would I have been spying on?

'Coffee, Senhor. Coffee. That is why we are nervous. That is why we have brought you here.'

I was even more perplexed. 'What about it?' I asked. 'I picked a few beans and drank lots of it with Elisa and her family. I didn't think that this was a crime.'

I had the impression of some surprise on his part at my naïvety, as if something that was obvious to him should therefore be obvious to everyone else, outsiders included. As he lit another cigarette and began to explain to me why I had ended up where I was, I remembered Sonia's words of caution about not taking Cuba at its face value. Besides the cheerfulness, the good humour and Caribbean levity, suspicion was present too, a result of the historical circumstances that had provoked such an attitude.

The previous year, my interrogator continued, not far from the very location where I had been picked up, the authorities had arrested some foreigners engaged in economic sabotage. They were found with a variety of coffee beans that they had planned to smuggle out of the country and on to Miami. At some covert research facility in the United States a strain of disease would be developed to attack Cuban coffee plantations. Undermining local production and depriving locals of their beloved national beverage was designed to create dissatisfaction and political dissent. I tried hard to disguise my incredulity at what he was telling me as he elaborated further.

'Did you know that our tobacco is targeted too? Our plantations are sprayed from the air by aircraft operating out of Florida with diseases that are designed to destroy our principal export. Why? Well, if we lose our tobacco industry, our enemies believe that our economy will decline even further and that people will rise up in revolt to remove our current leaders. That is why we have to be sure that, if we find someone in the mountains with no documents to prove who they are, we have to do everything we can to find out what they are doing there. I am sure you can understand why we have to be so careful.'

While I appreciated his lengthy explanation, his words only exacerbated my apprehension too. With the entire future of the country at stake I could be held for days if not weeks. Maybe I would be deported for being so foolish. The thought of the lecture I would receive from Sonia and her bosses when this unfortunate affair was over did little to reassure me that an easy resolution would materialize soon.

But half an hour later the same individual who had assumed responsibility for my case returned to the room where I was sitting, extended a friendly hand and told me I could go. Everything had been resolved. I was clearly not a spy, only someone who had foolishly forgotten to carry his documents around with him. Resigned to a considerably worse fate than such a slight admonition, I gratefully accepted his handshake and stuttered my apology. Had he managed to get through to Sonia or someone in the Ministry who had corroborated my story?

It turned out that Elisa had contacted the same uncle we had visited a few days previously. Family connections clearly accounted for a great deal. He had phoned the inspector of police in Guantanamo who in turn had phoned the inspector of police in Baracoa. The family credentials were impeccable. No one could accuse them of facilitating the visit of someone determined to undermine what they had all made sacrifices to protect. 'Please travel with you papers in future,' he concluded, as I exited the station.

Back in the car and despite my repeated apologies and obvious embarrassment Elisa did all she could to brush aside what had happened. It was nothing more than a small, unfortunate episode. Despite the stress and inconvenience, she urged me not to think badly of her compatriots. The story I had heard was substantially true. Cuba's enemies would stop at nothing to undermine the country and their leaders who had stood up to them.

On the outskirts of Baracoa and beyond the last police checkpoint at the edge of town, I wound down the window and took a deep breath of the cool evening air. 'Thank God they did not search my rucksack,' I said as I rummaged around to find what I was looking for.

'What is it?' Elisa asked as I extracted a small plastic bag I had placed in one of the pockets, a token of my visit to the mountains.

'Coffee beans,' I replied as I shook the contents out of the window.

EPILOGUE

The Blue Mountains of Jamaica were a brilliant green with occasional brown patches on the middle slopes where their famous coffee was grown. The contrast with the sweltering heat of Kingston was dramatic. In the space of only a few kilometres the temperature plummeted from a hot and humid thirty degrees along the coast to less than five at the highest point of the island. When a break in the clouds permitted, from that same summit one could look at the city below and imagine that its miles of overcrowded suburbs and shanty towns, its veins and arteries that transported a heavy and ponderous traffic, had been transformed into a more benign and considerate toy town.

In between my frequent travels around the Caribbean and my engagement with our projects for street children in the cities of Jamaica, Hagley Gap in the Blue Mountains was my favourite place to chill out. It had a quaint English feel to it, with tea gardens, a pub, a restaurant selling cottage pie and Guinness, and even a red postbox on its principal street. The trails through the surrounding forest could have been back home although the brightly coloured birds and a species of exotic butterfly that was reputed to be amongst the biggest in the world provided a reminder that unlike Scotland this was in the tropics. No matter the cold weather at this height, the pine trees here had never seen snow.

Despite the occasional need for a respite in 'little England' I had grown used to my routine: the nomadism that ferried me between the different islands every few weeks, the challenge of developing programmes of work in places that were new and unfamiliar, the space and time I had managed to find to interact with people from other cultures. In particular, the variety of my location appealed to me, the different geographies, histories and languages of the region that made it impossible to ever identify a solid and uniform Caribbean identity.

That contrast continually intrigued me. In Cuba there was a functioning Government that penetrated every part of people's personal and professional lives. I could not drive around the country without making a few phone calls and sometimes having to fill out a written application at the same time. Meanwhile, only a short distance away in Haiti, both because of recently flawed elections and a history of governance that aroused deep scepticism within its population, there seemed to be no Government in place for much of the time I was there. No one was in charge. When I asked my

Haitian colleagues as to where I needed to go to acquire formal permission to work in a particular place or sector they would scratch their heads, look confused and tell me that no one asked such a silly question. I should simply get on with the business of helping people and not waste my time pursuing an official endorsement that would never materialize.

Jamaica added another flavour when it came to acquiring permissions. Over and above the agreement required from a particular line Ministry in order to work in health, education or social welfare, local level approval was just as essential, at least in the kinds of places where we needed to work. Community representatives were not Government officials, politicians or anyone formally elected to promote their interests. I recalled one encounter when a member of my staff invited me to accompany her to an office in one of Kingston's informal suburbs, in order to have access to a large group of children who had ended up on the streets and were in need of our help. As we entered a building which had no formal identification of the responsible body housed here, she told me to keep quiet, to let her do all the talking and to nod or shake my head in whatever direction she instructed me. The meeting was presided over by one of the local 'dons', a gangster whose accompanying officials were men with guns and glittering jewellery. I barely understood any of the Jamaican patois that was exchanged but the smiles at the end of our meeting indicated that we had come to a successful conclusion, that and an offer to imbibe an illegal substance which was placed in front of me and which I politely and respectfully declined.

Once every six months I would return back to Zimbabwe. During the first few days of being back, my young son would watch me with wary eyes, occasionally venturing a shy smile whenever I managed to penetrate his reserve. But more difficult than the initial distance was breaking off the familiarity we had managed to find by the end of my visit. There were tears and wails whenever I packed my bags. Despite my promise that a time would come soon when we would be together as a family, our geographical separation for six years meant that I did not actually believe it. Openings in Zimbabwe for work in the career I had chosen were few and far between. And besides that, the job in my new location was rewarding, interesting and what I most wanted to do.

All of that changed during a phone call with my boss one day, part of our routine of keeping in touch once a month unless an emergency dictated a more specific communication. At the end of our exchange on financial figures, project reports and the interest of several donors in supporting our work, she added that there was a vacancy in the organization that I might be interested in pursuing.

'But I'm happy enough here,' I responded. 'I'm keen to continue for a few more years at least.'

'I think this one might change your mind. It's a

country directorship in Zimbabwe. If you got the job you could get back to your family.'

'Of course,' I replied, trying to sound more convinced and enthusiastic than I felt at that moment. 'That would be an added attraction. When's the deadline for making an application?'

'Well, you only have a few days left before it closes. If you want to go ahead, you need to phone the recruiting officer as soon as possible.'

In my favourite pub in the Blue Mountains where I had come the following day to mull over my decision, the unease I had felt when first alerted to the possibility of returning to Zimbabwe had not disappeared. For several years I had envisaged such a moment, when an opportunity would present itself to reclaim my family and return to a place that I could properly call home. I remembered Yasmine's final words when we had parted in Morocco, her admonition that while moving around had its attractions for a while it could not substitute for the stability of a family and a fixed location. I knew that at some stage I would have to make up my mind as to which direction I wanted my life to take. The problem was that I had not expected it to come just then, when I was unprepared, still unsure and not yet disillusioned with an itinerant lifestyle that continued to appeal to me.

Shouldn't I feel more enthusiastic that this was the right thing for me to do, I thought, before I contacted my home office to signal my interest?

And if I was successful in my application where was the certainty that regret wouldn't come later? While mindful of the fact that I had a duty to my family to be with them, especially if an opportunity for employment meant that I had every financial reason to do so, I wanted more than this as a justification for making such an important decision. Where was conviction when I needed it?

Then, as I sipped my Guinness and contemplated the panoramic view of the green hills and the blue sea below me, I recalled that in actual fact conviction and certainty had never been present around any of the choices I had previously made to significantly change my life. Travelling to Sudan, leaving Sudan, moving to Zimbabwe, leaving Zimbabwe, had never been accompanied by a one hundred per cent certainty that I was doing the right thing. I recalled the initial regret when leaving my family in Harare several years previously, the questions and doubts that had pestered me for several months as to whether I had made a good choice. Circumstances presented themselves for a decision to be made but leaving the past behind was never easy. The only imperative was not to shy away from something just because it was a break with what one had become familiar with, or because the future by definition could never be assured and predictable.

One month later I was back in the Blue Mountains, this time to say goodbye. My application had been successful and I had only a few days left before a flight to London and then on to Harare to assume my new post. The previous week I had bid farewell to colleagues in Haiti. The week before that I had parted from friends in Cuba to tears and hugs and requests to return some day.

'You must be looking forward to getting back to your family,' was the universal comment I received when I mentioned where I was headed.

'Of course,' I replied, 'although I'll be sad to leave such beautiful islands and good friends behind.'

The drive to Hagley Gap was as scenic as always: the pine forests emerging from the clouds, Kingston bay that sparkled blue and clear below me, the precipitous cliffs that marked the wilder northern coastline. 'This will be the last time you will ever see this place,' a niggling voice persisted under the high spirits I always had when making this excursion. But as the outer suburbs of the city relaxed into green countryside, I did not let that thought deflect me from enjoying the moment or undermining my acceptance of the new journey that lay ahead of me.